Spanish Phonology

GEORGETOWN STUDIES IN SPANISH LINGUISTICS SERIES
JOHN M. LIPSKI, SERIES EDITOR

El español en contacto con otras lenguas
Carol A. Klee y Andrew Lynch

Sociolingüística y pragmática del español
Carmen Silva-Corvalan

Sonido y sentido: Teoría y práctica de la pronunciación del español contemporáneo con audio CD
Jorge M. Guitart

Spanish Phonology: A Syllabic Perspective
Sonia Colina

Varieties of Spanish in the United States
John M. Lipski

Spanish Phonology

A Syllabic Perspective

SONIA COLINA

Georgetown University Press
Washington, D.C.

Chapters two and three are based on "Optimality-theoretic advances in our understanding of Spanish syllabic structure," in Fernando Martínez-Gil and Sonia Colina, *Optimality-Theoretic Studies in Spanish Phonology*, 2006, 564 pp. With kind permission by John Benjamins Publishing Company, Amsterdam/Philadelphia. www.benjamins.com

Extracts from Colina (2006b) appear in chapter 5. With kind permission by John Benjamins Publishing Company, Amsterdam/Philadelphia. www.benjamins.com

Georgetown University Press, Washington, D.C. www.press.georgetown.edu

Library of Congress Cataloging-in-Publication Data

Colina, Sonia.
 Spanish phonology:a syllabic perspective/Sonia Colina.
     p. cm.
 Includes bibliographical references and index.
 ISBN 978-1-58901-262-2 (pbk.:alk. paper)
 1. Spanish language--Phonology. 2. Spanish language--Syllabication. I. Title.
 PC4131.C58 2009
 461'.5--dc22

                                                              2008034758

A mis padres, Pilar Garea y José Colina

Contents

Examples and Figures

EXAMPLES

FIGURES

Acknowledgments

I would like to express my gratitude to numerous colleagues who have given me much advice throughout the years and have taught me a great deal about phonology, in particular José Ignacio Hualde and Fernando Martínez-Gil. For detailed comments and many hours of discussion on the content and analyses presented in this book, I would like to thank Iggy Roca and Carlos Eduardo-Piñeros. This book has also benefited from the comments of three anonymous reviewers and the assistance provided by Gail Grella and the editorial team of GUP. My gratitude goes to all of them. For their support of this project, I am indebted to Gail Grella and John Lipski.

Readers familiar with recent OT literature in Spanish phonology may recognize some of the ideas presented in parts of Chapter 2 and the beginning of Chapter 3. *Spanish Phonology: A Syllabic Perspective* has its origins in an overview article on Spanish syllabification published by the author (Colina 2006c) in the volume *Optimality-theoretic Advances in Spanish Phonology*. I would like to express my appreciation to John Benjamins for the publishing of that earlier work which served to lay the groundwork for the writing of this book.

I also acknowledge a sabbatical from the University of Arizona that permitted me to complete work on the current book. Readers are asked to consult my homepage, www.u.arizona.edu/~scolina, for any errata or additions to this text that were received too late to make it into print.

1

Introduction

1.1 AIM AND THEORETICAL FRAMEWORK

This monograph offers a comprehensive analysis of a variety of crucial issues in the phonology and morphophonology of Spanish: syllable types, syllabification algorithms, syllable repair mechanisms, syllable mergers, nasal assimilation, obstruent vocalization and spirantization, obstruent neutralization, glide formation, onset strengthening, aspiration, /r/ realizations, velarization, plural formation, word classes, and diminutives. The main goal of the book is to contribute to current understanding of important topics in Spanish phonology by addressing a wide range of phonological phenomena from a variety of dialects of Spanish.

The content is organized around the syllable. Books on Spanish phonology, be they textbooks or research monographs, often follow a sequential organization of content that covers the major phonological phenomena of the language followed by chapters on suprasegmentals like syllabification and stress. Since a great majority of phonological phenomena in Spanish cannot be described, nor accounted for, without reference to the syllable, these phenomena are presented here in their syllabic context, using the syllable as the overarching organizational principle. As it will be shown below, reference to syllabic structure is crucial as it serves to highlight the motivation shared by many phonological processes.

The book is written from the perspective of Optimality Theory (OT), one of the most, if not the most, influential theories of phonology today. Resorting to the syllable as the organizing principle for the book is very appropriate to an optimality-theoretic framework due to the centrality of the notion of parallel evaluation in OT. Parallel evaluation means that an account of an apparently segmental process cannot limit itself to segmental and featural constraints, but that syllabic, metrical, and prosodic constraints need to be brought into the picture simultaneously. Small areas of the phonology can no longer be neatly and conveniently dissected and separated for analysis without referring to relevant prosodic structure.

On a similar note, OT, being inherently typological, makes predictions about linguistic variation, therefore making the analysis of Spanish, with its numerous dialects, an excellent testing ground for the theory. This volume shows that our understanding of many difficult problems in Spanish phonology is improved within an optimality-theoretic approach: the book compares its analyses with those proposed previously, discussing difficulties faced by these analyses, as well as by different versions of OT, and identifying areas where there is still room for discussion and exploration. By covering issues in OT through the data and problems presented by one language and its dialects, *Spanish Phonology* will appeal to OT researchers and students familiar with the theory, but who are not experts in Spanish, as well as to Spanish linguists and graduate students who may not be well-versed in the intricacies of the theory.

Spanish Phonology is intended as core reading for advanced undergraduate and graduate-level phonology courses (including seminars) in Spanish linguistics, general linguistics, and OT, as well as related areas such as bilingualism, language acquisition, or speech and hearing. Because of its wide coverage, this monograph is a good point of departure for the study and teaching of many crucial issues of Spanish phonology, dialectal variation, and OT (e.g., postlexical resyllabification, /s/-aspiration, nasal velarization, diphthongs and hiatuses, glide formation, coda neutralization processes, stratal and nonstratal OT).

This book can be read at different levels of specialization. Advanced sections, identified by a gray vertical rule on the left and smaller type, can be skipped by researchers and students wanting to obtain a general understanding of the topic without affecting readability and coherence. Regarding constraints and constraint ranking, complete (and often complex) rankings are included, as are simplified rankings (in the form of Hasse diagrams or summarized crucial rankings) for readers interested only in the core aspects of the analysis. Rankings and constraints are also provided in each chapter.

Spanish Phonology has a number of special features designed with an educational purpose in mind. Addressing the needs of students and researchers in general phonology on the one hand, and Spanish linguists on the other, the book includes some study aids at the end of each chapter, with various sections aimed at improving understanding of the material:

1. *Study Questions* reviews selected topics covered in the book and poses questions that may not come to mind during the first reading of a chapter.

2. *Going Back to the Sources* lists the sources that were most influential in the writing of each chapter. This section will help the nonspecialist reader decide where to start when looking up the references mentioned in the book, and will also be useful for teachers who may want to design a more advanced course around this textbook by complementing and expanding its content with a more detailed reading of the relevant literature.

3. *Key Topics* contains a list of important topics covered from the perspective of Spanish phonology, as well as from that of general phonology (e.g., nasal assimilation, Richness of the Base).

4. *Topics for Further Research* includes suggestions for those who may want to pursue research in related topics. It helps students consider the areas that are still in need of further exploration and discussion in Spanish phonology. These sections will be useful to students and researchers in related areas, such as first and second language acquisition, phonetics, and dialectology, as they may suggest possible ways to contribute to phonological theory and Spanish phonology.

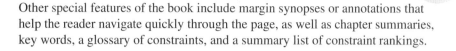

Other special features of the book include margin synopses or annotations that help the reader navigate quickly through the page, as well as chapter summaries, key words, a glossary of constraints, and a summary list of constraint rankings.

1.2 WHY THE SYLLABLE?

1.2.1 THE ROLE OF THE SYLLABLE IN PHONOLOGICAL THEORY

Since its introduction as a unit of phonological organization in the late seventies (Hooper 1976; Kahn 1976), the syllable has played an increasingly important role in phonological theory. The syllable allows the analyst to formulate generalizations that could not be easily expressed without it. For instance, consider some well-known processes of Spanish phonology, such as nasal velarization (e.g., /pan/ [paŋ] 'bread'), /s/-aspiration (e.g., /dos/ [doh] 'two'), voicing assimilation (e.g., /mismo/ [mizmo] 'same'), liquid gliding (e.g., /papel/ [papei̯] 'paper'), and nasal assimilation (e.g., /kanbio/ [kambi̯o] 'change'). Without referring to the syllable, the analyst would fail to grasp the common underlying motivation for those processes: the neutralization of contrasts in a weak syllabic position (coda). Similarly, phenomena like onset strengthening, in which a high vocoid is realized as a palatal obstruent in onset position (e.g., /kom-iendo/ [ko.mi̯en.do] 'eat-gerund' versus /kre-iendo/ [kɾe.ɟ̯en.do] 'believe-gerund') can be seen as the result of the onset preference for strong, less sonorous segments, an insight that would be entirely lost in a model of phonology without syllables.

The syllable is also relevant with respect to nonsegmental aspects of the phonology. For instance, many stress generalizations cannot be formulated without it. In Spanish it is well-known that lexical stress cannot be placed further to the left than the antepenultimate syllable (Harris 1983 and others; three-syllable window), *teléfono *télefono* 'telephone,' or further than the penultimate when the latter has a branching rhyme (Harris 1983; branching condition), *Venezuéla *Venézuela*. Phonotactic restrictions also hold over syllables and syllabic components with regard to the type and number of segments. For example, the ill-formed hypothetical *muersto* can only be explained as the result of an excessive number of segments in the rhyme (three being the maximum), given that /ue/ and /rs/ sequences are by themselves licit strings.[1]

The importance of the role played by the syllable in modern phonological theory increased exponentially with the advent of OT. The syllable is possibly the area of phonological inquiry that has attracted the most interest amongst OT practitioners and, as a result, it constitutes the focus of a significant body of OT research. All of the early OT studies contain large sections devoted to syllabification issues (cf. Prince and Smolensky 1993; McCarthy and Prince 1993a, 1993b). In Spanish, too, the first dissertations published within an OT framework were studies of syllabification and syllabification-related processes (Morales-Front 1994; Colina 1995). The amount of syllable-related OT research does not come as a surprise if one considers the ease with which syllable types illustrate optimality accounts of factorial typologies and how the syllable serves to exemplify the interaction of segments, moras, sonority, edges, and stress in OT.

1.2.2 OPTIMALITY THEORY AND SYLLABLE STRUCTURE

In addition to contributing to the development of OT, the syllable has benefited from advances in OT. In general terms, three areas of the theory that have proven useful for syllabic theory are

1. In OT, language-specific rules are replaced by universal constraints and language-specific constraint ranking. Consequently, syllable structure is the result of conflicting universal requirements on syllable structure prioritized differently across languages. An important consequence of this is that, by resorting to universal constraints, OT can formalize and account for the similarity of syllabification mechanisms in various languages in a much more principled way than the numerous language-specific syllabification rules of serial phonology. For example, most languages seem to have an *Onset Rule* that attaches one or more consonantal segments to the left of the nucleus. Yet, in order to capture the universal nature of this rule, a derivational model consisting of language-specific rules has to stipulate that the *Onset Rule* is universal. In OT, however, the universal preference for V.CV is the effect of a universal constraint, ONSET, which requires that all syllables have an onset, in combination with a universal dislike for codas captured by the constraint *CODA. Another important contribution of OT to the understanding of syllable structure is that constraints are violable under domination from a more highly ranked constraint. Hence not all languages and all syllables will have onsets—some languages will have onsetless syllables. The prioritizing of conflicting, violable, universal constraints in multiple rankings produces variation in syllable structure and syllabification.

2. In OT, constraints are of two types: those that require preservation of underlying contrasts (faithfulness constraints) and those that favor unmarked structure. Thus, syllable structure (i.e., a syllabified output) is the result of the interaction of universal faithfulness and markedness constraints. ONSET, for example, is a markedness constraint that states that the preferred syllable type is CV. If all syllable markedness constraints were always dominant across languages, languages would exhibit no marked syllable structure and the only syllable type would be CV. However, this is not so, because in order to be useful communication tools, languages need to express a large number of contrasts. In response to this functional need, faithfulness constraints require preservation of input form. Hence, inputs may consist of syllables without onsets. If the corresponding faithfulness constraint (DEP-IO, no epenthesis, or MAX-IO, no deletion) is ranked above markedness, the output and the language will permit onsetless syllables. If markedness is ranked above faithfulness (DEP-IO or MAX-IO), all syllables will have onsets. An important observation brought to light by OT is that when the faithfulness constraint(s) forcing violation of markedness is no longer relevant, unmarked structures will surface (McCarthy and Prince 1994). This phenomenon, known as "the emergence of the unmarked," has been shown to be true in adult phonology as well as in child and second language phonology. In Spanish hypochoristics, for instance, faithfulness to the underlying representation is no longer at stake because hypo-

choristic formation implies deletion by definition. CVC or CG(glide)V syllables, usually tolerated because of the domination of faithfulness over markedness constraints (*CODA, *COMPLEX-NUCLEUS), are truncated to CV when faithfulness is no longer dominant, for example, /daniel/ [daṇiel] > [dáni] 'Daniel' (Colina 1996; Piñeros 2000).

3. OT can satisfactorily explain *conspiracies*. Languages often have several rules that work toward a common goal. For instance, Spanish has a rule of diphthongization (i.e., syllable merger) of high vowels when preceded or followed by another vowel: *mi amigo* [mi̯a.mi.ɣo] 'my friend' (example 1.1). It also has a rule that resyllabifies a word-final consonant to the onset position of a vowel initial word: *tus amigos* [tu.sa.mi.ɣos] 'your friends' (example 1.2).

Example 1.1

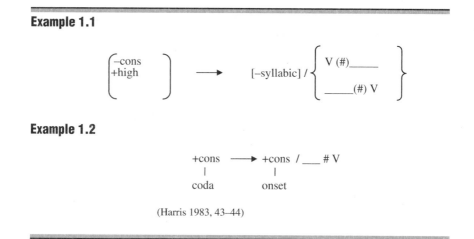

Example 1.2

(Harris 1983, 43–44)

Although not apparent from the format of the rules, examples 1.1 and 1.2 have the elimination of onsetless syllables as a common goal. Serial rules and derivational formalisms have been known to hide the real purpose behind rules, in what is usually referred to as "rule conspiracy" (Kenstowicz and Kisseberth 1979). OT, on the other hand, naturally and elegantly captures this purpose by means of interacting universal constraints. In the examples it is the domination of ONSET over other relevant constraints (e.g., ALIGN-LST, MAX-IOµ) that drives both resyllabification and syllable merger (diphthongization) in the outputs: ONSET satisfaction is obtained by misaligning word and syllable boundaries (ALIGN-LST violation) and by underparsing a mora (MAX-IOµ violation), respectively.

In sum, while syllable structure has been crucial in the development of modern phonology and in particular of OT, OT has in turn, and perhaps to an even greater extent, contributed to advancing our understanding of syllable structure, syllable-related processes, and the role of syllable structure in phonology.

1.3 CURRENT ISSUES IN OPTIMALITY THEORY AND SPANISH PHONOLOGY

Most readers will be familiar with the basics of OT, so I will not offer a detailed introduction to the theory. It is recommended that those who are not familiar with

OT first review Kager's overview (1999). In what follows I examine a few concepts within the theory that are more controversial, possibly less understood by some, or particularly relevant to the Spanish data and the discussion presented in this book. They will be discussed in more detail in the relevant sections of the book.

Correspondence theory and output-to-output constraints. The correspondence theory of faithfulness posits a correspondence relation from the input to the output of each one of its candidates, thus giving rise to IO (input-to-output) constraints. Correspondence can also be established between two outputs, a base and a reduplicant, a base and a truncated form, a base and a morphologically related form, morphologically related forms that are not derived, and lexically related outputs, among others (McCarthy and Prince 1995; Benua 1995; Kenstowicz 1996). The pertinent correspondence relations and constraints are generally referred to as output-to-output (OO), or more specifically, as Base-Reduplicant (BR), Base-Truncated form (BT), Base-Affixed form (BA), Uniform Exponence (UE), and so on, depending on the case. The condition for a non-input based correspondence relation is that the base has to be an independently occurring form of the language that contains a subset of grammatical features of the derived form (Kager 1999, 282). OO constraints become active in the presence of output-to-output correspondence and are ranked separately from their IO counterparts.

OO correspondence relations have been proposed for Spanish for hypochoristics (Colina 1996), vocoids (Colina 1999), plurals (Colina 2006b; Lloret and Mascaró 2006), diminutives (Colina 2003b; Lloret and Mascaró 2006), /s/-aspiration and prefixes (Colina 1997, 2002, 2006c). Faithfulness to the input often results in violations of markedness constraints; yet, when the influence of the input is not present, as in processes such as hypochoristics, truncation, and reduplication, unmarked structure surfaces. OO correspondence captures this fact in a direct manner by the ranking of markedness over OO faithfulness constraints. This phenomenon is usually referred to as "the emergence of the unmarked" (McCarthy and Prince 1994) and can be seen clearly in hypochoristic formation in Spanish: /daniel/ [da.ni̯él] > [da.ni] where the complex nucleus of the second syllable has been reduced to a single one (see Colina 1996).

Lexicon Optimization and Richness of the Base (RoTB) (Prince and Smolensky 1993; Kager 1999; McCarthy 2002). Another important notion within OT is the postulate of Richness of the Base, according to which there exist no restrictions or constraints affecting the input. In other words, the theory is entirely output-based, and the constraints and constraint rankings are sufficient to explain all outputs. This concept is often misunderstood as either questioning the need for underlying representations or entirely eliminating them. RoTB does not mean that no underlying representations are posited; rather, that the phonology must be able to deal with any potential input, selecting only the optimal output. Suppose there is a language X, in which *CODA is undominated. Language X may not have in its vocabulary the word /pat/, yet, when presented with this form, the phonology must be able to explain the output [pa] as the result of the domination of *CODA over MAX-IO.

Then the question arises that, if there is a rich base, which can potentially be anything, how is the learner going to select the correct underlying representation among such a number of possibilities? In absence of any evidence, the proposal is that the learner selects the input that most closely resembles the output. This is the learning strategy known as Lexicon Optimization. It will be shown at several points throughout this book that for the same output, given two possible inputs or more, the parse that most closely resembles the input is the one that incurs fewer violations (its violations will be a proper subset of the violations incurred by alternative underlying representations).

The derivational residue in OT: stratal versus nonstratal OT. Opacity is perhaps the most controversial area within OT (Kiparsky 1973). In derivational terms, I refer to opacity as those situations in which the context for the application of a rule is met but the rule fails to apply; or those in which the rule has applied despite the fact that the input no longer meets the rule's structural description, for example, coda aspiration in onset position in Spanish /las alas/ [la.ha.lah] 'the wings.' These types of data have proved very problematic for OT under an entirely parallel mode of evaluation in which, for instance, a constraint against coda [s] in Spanish should not affect a segment in an onset position, thus predicting the selection of the ill-formed output *[la.sa.lah]. One way to deal with these examples is by means of OO (Identity) constraints or alignment constraints (see chapter 4). Stratal OT (StrOT) (Bermúdez-Otero 1999, 2003, in press) has been proposed by some researchers as another way to address opacity within OT, suggesting that a limited and restricted number of strata are necessary even in OT. In StrOT some constituents in the morphosyntactic structure of a linguistic expression (stem, word, and phrase) define phonological domains; phonological domains may in turn invoke different rankings of the constraint set (CON), which are said to belong to different levels (stem, word, and phrase). In StrOT the output of the stem level constitutes the input to the word level, and the output of the word level serves as input for the phrase level.[2]

A more recent proposal, OT with candidate chains (OT-CC) (McCarthy 2007), accounts for opacity through a synthesis of OT and derivations in which a candidate consists of a surface form and a series of intermediate forms. The combination of derivations and OT proposed by OT-CC appears to be unnecessary to account for the Spanish data (cf. chapter 4); however, McCarthy (2007) argues that some types of opacity (not found in Spanish) cannot be satisfactorily explained on the basis of OO constraints or StrOT.

Variation and constraint ranking. Language variation is a recurrent topic throughout this book, where dialectal variation in a particular set of data is accounted for through variations in constraint ranking. Some examples of this involve coda obstruents (chapter 2), syllable merger in Chicano and Peninsular Spanish (chapter 3), /s/-aspiration (chapter 4), and plurals in standard dialects and in Dominican Spanish (chapter 5).

Nondialectal variation, although also generally explained as the result of differences in constraint rankings, is somewhat more challenging for OT, necessitating additional refinements beyond the notion of constraint re-ranking. One theory of intraspeaker (dialect-internal) variation within OT is partial ordering theory (Reynolds 1994; Anttila and Cho 1998; Nagy and Reynolds 1997; McCarthy 2002 and references therein). Partial ordering theory views a particular grammar as a partial ordering of constraints in which constraints that conflict may be in free ranking with respect to one another, leading to variation in the output. Each input-to-output mapping is obtained by applying a totally ordered hierarchy of constraints that is randomly sampled from the total orderings that are consistent with the grammar.

Another proposal for dealing with variation that does not include unranked constraints is that of Stochastic OT (Boersma and Hayes 2001). Stochastic OT proposes the notion of continuous ranking scales, where constraints are said to be associated with ranges of values rather than with single points. Variation is the result of overlapping ranges. Stochastic OT appears to have the potential to

explain complex types of noncategorical variation, possibly even the type of sociolinguistic variation revealed by phenomena like /s/-aspiration or intervocalic /d/
deletion in Spanish. I will return to this topic in chapter 6.

1.4 THE PHONOLOGICAL SYSTEM OF SPANISH: FEATURAL REPRESENTATION

I adopt the hierachical organization of features in example 1.3 (Clements 1985;
Sagey 1986; Halle 1995; Hualde 1989a; Núñez-Cedeño and Morales-Front
1999). Features not relevant for the discussion in this book are not mentioned.

The geometrical organization of features in example 1.3 differs from that in
Hualde (1989a) by placing [consonantal] and [sonorant] directly under the root
node. The argument for this is that these features are major class features not
affected by assimilation in Spanish, as well in other languages. The placement of
[continuant] and [lateral] is controversial. For Spanish, Núñez-Cedeño and
Morales-Front (1999) place these two features under the root note, whereas
Hualde (1989a) puts them under the supralaryngeal node, along with all manner
features. The distinction has no bearing on the analyses presented, so I will not
belabor the point.

The relevant phonemes and allophones of Spanish are introduced along
with the data throughout the book. Those readers who would like an overview of
the sounds of Spanish are referred to Hualde (2005, 8–9). The phonetic symbols
used throughout follow the International Phonetic Alphabet (IPA) except for the
following:

  [y] = palatal fricative

  [j] [w] = onset (nonmoraic) high vocoids preceded by a tautosyllabic consonant

  [i̯] [u̯] = high glides parsed in the nucleus or in the rhyme

  [č] = voiceless alveopalatal affricate

1.5 OVERVIEW OF THE BOOK

In addition to this introduction, the book contains four chapters and a conclusion
(chapter 6).

Chapter 2 presents an account of the basic syllable types of Spanish from an
optimality-theoretic perspective and compares it to rule-based models. The analysis proposed also captures generalizations about the specific segments parsed in
each syllabic position in terms of sonority hierarchies and syllabic markedness
constraints, examining and explaining segmental restrictions on the onset,
nucleus, and coda. The topics of diphthongs, hiatuses, and the status of glides are
included, as well as coda neutralization phenomena in various dialects. Preservation of point of articulation in coda obstruents, nasal assimilation, word-final
codas, and the selection of the target of deletion in complex codas are additional
phenomena covered in this chapter.

Chapter 3 reviews syllabification across words, focusing on consonant resyllabification and syllable merger (diphthongization). A derivational account of
resyllabification is summarized and compared to an optimality-theoretic account.

Example 1.3

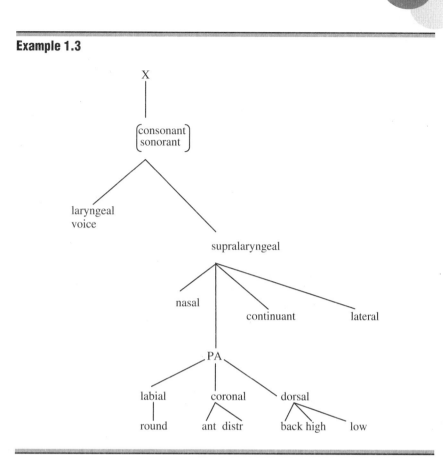

The OT account is shown to bring forth an important insight regarding resyllabification, namely, that alignment of the syllable with the word can be sacrificed in order to provide an onset for a vowel-initial word. A significant part of this chapter deals with OT analyses of syllable mergers in Peninsular and Chicano. The proposed analyses are shown to be able to incorporate dialectal differences (e.g., gliding of mid vowels versus raising of mid vowels; gliding of only the first vowel in the sequence versus gliding of the least sonorous vowel) in a direct way not available to derivational analyses.

Chapter 4 reviews derivational proposals for domain of syllabification and the interaction of syllabification with morphological operations, such as suffixation, prefixation, and compounding. An OT account is presented that obviates the need to define domain of syllabification through the use of general mechanisms, namely, universal constraints and language-specific ranking previously motivated for the language. No extrinsic ordering of phonological rules and morphological operations rules is necessary either.

Chapter 5 focuses on epenthesis and deletion phenomena, such as those traditionally known as final epenthesis, plural epenthesis (in standard and nonstandard dialects), initial epenthesis, diminutive epenthesis, and deletion and neutralization of coda consonants. OT accounts are proposed and compared with serial analyses. Some of the innovative proposals presented are:

- There is no active process of final epenthesis, only word-final coda deletion or neutralization.

- Plural epenthesis reflects the emergence of the unmarked with respect to the constraint against coda consonants (*CODA).

- Plural epenthesis is shown to account for pluralization in general dialects and in other dialects, like Dominican Spanish (double plurals). In Dominican, double plurals are argued to result from normal pluralization mechanisms in conjunction with restrictions on coda obstruents (/s/-deletion and -aspiration) and the need for overt realization of morphemes in prominent positions.

NOTES

1. *st-* is not an acceptable onset cluster in Spanish.
2. Other accounts of opacity effects within OT using a modular architecture similar to that of Lexical Phonology are proposed by Kiparsky (2003). See also McCarthy's discussion of the topic (2002, 185) for additional references.

2

Syllable Types and Phonotactics

2.1 BASIC SYLLABLE TYPES

In purely descriptive terms, most dialects of Spanish have the syllable types in example 2.1:

Example 2.1   **Basic syllable types in Spanish**

a.	V	*a*.la	'wing'
b.	CV	a.*la*	'wing'
c.	CVC	*pan*	'bread'
	CVG	*soy*	'I am'
d.	VC	*un*	'one'
	VG	h*ay*[1]	'there is'
e.	CCV	*flo*.tar	'float'
f.	CCVC	*tren*	'train'
	CCVG	*plei*.te.ar	'to fight'
g.	VCC	*ins*.truir	'instruct'
	VGC	*aus*.tral	'austral'
h.	CVCC	*pers*.pec.tiva	'perspective'
	CVGC	*caus*.ti.co	'caustic'
i.	CCVCC	*trans*.por.te	'transportation'
	CCVGC	*claus*.tro	'cloister'

Postvocalic glides can follow the nucleus, as in the second examples in (c, d, f, g, h, i); prevocalic glides are also possible as long as the entire rhyme does not contain more than three segments; that is, prevocalic glides are acceptable in open syllables and in syllables closed by a single consonant or glide (Harris 1983). Note that the term *glide* is used in this book as a convenient label to refer to a surface [–syllabic] vocoid that either accompanies a vowel in the nucleus (parsed as part of a complex nucleus) or is parsed in a syllable margin; use of the term *glide* in this fashion is neutral with regard to the phonemic or nonphonemic status of these segments in Spanish, a rather controversial matter (see below on the diphthong/hiatus contrast). The term *vocoid* is also used to mean a vowel or glide, that is, a [–consonantal] segment that could be [+syllabic] or [–syllabic].

In OT, the possible syllable types for any one language (including Spanish) are the result of the interaction of universal violable constraints. Constraints are of two types: markedness and faithfulness. Markedness constraints favor unmarked structures over marked ones, and faithfulness constraints try to preserve lexical contrast through congruity of outputs to their inputs. There is a limited number of constraints present in all languages, which explains why possible syllable types constitute a limited inventory from which all languages draw their syllable templates. Given these assumptions about the universal nature of constraints, the analyst must demonstrate that the relevant constraints are truly universal (see Kager 1999 for detailed justification).

A universal of syllable typology is that all languages prefer syllables that start with a consonant (onset) and end in a vowel, CV thus being the preferred, unmarked syllable type. While some languages allow codas, none requires them; similarly, some languages allow onsetless syllables, but none forbids onsets. In sum, there are no languages that require codas and forbid onsets.[2] Complex syllabic constituents are universally more marked than singletons: There is no language that has complex onsets, codas, or nuclei and lacks single segment onsets, codas, and nuclei. The reverse is also true: There exist languages that ban complex subsyllabic components but allow singletons. Thus, OT argues for the syllabic markedness universal constraints in examples 2.2 and 2.3:

Example 2.2

ONSET: No vowel-initial syllables.

*CODA: Syllables cannot end in a coda.

Example 2.3

*COMPLEX ONSET: No more than one segment in the onset.

*COMPLEX CODA: No more than one segment in the coda.

*COMPLEX NUCLEUS: No more than one segment in the nucleus.

On the basis of proposals by Itô and Mester (1994) and McCarthy and Prince (1993a), Piñeros (2001) formulates ONSET and *CODA in terms of alignment, as in (a) and (b) in example 2.4, respectively:

Example 2.4

a. ALIGN-L(σ,C): Every syllable must have a consonant at its left edge.

b. ALIGN-R(σ,V): Every syllable must have a vowel at its right edge.

> In addition to the alignment version of ONSET and *CODA in example 2.4
> (syllable-to-segment alignment), Piñeros introduces their segment-to-syllable
> counterparts:

Example 2.5

a. ALIGN-L(C,σ): Every consonant must be aligned with the left edge of the syllable.

b. ALIGN-R(V,σ): Every vowel must be aligned with the right edge of the syllable.

> The segment-to-syllable alignment constraints in example 2.5 regulate seg-
> ment distribution over the syllable, capturing the consonantal preference for
> the onset and the preference of vowels for the right edge of a syllable.
>
> I am not aware of the existence of any empirical arguments in favor of the align-
> ment over the markedness proposal, so I take the alignment and non-alignment
> versions of the constraints to represent alternative ways of formalizing the same
> content. I use the ONSET and *CODA labels because of typographical conve-
> nience and because they are perhaps better known in the literature. I will return
> to this topic in section 2.2.

As far as faithfulness, the relevant constraints in example 2.6 refer to the need to
avoid deletion (MAX-IO) and epenthesis (DEP-IO) of input segments:

Example 2.6   Basic segmental faithfulness constraints

MAX-IO: Every segment present in the input must have a correspondent in the
output.[3]

DEP-IO: Every segment present in the output must have a correspondent in the
input.

FAITH: (cover term for all faithfulness constraints)

Spanish allows onsetless syllables as well as syllable codas. Therefore, ONSET and
*CODA must be dominated by faithfulness constraints: FAITH >> ONSET, *CODA.

   In example 2.7, candidates with epenthesis and deletion violate the top-
ranked FAITH because they alter the input representation either by inserting an
element that is not present in the input (epenthesis, (b)) or deleting an input
phone (d). (a) and (c) violate ONSET on account of one and two onsetless syllables respectively. By syllabifying the intervocalic consonant with the second
vowel, (a) incurs only one ONSET violation; it also avoids the *CODA mark of (c).

Example 2.7   /ala/ [a.la] 'wing'

	FAITH	ONSET	*CODA
a. ☞ a.la		*	
b. ta.la	*!		
c. al.a		**!	*
d. la	*!		

Example 2.8   /poner/ [po.ner] 'put'

	FAITH	ONSET	*CODA
a. ☞ po.ner			*
b. po.ne.ɾe	*!		
c. pon.er		*!	**
d. po.ne	*!		

Therefore, although not perfect, (a), with only one ONSET violation, is the optimal candidate and the output.

Evaluation proceeds similarly in example 2.8 in which (a), [poner][4], is the best candidate because (b), [ponere], attempts to get rid of the coda consonant through epenthesis and violates the more highly ranked FAITH. (d) encounters the same fate given that there is deletion of the final consonant (a consonant present in the input is absent in the output). Finally, (c) incurs an unnecessary violation of ONSET and is therefore eliminated. Note that it could be argued that word-initial onsetless syllables (*a.la*) are not the result of faithfulness, but the effect of an alignment constraint that bans insertion in word-initial position.

Example 2.9

ALIGN-L: The left edge of the grammatical word coincides with the left edge of the prosodic word (Kager 1999, 111).

However, ALIGN-L cannot be the constraint responsible for the well-formedness of onsetless syllables in Spanish (to the exclusion of faithfulness), as onsetless syllables are also possible in word-internal position, *ma.re.a* 'tide,' *ve.o* 'I see.'

As mentioned above, Spanish also allows complex onsets and codas, which suggests that FAITH dominates the markedness constraints prohibiting onset and coda clusters, *COMPLEX ONSET and *COMPLEX CODA.

Onset maximization

*CODA in turn must dominate *COMPLEX ONSET given that word-internal onset clusters are preferred to the parsing of the consonants in the coda and the onset of two adjacent syllables, as in example 2.13 (cf. *onset maximization* in derivational approaches).

Figures 2.1 and 2.2 show how a derivational account explains onset preference and onset maximization (for an alternative derivational account see Harris 1983). An Onset Rule ordered before a Coda Rule accounts for the syllabification of an intervocalic consonant with the second vowel (V.CV). This is captured in OT through the presence of the universal nonconflicting constraints ONSET and *CODA.

Example 2.10

FAITH >> *COMPLEX ONSET, *COMPLEX CODA

Example 2.11 /broma/ [bɾo.ma] 'joke'

	FAITH	*COMPLEX ONSET
a. ☞ bɾo.ma		*
b. ɾo.ma	*!	
c. be.ɾo.ma	*!	

Example 2.12 /insto/ [ins.to] 'I urge'

	FAITH	*COMPLEX CODA
a. ☞ ins.to		*
b. in.to	*!	
c. is.to	*!	
d. i.nes.to	*!	
e. in.se.to	*!	

Example 2.13 /potro/ [po.tɾo] 'young horse'

	*CODA	*COMPLEX ONSET
a. ☞ po.tɾo		*
b. pot.ɾo	*!	

Derivational approaches explain onset cluster preference by ordering a Complex Onset Rule ("attach a second consonant to the left of the onset") before the Coda Rule, which says, "Adjoin a coda to the right of the nucleus" (Hualde 1991) (see chapter 3 for more detail on syllabification rules in derivational approaches to syllabification). Yet, as seen in figures 2.1 and 2.2, rule ordering in itself is not sufficient as not all consonants are acceptable clusters. Rule 4 in figure 2.2 must be prevented from applying to avoid an ill-formed cluster *[nsa]. A stipulation, condition, or filter must be added so that the Complex Onset Rule applies only when the resulting cluster would be well-formed. This solution is problematic because the condition cannot be directly incorporated into the rule-based approach.

As will be shown in section 2.2, OT can incorporate segmental restrictions through markedness constraints and constraint ranking. Notice also that because onset maximization is the result of the language-specific ranking of universal constraints, the OT account is superior to derivational ones in which language-specific rules (suspiciously similar in many languages) apply in a language-specific order. Derivational models in which rules are language-specific cannot explain why most languages seem to have Onset and Complex Onset Rules, unless universal rules were to be proposed alongside language-specific ones. This maneuver complicates the theory unnecessarily as universal rules would be required in addition to language-specific rule ordering and language-specific rules.

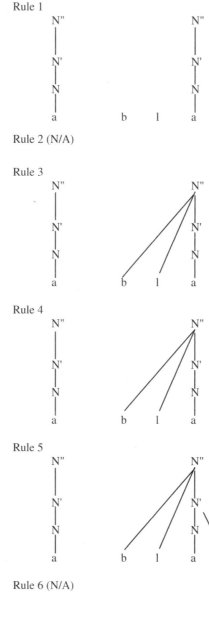

Spanish syllabification rules
(Hualde 1991)[5]

Rule 1

1. Node projection:
Mark vowels as syllable heads,
create N nodes, and project N'
and N" nodes.

Rule 2 (N/A)

2. Complex nucleus:
Adjoin a prevocalic glide
under the N" node.

Rule 3

3. CV rule:
Adjoin a consonant to the left of
the nucleus under the N" node.

Rule 4

4. Complex onset:
Adjoin a second consonant under
the N" node if the result would
be a permissible onset cluster
(stop or /f/ + liquid, except */dl/
and (*) /tl/).

Rule 5

5. Coda rule:
Adjoin a segment to the right
of the nucleus under N'.

Rule 6 (N/A)

6. Complex coda:
Adjoin a consonant to the right
of a glide under N'.

Rule 7 (N/A)

7. /s/-Adjunction: Adjoin /s/
under N'.

Figure 2.1 Onset maximization.

Templatic syllabification accounts associate segments to a language-specific
syllabic template (Itô 1986, 1989; Crowhurst 1992), such as CCVCC. Association of segments to the syllabic template can proceed from right to left and
from left to right. The directionality of syllabification (right to left in Spanish) accounts for onset maximization. In addition to the problem mentioned

Rule 1

Rule 2 (N/A)

Rule 3

Rule 4 (N/A)

Rule 5

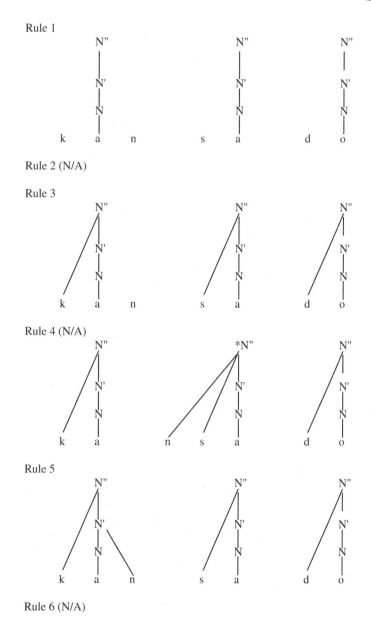

Rule 6 (N/A)

Rule 7 (N/A)

Figure 2.2 No onset maximization

above regarding well-formedness of complex onsets, templatic accounts of Spanish syllabification have the additional complication of requiring level-specific directionality: In other words, for some analyses, directionality of syllabification must be different for the lexical and postlexical level. For instance, in some analyses, association to a CCVCC template must be from left to right postlexically in order to obtain epenthesis to the right of the cluster in [ma.ðɾe] versus *[ma.ðeɾ] 'mother'; however, lexically, onset maximization requires right to left syllabification: [a.βlar] versus *[aβ.lar] 'to talk' (Crowhurst 1992, 239).

Complex nuclei: diphthongs

Spanish allows prevocalic and postvocalic glides. Postvocalic glides are in the coda (Hualde 1991) and prevocalic glides are part of the nucleus (not onset), which suggests that *COMPLEX NUCLEUS must be violated in the case of rising diphthongs (e.g., /pierde/ [pi̯érðe]), and *CODA or *COMPLEX CODA must be violated in the case of falling diphthongs. I return to this topic in section 2.2.1.

Example 2.14 shows a summary of the constraints and constraint rankings proposed so far, including a Hasse diagram in which ranking relations are represented by means of straight lines connecting dominating and dominated constraints. Constraints not connected by lines are not crucially ranked.

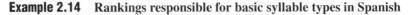

Example 2.14   **Rankings responsible for basic syllable types in Spanish**

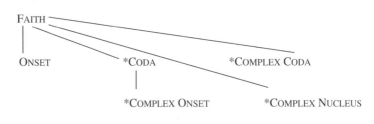

Descriptive facts	Ranking
coda clusters	FAITH >> *COMPLEX CODA
complex nuclei	FAITH >> *COMPLEX NUCLEUS
onset maximization	*CODA >> *COMPLEX ONSET
onsetless syllables	FAITH >> ONSET
V.CV	ONSET, *CODA

In sum, one important advantage of an OT account of the basic syllabic typology of Spanish is that it is obtained by permutations of a few basic universal constraints rather than a listing of syllable types or language-specific templates. In other words, the universal nature of constraints exhibits greater explanatory power than the purely descriptive list given in example 2.1 or the language-specific rules and templates of derivational accounts.

2.2 SEGMENTS AND THE SYLLABLE

Despite its general explanatory adequacy and ability to account for basic syllable types and templates, careful consideration reveals that the general ranking in example 2.14 is not sufficient to account for all the facts. Not all consonant clusters in VCCV sequences are parsed in the same syllable, *par.te* **pa.rte* 'part'; similarly, although Spanish allows consonants in the coda, not all codas are acceptable in all dialects, *club* *[klub] 'club.' In addition, not all consonants can fill C positions; for instance, *[npa] is not an acceptable syllable despite the ranking FAITH >> *COMPLEX ONSET. It is therefore obvious that syllabic constraints that refer to subsyllabic components and number of segments are not sufficient. Minimally, generalizations about the specific segments parsed in each of those positions must be accounted for, as well as the order of segments within the syllable. In broad terms, two areas need to be addressed: sonority (section 2.2.1) and the parsing of segment types in subsyllabic constituents (section 2.2.2).

2.2.1 THE SONORITY CONTOUR

Syllables exhibit a contour based on the universal sonority scale in example 2.15, according to which the syllable rises in sonority towards the nucleus (the most sonorous point) and then decreases towards the coda (Clements 1990; Sonority Sequencing Principle). Segments are ranked according to sonority in the universal sonority scale:

Example 2.15

Obstruents < Nasals < Liquids < Glides < Vowels

For Spanish, Martínez-Gil (1996, 1997) has proposed a subset of distinctions that separates obstruents into stops and fricatives:

Example 2.16

Stops < Fricatives < Nasals < Liquids < Glides < Vowels

In most dialects of Spanish, stops, fricatives, and nasals are possible onsets, but glides and vowels are not. Only vowels are possible nuclei (glides are well-formed in prevocalic position). All segment types can be parsed in the coda except for vowels.

Pre-OT models of phonology express these facts in the form of descriptive generalizations, language-specific rules ("mark vowels as syllable heads"), or restrictions on the application of certain rules (Harris 1983, 1989a, 1989b; Hualde 1991, 1999a). Additional rules are required to express repair mechanisms. The role of sonority is recognized, but sonority scales constitute separate, external mechanisms and are not formalized into the theory.

Sonority as harmonic alignment of prominence scales

An optimality-theoretic framework, however, captures the generalizations that relate syllabic positions with sonority classes in a straightforward manner by means of universal scales and constraint hierarchies. The syllable position prominence scale (Nucleus > Coda > Onset) can easily be combined with the sonority scale (via harmonic alignment) to produce a constraint hierarchy (McCarthy 2002, 21). The most prominent syllable position (Nucleus) is aligned with the most sonorous segment (Vowel) and vice versa, so that the most highly ranked constraint is the one that penalizes parsing the most sonorous segment in the least prominent position.

Example 2.17 **Harmonic alignment of prominence scales (sonority and syllabic prominence)**

Nucleus > . . . . . > Onset

Vowel > . . . . . > Obstruent

The ranking of faithfulness constraints with regard to the sonority scale (hierarchy of markedness constraints) determines whether violations can be forced through

Example 2.18   **Constraint hierarchy**

*NUC/obstruent >> . . . . >> *NUC/vowel

*ONSET/vowel >> . . . . >> *ONSET/obstruent

domination, thus explaining language variation (language-specific ranking) in an otherwise universally fixed hierarchy. The fact that in Spanish only a vowel can be the sole segment in the nucleus is the result of the ranking in example 2.19, as a vowel will always be a better nucleus than a glide (i.e., *NUC/glide dominates *NUC/vowel), and the constraints against parsing other non-vocalic segments in the nucleus dominate FAITH.

Example 2.19   **Segment types in the nucleus**

*NUC/obstruent >> *NUC/nasal >> *NUC/liquid >> FAITH >> *NUC/glide >> *NUC/vowel

This is not the case in languages that allow syllabic liquids and nasals, like English. In English a liquid or nasal can serve as a syllable nucleus if no vowel is available. The domination of FAITH over *NUC/nasal >> *NUC/liquid guarantees the parsing of a nasal or liquid in the nucleus rather than deletion or vowel epenthesis.

Example 2.20

*NUC/obstruent >> FAITH >> *NUC/nasal >> *NUC/liquid >> *NUC/glide >> *NUC/vowel

With respect to the onset position, Spanish sonorants and obstruents can appear in the onset, but obstruents are preferred. Vowels cannot be in the onset and therefore *ONSET/vowel must be undominated, as in example 2.21. In many dialects glides are also banned from the onset, motivating their ranking in example 2.21. I return to the topic of glides later in this chapter.

Example 2.21   **Segment types in the onset**

*ONSET/vowel >> *ONSET/glide >> FAITH >> *ONSET/liquid >> *ONSET/nasal >> *ONSET/obstruent

In the coda, as sonority decreases from the nucleus, more sonorous sonorants are preferred to obstruents as shown in example 2.22.

The domination of FAITH over the other constraints reflects the fact that in some dialects of Spanish all segments, except for vowels, can appear in the coda. Dialectal variation in this regard usually corresponds to variation in the ranking of FAITH with regard to the other constraints (see below for more on this topic). Vowels are more sonorous than glides, and therefore *CODA/vowel should be the lowest ranked constraint in example 2.22. Yet, since *CODA/vowel is also domi-

Example 2.22   Segment types in the coda

FAITH >> *CODA/obstruent >> *CODA/nasal >> *CODA/liquid >>
*CODA/glide >> *CODA/vowel

nated by FAITH, vowels should be well-formed in the coda. The explanation for this apparent conundrum rests in that, while there is a universal constraint that bans codas (*CODA), there is none that prohibits nuclei; since vowels are the best possible nuclei (low ranking of *NUC/vowel), vowels will always be parsed in the nucleus and never in the coda.

> In an alignment format (Itô and Mester 1994; McCarthy and Prince 1993a), the onset and coda markedness hierarchies in examples 2.21 and 2.22 correspond to the hierarchy ALIGN-L(Obstruent,σ) >> ALIGN-L(Nasal,σ) >> ALIGN-L(Liquid,σ) (Piñeros 2001). Piñeros does not contain separate hierarchies for the onset and the coda, on the assumption that all consonants try to align with the onset position (thus eliminating the need for a separate *CODA constraint). The difficulty with Piñeros's proposal is that it does not allow for coda glides, which are in fact much better aligned with the coda than with the onset in Spanish. Piñeros assumes that postvocalic glides are part of the nucleus (see below for arguments that support their parsing in the coda).

In Spanish, postconsonantal prevocalic glides are part of the nucleus and postvocalic glides are normally considered to be in the coda.

Parsing of prevocalic glides

> The specific parse attributed to prevocalic glides has important consequences for all areas of phonology, in particular for experimental research in acquisition and other related areas, given that mistaken assumptions would have serious consequences for experimental design and data collection. Solid arguments exist in favor of the nuclear status of prevocalic glides:
>
> (a) In the Montañés dialects of Cantabrian Spanish mid vowels are raised to high if the stressed syllable contains a high vowel ([kuxiría] 'I would take' versus [koxeré] 'I will take'), or a prevocalic glide ([kuxi̯eɾa] 'I took' (subjunctive)). Since the trigger of harmonization must be stressed, prevocalic glides must bear stress, and therefore (assuming that stress is assigned to nuclei) prevocalic glides must be part of the nucleus (Hualde 1991, 479). Postvocalic glides do not trigger mid vowel raising ([afloxe̯is] 'you-plural loosen' (subjunctive)) and must therefore be in the coda.
>
> (b) A rhyme in Spanish can contain at most three segments; a syllable can have up to five segments, when two of those are in the onset (Harris 1983). On the basis of those facts, the only way to explain the ill-formedness of the hypothetical *muersto versus cliente 'client' is to assume that the prevocalic glide in *muersto is in the rhyme (thus in the nucleus, given its prevocalic position) (Harris 1983).
>
> (c) Spanish has one well-known restriction on identical voicoids in the rhyme: *ii, *uu, *ji, *ij, *wu, *uw (Harris 1983). Thus, the only way to account for the ill-formedness of two high front segments in *escritori-ito

'desk' (diminutive) is to assume that they are both in the rhyme (nucleus), rather than in the onset and rhyme. The form of *tramoy-ista* 'trickster' is acceptable because the first high segment occupies the onset, as demonstrated by its consonantization (Harris and Kaisse 1999, 128)

| *tramoy-a* | 'trick' | *tramoy-ista* | 'trickster' |
| *escritori-o* | 'desk' | **escritoriito, escritorito* | 'desk-DIM' |

(d) In hypochoristic formation, segments parsed in the onset cannot become nuclear in the hypochoristic (e.g., *Petronio, Petro *Petr*). Prevocalic glides, however, are copied as a full vowel in nuclear position, as in [da.nįél] [dani] (Colina 1996; Núñez-Cedeño and Morales-Front 1999).

The syllabic affiliation of postvocalic glides is not as problematic as that of prevocalic glides and, as a result, it has not received as much attention. Whether they are part of the nucleus or the coda, postvocalic glides are in the rhyme and have similar status regarding other phonological processes such as stress computation. A strong argument in favor of the coda affiliation of postvocalic glides is related to the fact that only sonorants or [s] are allowed after a coda glide, *vein.te* 'twenty,' *béis.bol* 'baseball.' Since coda obstruents other than [s] are acceptable in many varieties of Spanish, *ob.soleto* 'obsolete,' *dig.no* 'worthy' (see section 2.2.2), the only way to account for their ill-formedness after a glide is to assume that the glide is the first segment of the coda and the restrictions on the consonant following it are in fact restrictions on coda clusters.

Complex nuclei and prevocalic glides

Given their nuclear status, prevocalic glides incur a *COMPLEX NUCLEUS violation as in (a) in example 2.24, in addition to a violation of *NUC/glide. This is done in order to avoid violating the more highly ranked ONSET, as in (b).

Example 2.23

*ONSET/glide, ONSET >> *COMPLEX NUCLEUS, *NUC/glide

Example 2.24   /pierde/ [pįér.ðe] 'he loses'

	*ONSET/glide	ONSET	*COMPLEX NUCLEUS	*NUC/glide
a. ☞ pįér.ðe			*	*
b. pi.ér.ðe		*!		
c. pjér.ðe	*!			

The undominated constraint *ONSET/glide guarantees that the glide is not parsed in the onset in (c) of example 2.24.[6] [j] is used in (c) and in the rest of this chapter to represent an onset glide, thus graphically distinguishing it from a nuclear glide, as in (a). Nuclear or coda glides are represented with a diacritic under the vowel, as in (a). Glides cannot be parsed as the sole segment in the nucleus. However, no additional constraint is necessary at this point since glides are in the nucleus only under ONSET domination; therefore, the resulting glide is always preceded or followed by a vowel.

The careful reader will have noticed that the tableau in example 2.24 makes no mention of moraic structure. Assuming that vowels are underlyingly specified as moraic, for an underlying vowel to be parsed as part of a complex nucleus and also satisfy ONSET, its input mora must not be present in the output, thus incurring a violation of FAITH, or more specifically MAX-IOμ (a mora present in the input must have a correspondent in the output) (example 2.25).

Example 2.25   Diphthongization

*ONSET/glide, ONSET >> *COMPLEX NUCLEUS, *NUC/glide, MAX-IOμ

Despite the working assumption that vowels are underlyingly specified as moraic, nothing in the analysis presented here hinges upon that. Alternatively, a constraint requiring the presence of one moraic segment in the nucleus and its domination over DEP-IOμ (a mora in the output must have a correspondent in the input) would select an output in which the nucleus contains a vowel associated with a mora. In example 2.24 this would be [e] as it is the segment with greatest sonority. The high vocoid would be non-moraic and parsed in the nucleus as the result of trying to avoid violations of the highly ranked *ONSET/glide and ONSET. A third possibility of analysis is one in which no moraic information is present in the underlying representation (except for segments lexically marked as such, like exceptional hiatuses), since Spanish does not make use of the distinction between short and long segments (i.e., geminate consonants versus singletons, long versus short vowels). Association of segments to moras would be determined by the constraints and constraint ranking: a constraint requiring syllables to have at least one mora and a hierarchy of constraints like the one in example 2.20 that would select the best segment for moraic association.

The idea that moraic structure in Spanish can be determined through the constraints and constraint ranking is allowed in OT under the postulate of Richness of the Base (RoTB) (McCarthy 2002). According to RoTB, the phonology places no restrictions on the form of underlying representations, as it is the constraints and constraint ranking that are entirely responsible for the selection of the optimal candidate. In other words, the correct output will be selected by the constraint hierarchy independently of the form of the underlying representation. Additional examples of the implications of RoTB for an OT analysis of the phonology of Spanish will be presented throughout this volume (cf. for instance, examples 2.44 and 2.45).

Is Spanish quantity sensitive?

Prevocalic and postvocalic diphthongs raise some interesting questions regarding their moraic status (Harris 1983; Carreira 1988; Rosenthall 1994). Harris notes that prevocalic glides behave like postvocalic ones in that they are incompatible with antepenultimate stress (branching condition), thus suggesting moraicity and quantity-sensitive status for Spanish (like heavy syllables, they attract stress). Yet, whether Spanish can be considered quantity sensitive is still an open question, as shown by work that argues that the restrictions on antepenultimate stress could be the result of a historical gap (no such forms existed in Latin, and Spanish kept lexical stress in the same position it had in Latin) and not a true restriction on stress computation

(Roca 1988; Hualde 1999b). This is particularly relevant to rising diphthongs, given that many of these result from the diphthongization of a Latin
open mid vowel in a stressed position. Postvocalic glides also differ from
prevocalic ones in that, independently of their syllabicity, they can acquire a
mora through Weight-by-Position.[7] In other words, there exists no clear evidence that the lack of antepenultimate stress with a branching penultimate
responds to quantity sensitivity in Spanish and not to a gap in the lexicon (for
historical reasons); therefore, the analysis of prevocalic and postvocalic
glides as nonmoraic vocoids is well supported.

**Diphthong-
hiatus contrast**

Some Spanish dialects have a lexical contrast between diphthongs and
hiatus, *Luí.sa* versus *Su.í.za* 'Switzerland' (Hualde 1997, 1999b, 2002;
Colina 1999). In a limited number of examples, a hiatus is found instead
of the expected diphthong, thus giving rise to a few near-minimal contrasts like the one above. Some hiatuses can be explained through (a) anal-
ogy, when a high vocoid is stressed in a morphologically related word
(e.g., *v*[i.á.]*ble* 'viable,' cf. *vía* 'way'); or (b) the presence of an interven-
ing morphological boundary, such as a prefix or suffix (*bi-, -oso, -al, -ario*),
as in *man*[u.a]*l* 'manual.' The remaining cases constitute a restricted list
that must be marked as exceptional in the lexicon, despite the presence of
some tendencies, such as hiatus being favored after a word initial trill and
disfavored after a velar (Hualde 1999b). In sum, I subscribe to work by
Hualde (1997, 1999b) and Roca (1991, 1997, 2006) that argues that these
contrasts are lexically determined, and therefore, Spanish does not have an
underlying contrast between glides and vowels (contra Harris 1969,
1989a; Hualde 1991, 1994). Some of the arguments in favor of the contrast are crucially dependent on rule ordering, for instance, for */sá.u.ri.o/
[sáu̯.ri̯o] 'saurus' not to violate the three-syllable window, one of the two
glides needs to be underlying (Roca 2006). This argument, however, loses its
strength in a parallel model in which the output [sáu̯.ri̯o] is stressed on the
penultimate syllable and does not violate the three-syllable window (Hualde
1999b).

**Onset
strengthening**

Given the high ranking of *ONSET/glide in most dialects, glides cannot be parsed
in the onset. However, an underlying vocoid can be forced into the onset (thus
satisfying ONSET) through faithfulness violations of MAX-IOμ and IDENT(cons)
(e.g., /kom-iendo/ [ko.mi̯én̯.do] 'eat-gerund' versus /kre-iendo/ [kre.yen̯.do]
'believe-gerund').

Example 2.26

IDENT(cons): A segment's input specification for the feature [consonantal] must
match that of the output.[8]

Example 2.27 Onset strengthening

*ONSET/glide, ONSET >> MAX-IOμ, IDENT(cons)

Example 2.28 shows that the process traditionally known as onset strengthening,
in which a high vocoid in the onset becomes a palatal fricative, is simply the
result of trying to satisfy ONSET while also avoiding violations of the highly

Example 2.28 /kre-iendo/ [kɾe.yen̦.do]

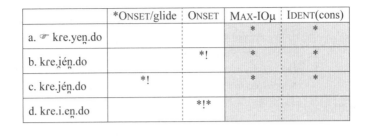

	*ONSET/glide	ONSET	MAX-IOμ	IDENT(cons)
a. ☞ kɾe.yen̦.do			*	*
b. kɾe.i̯én̦.do		*!	*	*
c. kɾe.jén̦.do	*!		*	*
d. kɾe.i.en̦.do		*!*		

ranked markedness constraint that penalizes glides in the onset (*ONSET/glide).
Faithfulness violations are preferred. Parsing the glide in the onset (c) or in the
nucleus (b) incurs violations of top-ranked *ONSET/glide and ONSET. A candidate like (d), in which /i/ is a vowel, is ruled out because of two ONSET violations.
The fricative in (a) is a better option since, by changing its stricture and underparsing a mora, it only violates the low-ranked faithfulness constraints
IDENT(cons) and MAX-IOμ.

   An OT analysis of this kind, because of its parallel nature, does not encoun-
ter the problems of causality faced by derivational, serial models. Serial analyses
of onset strengthening are indeterminate as to whether a glide becomes an
obstruent after it has moved into the onset position, or whether it moves to the
onset as a result of its becoming an obstruent and no longer being acceptable in
the nucleus (Hualde 1991).

> A similar OT analysis of onset strengthening can be found in Roca (2005).
> Under the view that there are no glides in Spanish (Roca 1997), Roca's anal-
> ysis relies on the constraint *H/O (no high vowels in the onset) instead of
> *ONSET/glide. The crucial difference between Roca's and the current analy-
> sis rests in that his does away with the notion of glide. The present analysis
> argues that regardless of the phonemic status of glides in Spanish, possible
> output candidates with a glide (i.e., a nonsyllabic, nonconsonantal vocoid)
> need to be evaluated and ruled out. Furthermore, since the postulate of Rich-
> ness of the Base does not allow any restrictions on the form of the UR, there
> must be some constraint that rules out this segment in the output, indepen-
> dently of the shape of the phonemic inventory of Spanish.

> It was mentioned above that most dialects of Spanish have onset strength-
> ening, due to the prohibition against onset glides (i.e., nonconsonantal
> segments in the onset). However, some dialects, including some spoken in
> the southwestern United States, do not have onset strengthening. Instead,
> they allow onset glides, as in [ma.jo] 'May' (Canfield 1981; Alvar 1996).
> These facts suggest the ranking ONSET >> *ONSET/glide, IDENT(cons) for
> the relevant dialects.

As seen above in examples 2.25, 2.27, and 2.28, moraic structure interacts with
syllabic constituency and the sonority hierarchy ranking. Cross-linguistically,
nuclei are always moraic, onsets always nonmoraic, and codas can be moraic or

nonmoraic. Faithfulness (MAX-IOμ, IDENT(cons)) and markedness violations (*COMPLEX NUCLEUS) can be incurred under pressure from more highly ranked constraints (e.g., ONSET). In Spanish, high vocoids become fricatives, and complex nuclei and codas (vowel + glide, glide + vowel) are allowed to avoid onset violations, for example, in diphthongization in *diario* [di̯a.ri̯o] 'diary' and onset strengthening in example 2.28. A complete account of these processes, however, also needs to explain the selection of the nonmoraic vocoid. While derivational models simply refer to the degree of sonority (the least sonorous vocoid is the one that becomes a glide or is the least likely to be associated with a mora), an OT analysis can elegantly formalize this generalization by means of a constraint hierarchy based on the universal sonority scale, in which low vowels are the most sonorous, and high vowels are the least sonorous.

Accounting for the nonmoraic part of a diphthong

In example 2.29b all constraints require vowels to be moraic, but the most highly ranked constraint requires that the most sonorous vowels be moraic, and the lowest ranked constraint requires that the least sonorous be moraic. The same constraint hierarchy can be formulated using negative constraints, where the ranking is reversed, and the constraint that penalizes association of a mora to the least sonorous vowel is the highest ranked, while the one that penalizes moraic low vowels is the lowest ranked, as in example 2.29c.

Example 2.29

a. *ONSET/glide, ONSET >> *COMPLEX NUCLEUS, *MAX-IOμ

   *ONSET/glide, ONSET >> * IDENT(cons), *MAX-IOμ

b. low/μ >> mid/μ >> hi/μ

c. *hi/μ >> *mid/μ >> *low/μ

High vocoids are more likely to be nonmoraic than mid vocoids, since their moraicity incurs a higher constraint violation; for the same reason, mid vocoids are also more likely to be nonmoraic than low vocoids. Taking into consideration that the motivation behind diphthongization is to avoid an onsetless syllable by creating a complex nucleus (ONSET >> *COMPLEX NUCLEUS), the gliding generalization can be obtained in a straightforward manner through ranking permutations of ONSET with respect to the hierarchy in example 2.29b, as seen in example 2.30.

Example 2.30   Glide formation and vowel height

low/μ >> mid vowel/μ >> ONSET >> hi/μ (no mid glides, only high glides)

low/μ >> ONSET >> mid vowel/μ >> hi/μ (no low glides, only high and mid glides)

All Spanish vowels except for /a/ can be nonmoraic. Although ONSET >> low/μ >> mid vowel/μ >> hi/μ is a possible ranking, it will fail to produce a low glide because, in a V_1V_2 sequence in which the V_1 and V_2 are nonidentical, it will never be necessary to underparse the mora of a low vowel in order to satisfy ONSET, as either a mid or a high vowel (a better option) will always be available.

Identical vowels satisfy ONSET by deletion or coalescence, and thereby also satisfy an Obligatory Contour Principle(OCP)-type constraint. Finally, one must also recall that nuclei with more than one syllabic segment (VV rather than GV) are not possible in Spanish, which indicates that the constraint responsible is undominated. The topic of diphthongization (vowel merger) will be treated again in more detail in chapter 3.

Sonority and non-nuclear clusters

Before concluding this section, a few words must be said about the sonority of non-nuclear clusters. Onset and coda clusters must obey the sonority sequencing principle (SSP), and, therefore, onset clusters that do not increase in sonority or coda clusters that do not decrease in sonority are not allowed. The relevant constraint, SON-SEQ (Kager 1999) (complex onsets rise in sonority, and complex codas fall in sonority), is undominated, *pa.rte* 'part.' In addition, the two segments of an onset cluster cannot be too close in sonority, *fu.tbol* 'soccer.' One of the members must be a plosive or /f/ and the other a liquid; for example, *broma* 'joke,' *prima* 'cousin,' *tren* 'train,' *drenar* 'drain,' *grande* 'big,' *creer* 'to believe,' *blando* 'soft,' *planta* 'plant,' *glotón* 'glutton,' *cloro* 'chlorine,' *flaco* 'skinny,' *frito* 'fried.'[9]

In pre-OT models, this generalization was expressed as a condition on the application of a Complex Onset Rule that attached a second consonant to the left of an already existing onset. A ban on adjacency (members of an onset cluster cannot be adjacent on the sonority scale) or a number reflecting the distance on the sonority scale between the two members of the cluster was used to capture the sonority distance required for the Complex Onset Rule to apply (Harris 1983, 1989b). In OT the onset cluster generalization is captured by a sonority distance constraint known as Maximal Sonority Distance (MSD) that requires the first member of the cluster to be drawn from the set of the least sonorous permissible onsets and the second from that of the most sonorous permissible onsets, thus maximizing the sonority distance between the two. In other words, the MSD constraint requires that there exists the maximum sonority distance between possible onset segments (Colina 1995; Martínez-Gil 1997).[10]

Which segments are possible onsets is reflected in the sonority constraint hierarchy in example 2.21, repeated here as example 2.31, where *ONSET/obstruent is divided into *ONSET/stop and *ONSET/fricative.

Example 2.31

*ONSET/vowel >> *ONSET/glide >> FAITH >> *ONSET/liquid >> *ONSET/ nasal >> *ONSET/fricative >> *ONSET/stop

---

The class of obstruents needs to be divided into *ONSET/fricative and *ONSET/stop to rule out fricatives as the first member of an onset cluster. Since, in addition to stops, /f/ can also be the first member of the cluster, /f/ must somehow be grouped with stops according to sonority. Martínez-Gil demonstrates this possibility by positing that stops and /f/ belong to "the class of obstruents that lack the specification [+continuant]." The feature [+continuant] contributes to sonority in Spanish and thus serves to separate on the sonority scale the obstruents that do not contain [+continuant] in their underlying representation (stops and /f/) and those that do and therefore exhibit higher sonority (fricatives) (Martínez-Gil 2001, 217). Martínez-Gil convincingly argues that /f/ does not need to be underlyingly specified as [+continuant] because no language has a phonemic contrast between labiodental stops and labiodental fricatives.[11]

Given that MSD is a violable universal constraint, the prediction is that it should be able to undergo violation under domination. This is precisely what happens in most varieties of Spanish. MSD is dominated by the constraint(s) responsible for obstruent spirantization, which requires voiced obstruents to be fricatives when preceded by a [+continuant] sound, for instance, /ablar/ [a.βlar] 'to speak,' /ago/ [aɣo] 'I do.'[12] (See Piñeros 2001 for an optimality-theoretic analysis of spirantization in which an ease of articulation constraint is responsible for voiced spirants in the output when preceded by another [+continuant] segment.)

> A different ranking of MSD is evidenced by Chilean Spanish. As noted by Martínez-Gil (1996, 1997), Chilean Spanish avoids spirant-liquid clusters by means of vocalization and coda parsing of the first member of the cluster, /logro/ [loṷ.ro] *[lo.ɣro] 'achievement.' This indicates that MSD dominates the IDENT constraints responsible for vocalization. The MSD analysis explains the contrast between voiced and voiceless stops: Since only voiced stops undergo spirantization, MSD violations will only be incurred by voiced stop + liquid clusters.

MSD also dominates other constraints such as DEP-IO, the anti-epenthesis constraint in example 2.34, given that [ezlaβo] is preferred to [slaβo] as the output of /slabo/ (cf. *Yugoslavo ~ eslavo* 'Yugoslavian' ~ 'Slav'). (See section 5.1.4 for more on initial epenthesis.)

2.2.2 SEGMENTS AND SYLLABIC POSITIONS

Sonority, subsyllabic constituency, and moraic structure cannot explain all the descriptive facts of Spanish syllabification. Harris (1989a, 155) says that the sonority scale "must be supplemented by language-particular restrictions of some kind." In this chapter I show that there is no need for language-particular restrictions or descriptive conditions on permissible phonemes; instead, those generalizations can be captured by the language-specific ranking of conflicting universal markedness and faithfulness constraints. Since no additional constraints or rankings are necessary to account for onset and nucleus segments, other than those in section 2.2.1, I focus on coda segments.

2.2.2.1 SEGMENTS IN THE SYLLABLE CODA

2.2.2.1.1 WORD-MEDIAL CODAS

Serial analyses of Spanish syllabification contain descriptive statements that list the consonants that are well formed in the coda. Although a descriptive generalization of the data is always a good starting point, the problem with that type of analysis is that it does not move beyond the level of description. As indicated above with regard to onset clusters, derivational models of syllabification must tack these generalizations onto syllabification rules like the Coda Rule: "Adjoin a coda to the right of the nucleus. *Possible codas are . . .* " I will show that in OT these conditions are simply the result of the interaction of universal markedness and faithfulness constraints. The list of licit coda segments can thus be obtained through constraint interaction. I will state the generalizations and then show how OT formalizes them.

Most Spanish dialects allow the following word-internally in coda position: nasals with the same point of articulation as the following consonant, *cambio* [kambi̯o] 'change'; /l/ or /r/ (neutralized in some Caribbean dialects), *malta* 'malt,' *marca* 'mark'; /s/, *pista* 'clue'; and /θ/, *pi[θ]ca* 'pinch' (in dialects with /θ/ in their inventories). Coda stops, lost at one point in the history of the language, have been recovered in some dialects in formal registers and under the influence of spelling. In these cases, however, [voice] and [continuant] are neutralized, hence there is no contrast possible between the coda obstruents in *concepción* 'conception' and *obsesión* 'obsession'; *étnico* 'ethnic' and *administrar* 'to administer'; *técnica* 'technique' and *dogmático* 'dogmatic' (Alonso 1945; Hualde 1989a).

Since Spanish has codas, *CODA must be dominated. I focus on obstruents first, then later move to sonorants. According to the sonority hierarchy in example 2.32, obstruents make the worst codas. This is in agreement with the descriptive facts for Spanish.

Example 2.32

*CODA/obstruent >> *CODA/nasal >> *CODA/liquid >> *CODA/glide[13]

Deletion of coda obstruents

Many dialects, such as rural varieties of Peninsular, Latin American Spanish, and Chicano Spanish, do not allow coda obstruents, often avoiding them through deletion. In those cases, the ranking must be as follows:

Example 2.33

*CODA/obstruent, DEP-IO >> MAX-IO

Example 2.34

MAX-IO: Every segment present in the input must have a correspondent in the output.

DEP-IO: Every segment present in the output must have a correspondent in the input.

Example 2.35   /obsoleto/ [osoleto] 'obsolete'

	*CODA/obstruent	DEP-IO	MAX-IO
a. ☞ o.so.le.to			*
b. ob.so.le.to	*!		
c. o.be.so.le.to		*!	

As seen in example 2.35, candidates that either preserve or avoid the coda obstruent through epenthesis—(b) and (c), respectively—are ruled out because they incur violations of the top-ranked constraints *CODA/obstruent and DEP-IO.

Formal varieties of Spanish (Hualde 1991) that retain coda obstruents exhibit the ranking in example 2.36, thus selecting [ob.so.le.to] as the output (*CODA/obstruent violation) in example 2.37:

Example 2.36

DEP-IO, MAX-IO >> *CODA/obstruent

Example 2.37   /obsoleto/ [oBsoleto]

	MAX-IO	DEP-IO	*CODA/obstruent
a. o.so.le.to	*!		
b. ☞ oB.so.le.to			*
c. o.Be.so.le.to		*!	

Despite the preservation of the obstruent, these dialects exhibit featural neutralizations in voice and continuancy (Hualde 1989a). In other words, the featural specification of the obstruent is altered with regard to the features [voice] and [continuant], incurring one or more faithfulness violations. The relevant faithfulness constraint is IDENT(feature) and its more specific versions IDENT(voice) and IDENT(continuant).

Example 2.38

IDENT(feature): A segment's input specification for a specific feature must match that of the output.

IDENT(voice): A segment's input specification for [voice] must match that of the output.

IDENT(continuant): A segment's input specification for [continuant] must match that of the output.

In this section uppercase will be used to abstract away from continuancy, when the [+/– continuant] specification is not directly relevant to the analysis. B stands for a bilabial voiced obstruent, and P is a bilabial voiceless obstruent; D and T are dental obstruents (voiced and voiceless), and G and K are their velar counterparts.

For voicing neutralization, the output may reveal obstruent devoicing (/digno/ [dikno] 'worthy') or assimilation (/futbol/ [fuðβol] 'soccer'). Since sonorants are not affected by devoicing, especially because voiceless sonorants are phonetically and typologically marked, a markedness constraint against voiceless sonorants, *SONORANT[–voice], must be undominated.[14] However, for nonsonorants, the unmarked voice specification for a coda is voiceless: *CODA[+voice] (voiceless codas are unmarked). *CODA[+voice] must dominate the relevant faithfulness constraint, IDENT(voice), so that it is possible to change input voice specifications, and, if necessary, to obtain a voiceless obstruent in the output. In sum, the relevant ranking for obstruent devoicing is:

Example 2.39   Obstruent devoicing in coda position

*SONORANT[−voice] >> *CODA[+voice] >> IDENT(voice)

As seen in example 2.40, the candidate with a voiced obstruent, (b), although faithful to the input, fails because it incurs a violation of the more highly ranked constraint against voiced codas.

Example 2.40   Obstruent devoicing in coda position
              /digno/ [diKno]

	*CODA[+voice]	IDENT (voice)
a. ☞ diK.no		*
b. diG.no	*!	

Voice assimilation of coda obstruents responds to the domination of the constraint that requires adjacent segments to agree with respect to voice, AGREE(voice), over IDENT(voice).

Example 2.41   Voice assimilation in coda position

AGREE(voice): Adjacent segments share the same specification for the feature [voice] (Lombardi 1999).

AGREE(voice) >> IDENT(voice)

Example 2.42   Regressive voice assimilation of coda obstruents
              /futbol/ [fuDβol]

	AGREE(voice)	IDENT(voice)
a. ☞ fuDβol		*
b. fuTβol	*!	

In example 2.42, (a) is a better candidate than (b) because it satisfies the dominating constraint AGREE(voice) by adopting the [+voice] specification of the following consonant.[15]

Free variation between coda devoicing and voicing assimilation

There exists variation, even within speakers, between obstruent devoicing and voice assimilation, for instance, /futbol/ [fuDβol] ~ [fuTβol] (Alonso 1945; Alarcos 1965; Quilis 1993; Navarro Tomás 1980; Hualde 1989a). In OT, free variation is generally accounted for through unranked constraints. In the case at hand, the ranking of AGREE(voice) with respect to *CODA[+voice] is not fixed. When AGREE(voice) and *CODA[+voice] are in conflict, the speaker must rank them, but since the ranking is not fixed, sometimes AGREE(voice) will be ranked higher, whereas other times *CODA[+voice] will come out on top.

Example 2.43   **Different outcomes of voice neutralization in coda**
                    obstruents: coda devoicing
                    /futbol/ [fuTβol]

	*CODA[+voice]	AGREE(voice)	IDENT(voice)
a. fuDβol	*!		*
b. ☞ fuTβol		*	

In example 2.43 the output (b) exhibits coda devoicing because *CODA[+voice]
is more highly ranked than AGREE(voice). A violation of *CODA[+voice] elimi-
nates the candidate with voice assimilation, (a).

Example 2.44   **Different outcomes of voice neutralization in coda**
                    obstruents: voice assimilation
                    /futbol/ [fuDβol]

	AGREE(voice)	*CODA[+voice]	IDENT(voice)
a. ☞ fuDβol		*	*
b. fuTβol	*!		

Example 2.44 reveals the opposite situation of that in example 2.43. The need to
agree in voicing is more important than having a voiceless coda. Therefore, the
candidate with assimilation, (a), whose highest ranked violation is
*CODA[+voice], is the winner and the output.

Example 2.45   **/fudbol/ [fuDβol] (assuming [+voice] in the input UR)**

	AGREE(voice)	*CODA[+voice]	IDENT(voice)
a. ☞ fuDβol		*	
b. fuTβol	*!		*

Example 2.45 is included to show that the results of evaluation would be the
same regardless of the voice specification of the input. The relevant constraints
and their ranking alone are responsible for the selection of the output, so much so
that the correct output will be selected independently of the form of the underlying representation, as illustrated by examples 2.44 and 2.45 (McCarthy 2002;
Richness of the Base).

Voicing assimilation only affects coda obstruents, so an obstruent in an onset
cluster does not assimilate in voicing to the following sonorant, *apretar* [a.pre.tar]
*[a.Bre.tar] 'to tighten.' This suggests that a more specific IDENT[ONSET](voice)
dominates AGREE(voice).

When the demands of AGREE(voice) and *CODA[+voice] are not in
conflict—that is, when the onset consonant following the coda is voiceless and
voice assimilation would result in a voiceless consonant—there is rarely any

alternation, as predicted: "*Las sordas resultan prácticamente obligatorias si la consonante siguiente es una oclusiva sorda.*" 'Voiceless segments are practically required if the following consonant is a voiceless stop' (Hualde 1991, 33; translation mine). This is demonstrated in examples 2.46 and 2.47, where the output is invariantly [opsoleto], regardless of the ranking of AGREE(voice) and *CODA[+voice]. As mentioned above, P stands for a voiceless labial obstruent unspecified for continuancy, while B is its voiced correspondent.

Example 2.46   /obsoleto/ [oPsoleto]

	AGREE(voice)	*CODA[+voice]	IDENT(voice)
a. ☞ oPsoleto			*
b. oBsoleto	*!	*	

Example 2.47   /obsoleto/ [oPsoleto]

	*CODA[+voice]	AGREE(voice)	IDENT(voice)
a. ☞ oPsoleto			*
b. oBsoleto	*!	*	

Continuancy neutralization

Examples 2.39–2.47 focus on voicing, abstracting away from continuancy. Coda obstruents in this dialect of Spanish also show neutralization in continuancy, surfacing as either stops or fricatives. An OT explanation for the alternation lies in the fact that, by ranking markedness over faithfulness, preservation of a contrast is no longer important and the default unmarked structure is preferred. On the basis of the sonority hierarchy in example 2.16, a coda fricative is less marked than a stop, /futbol/ [fuðβol].[16]

Example 2.48

Markedness >> IDENT(continuant)

*CODA/stop >> *CODA/fricative, IDENT(continuant)

However, in strong positions or positions of prominence (stressed syllable, focus position, emphasis, etc.), a stop is preferred for phonetic reasons. I use the cover term IDENT-PROMINENCE[–cont] to refer to the default status of stops in prominent positions. IDENT-PROMINENCE[–cont] dominates *CODA/fricative, so that in a position of prominence a stop will be selected over a fricative, [futβol] (emphatic, as in *Dije fútbol, no tenis*, 'I said football, not tennis').

Example 2.49

IDENT-PROMINENCE[–cont] >> *CODA/stop >> *CODA/fricative, IDENT(continuant)

General account of coda effects

To recapitulate: An OT analysis makes the prediction that, under the general ranking Markedness >> Faithfulness, there will be various ways to satisfy *CODA/obstruent, since there are various types of faithfulness constraints that could be violated (e.g., whole segment, featural identity). Such a prediction is borne out by cross-dialectal Spanish data. In addition to the deletion of coda obstruents, and voice and continuancy neutralizations, some Spanish dialects avoid marked codas by incurring other faithfulness constraint violations: For instance, aspirating dialects eliminate coda /s/ by deleting the supralaryngeal node of /s/ and incurring a faithfulness violation (MAX-IO(SL)), [meh] < /mes/ 'month' (see section 4.2.1); others vocalize obstruents through IDENT(stricture) violations (Martínez-Gil 1997; Piñeros 2001), /adkirir/ [aɨkirir] 'acquire,' and velarize or absorb coda nasals into the nucleus by failing to parse several features, /sinko/ [siŋko] ~ [sĩko] 'five' (Piñeros 2006).

As demonstrated by the analysis of obstruent coda deletion, and voice and continuancy neutralizations, an OT account can uncover the hidden motivation behind all these processes (to eliminate a marked structure or a coda obstruent) in a way not possible under a serial analysis that lists them as separate rules targeting the coda position.

Obstruent codas and point of articulation

Before concluding the account of obstruents in coda position, it is important to bring to the reader's attention one last generalization with regard to the place features of coda obstruents. Unlike sonorants, which are usually coronal, obstruents in coda position retain their point of articulation in many dialects: /fuDbol/ ~ [fuðβol] ~ [futβol] *[fupβol] *[fuββol]; /oBsoleto/ [opsoleto] ~ [oɸsoleto] *[oðsoleto] *[otsoleto], see example 2.52b. This suggests the high ranking of a constraint that requires preservation of place features in obstruents regardless of syllabic affiliation or place contrast neutralization (a well-known tendency of codas).

Since coda nasals in Spanish tend to be realized as coronals or to assimilate to the point of articulation of the following consonant—*sin* [sin] 'without,' *también* [tam.bi̯én] 'also,' *tonto* [ton̪.to] 'silly,' *tango* [taŋ.go] 'tango'—it can be concluded that faithfulness to place features is not as important for sonorants as it is for obstruents. Ranking the more specific IDENT^{OBSTR}(place) over the general IDENT(place) will suffice to obtain this effect without requiring an additional constraint that refers to sonorants (IDENT(place) is independently justified). Despite the restrictions on point of articulation in the coda (CODA COND), segments need place features; therefore HAVE PLACE must dominate CODA COND.

Example 2.50

IDENT^{OBSTR}(place): The place features of an obstruent in the input must match those of the output.

IDENT(place): The place features of a consonant in the input must match those of the output.

CODA COND: A coda cannot license place features.

HAVE PLACE: All segments must have place features.

Example 2.51

IDENT^{OBSTR}(place), HAVE PLACE >> CODA COND, IDENT(place)

Example 2.52   /obsoleto/ [opsoleto] ~ [oɸsoleto]

	IDENT^{OBSTR}(place)	HAVE PLACE	CODA COND	IDENT(place)
a. ☞ opsoleto ~ oɸsoleto			*	
b. otsoleto	*!		*	*

Some dialects do neutralize the point of articulation (PA) of obstruents: velar/glottal in Caribbean varieties, /submarino/ [sukmaɾino]; coronal in Mexican, /pepsi/ [petsi]; and in some Peninsular dialects, in which coronal [θ] is the default coda obstruent, /aktor/ [aθtor]. These dialects would rank IDENT^{OBSTR}(place) low in the hierarchy.

Nasal and lateral assimilation

In the case of sonorants, given that IDENT(place) is low-ranked, HAVE PLACE will be satisfied by selecting the place features that are ranked lowest in the place hierarchy and are therefore the least marked (i.e., coronal).

Example 2.53

a. Place Hierarchy: *DOR >> *LABIAL >> *CORONAL

b. HAVE PLACE >> *DOR >> *LABIAL >> *CORONAL >> IDENT(place)

Nasals and laterals take their place features from the following consonant through assimilation, thus satisfying CODA COND and HAVE PLACE simultaneously. Place features are obtained and licensed through the onset.

Example 2.54   /tango/ [taŋgo]

	IDENT^{OBSTR}(place)	HAVE PLACE	CODA COND	IDENT(place)
a. ☞ taŋgo				*
b. tango			*!	
c. tamgo			*!	*

In example 2.54, candidates (b) and (c) violate CODA COND by having their own coronal and bilabial points of articulation rather than sharing that of the following velar through assimilation like the optimal candidate, (a). For ease of presentation, an underlying coronal point of articulation is assumed in example 2.54. This assumption has no bearing on the results of candidate evaluation. As with obstruent voicing, different assumptions about the nature of the underlying representation result in the selection of the same optimal candidate (McCarthy 2002; Richness of the Base). Positing an alternative underlying representation with no specified point of articulation would also select (a) as the winner; in addition, (a), (b), and (c) would contain no IDENT(place) violations, and (b) and (c) would have marks for DEP(place), which forbids insertion of place features where there are none in the underlying representation. In absolute word-final position, before a vowel, and before a pause, where the nasal cannot obtain its point of articulation by sharing that of the following consonant, coronal is selected as the least marked point of articulation. Due to the domination of HAVE PLACE over CODA COND, the nasal consonant must have a point of articulation despite incurring a violation of CODA COND (see examples 2.51 and 2.53). As shown below in examples 2.55 and 2.56, noncoronal obstruents are often deleted in the same word-final context.

> In some dialects (Northwest Spain, Caribbean Spanish), coda nasals are realized with a velar point of articulation or become absorbed by the previous vowel, /pan/ [paŋ] 'bread.' It can be argued that those forms satisfy both HAVE PLACE and CODA COND by sharing the dorsal articulation of the preceding vowel. Piñeros (2006) presents an analysis of these phenomena in which place assimilation, velarization, and absorption are steps in a larger scale process aiming at incorporation of the nasal consonant into the structure of the nuclear segment for the sake of segment-to-syllable alignment (coda reduction or elimination, in our terms). A similar argument could be made for coda /s/-aspiration.

2.2.2.1.2 WORD-FINAL CODAS

In word-final position only coronal consonants are possible: the sonorants /l/, /n/, and /r/ (*papel, camión, amor*) and the obstruents /s/, /θ/ (*mes, pez*), and /d/ (*virtud*).[17] /d/ can be realized as [ð], [θ], [t], or be deleted. Other consonants are rare and may appear in unassimilated borrowings, *club, frac, bulldog, album, chef* (Hualde 1999a). Except for the behavior of obstruents, these facts are generally in agreement with the account of word-medial codas in section 2.2.2.1.1. Although word-medial stops and fricatives are acceptable in some dialects, as shown above, word-final obstruents are unusual in all dialects (with the exception of /s/).

Word-final epenthesis and deletion

    As mentioned above, noncoronal word-final obstruents are rare and they tend to appear in borrowings. The absence of word-final obstruents in the native lexicon is related to the fact that those segments were repaired at one point in the history of the language through epenthesis, so many of these forms are [e]-final today. At the point that epenthesis was operative, the ranking would have been *CODA/obstruent, MAX-IO >> DEP-IO. I argue that the present ranking, however, is *CODA/obstruent, DEP-IO >> MAX-IO, as demonstrated by the outputs of foreign words, *club* [klu], *frac* [fra] (see chapter 5 for more on the topic of final epenthesis). More specifically, since only noncoronal obstruents are affected (coronal obstruents are well-formed), the ranking must be as in example 2.55.

Example 2.55   **Noncoronal coda obstruents are deleted (rather than altering place features). Coronal coda obstruents are retained.**

*CODA/obstruent, DEP-IO >> MAX-IO

IDENT^{OBSTR}(place), HAVE PLACE >> *DOR >> *LABIAL >> MAX-IO >> *CORONAL, IDENT(place)

Example 2.56   /klub/ [klu]

	Ident^{Obstr} (place)	Have place	*Dor	*Labial	Max-IO	*Cor	Ident (place)
a. ☞ klu					*		
b. kluD	*!					*	*
c. klut	*!					*	*
d. kluB				*!			

Example 2.57   /θenit/ [θéniT]

	Ident^{Obstr} (place)	Have place	*Dor	*Labial	Max-IO	*Cor	Ident (place)
a. ☞ θéniT						*	
b. θéni					*!		
c. θéniP	*!			*			*

That some varieties of Spanish tend to preserve word-medial noncoronal coda obstruents can be explained by restricting the relevant ranking to Latinate words (nativized forms, part of the Spanish lexicon) in formal contexts.

Example 2.58   **Preservation of the place features of word-internal noncoronal coda obstruents in Latinate words (formal context)**

Ident^{Obstr}(place), Have place, Max-IO, Dep-IO >> *Dor >> *Labial >> *Coronal, Ident(place) (Latinate words)

2.2.2.1.3 COMPLEX CODAS

Spanish has coda clusters and therefore *Complex Coda must be dominated by faithfulness constraints. Nonetheless, since not all coda clusters are possible, additional constraints must be involved. Most coda clusters contain a coda consonant or glide + /s/. /s/ is well known to have a special status cross-linguistically that allows its adjunction to other segments, even in violation of sonority. I will therefore not delve into this topic and will simply treat these clusters as exceptional. Codas consisting of a glide + /s/, *dais* 'you give,' or a glide + coronal sonorant, *veinte* 'twenty,' *aunque* 'although,' conform to the sonority contour and to the coda markedness hierarchy that prefers coronal sonorants. Only /s/ is allowed after another consonant in a coda cluster (Hualde 1999a, 17), *biceps* [biseps] 'biceps,' *torax* [toɾaks] 'thorax.' In fast speech, these clusters are usually simplified to [bises] and [toɾas], suggesting the ranking in example 2.59:

Example 2.59

*Complex Coda >> Max-IO

Yet example 2.59 alone is not sufficient as it does not dictate which consonant in the cluster will delete (*[bisep], *[torak]). In an OT account, the universal sonority constraint hierarchy will select the correct output, always deleting the least sonorous consonant, as the constraint that bans its association to the coda will be ranked higher than those against more sonorous codas (see also example 2.22).

Example 2.60

*COMPLEX CODA >> *CODA/stop >> MAX-IO >> *CODA/fricative >>
*CODA/nasal >> * CODA/liquid >> *CODA/glide[18]

Selection of target of deletion in a coda cluster

A serial analysis, however, faces a serious obstacle in trying to account for the same facts. It cannot satisfactorily explain the selection of the segment targeted for deletion. Harris (1983) argues that in *esculp-tor* 'sculptor,' [p] is deleted to get [esku̯ltor] because it cannot be syllabified in the coda or in the onset. Yet, according to that, [ekspresiðente] 'ex-president' should be simplified as *[ekpresiðente] rather than [espresiðente] because [s] cannot be syllabified in the coda or in the onset. Adopting a similar position to that of Harris (1983), Hualde (1991, 485) tries to solve the problem by proposing a rule of /s/-adjunction ("adjoin /s/ under N") (also in Harris 1983) followed by another rule that deletes a stop in a stop + /s/ cluster.[19] This solution, however, is somewhat ad hoc and language-specific. In sum, it becomes apparent that serial models cannot formalize the purpose behind the rules—that is, the selection of the best coda (or deletion of the worst member of the cluster). In an OT account, this outcome is a natural consequence of the integration of universal markedness (i.e., the universal sonority constraint hierarchy) in the OT formalism. The ranking of faithfulness constraints with regard to the sonority scale determines whether markedness or faithfulness violations will occur and which segment will be the target of the repair mechanisms (e.g., deletion, feature modification).

A more detailed analysis of deletion in complex codas is provided within the context of repair mechanisms in chapter 5.

2.3 SUMMARY

This chapter presents an OT account of the basic syllable types of Spanish. The main advantage of an OT analysis of the basic syllabic typology of Spanish is that it is obtained by permutations of a few basic universal constraints rather than a listing of syllable types or language-specific templates.

Spanish generally allows onsetless syllables, as well as syllable codas and complex onsets and codas, which suggests that ONSET, *CODA, *COMPLEX ONSET, *COMPLEX CODA must be dominated by faithfulness constraints. *CODA in turn must dominate *COMPLEX ONSET given that word-internal onset clusters are preferred to the parsing of the consonants in the coda and the onset of two adjacent syllables (cf. *onset maximization* in derivational approaches). COMPLEX NUCLEUS is also dominated since the language has rising diphthongs (prevocalic glides).

The OT analysis proposed captures generalizations about the specific segments parsed in each syllabic position in terms of sonority hierarchies and syllabic markedness constraints. In most dialects of Spanish, stops, fricatives, and nasals are possible onsets, but not glides or vowels. Only vowels are possible nuclei (glides are well-formed in prevocalic position). Some segmental modifications (IDENT violations) are possible in order to create a CV syllable (satisfy ONSET), such as in onset strengthening and in the gliding of vocoids (prevocalic and postvocalic glides, diphthongization). All segment types can be parsed in the coda except for vowels.

In serial phonology the role of sonority is recognized, but sonority scales cannot be formalized into the theory and constitute separate, external mechanisms. On the other hand, an optimality-theoretic framework captures the generalizations that relate syllabic positions with sonority classes in a straightforward manner by means of universal scales and constraint hierarchies. The ranking of faithfulness constraints with regard to the sonority scale (hierarchy of markedness constraints) determines whether violations can be forced through domination, thus explaining language variation (language-specific ranking) in an otherwise universally fixed hierarchy.

Serial analyses of Spanish syllabification contain descriptive statements that list the consonants that are well-formed in the coda. In OT, licit coda segments are the result of constraint interaction. Many dialects of Spanish delete coda obstruents, indicating that MAX-IO must be dominated by *CODA/obstruent. Other dialects exhibit featural neutralizations in voice and continuancy (Hualde 1989a), the relevant ranking for obstruent devoicing being *SONORANT[–voice] >> *CODA[+voice] >> IDENT(voice). Voice assimilation of coda obstruents responds to the domination of AGREE(voice) over *CODA(voice). An OT explanation for neutralization in continuancy lies in the fact that by ranking markedness over faithfulness (IDENT(continuant)), preservation of a contrast is no longer important, and the default, unmarked structure—also a stop in prominent positions—is preferred.

The OT analysis also explains preservation of point of articulation in coda obstruents, nasal assimilation, word-final codas, and the selection of the target of deletion in complex codas.

STUDY QUESTIONS

1. How do faithfulness and markedness constraints interact to obtain the main syllable types in Spanish?

2. How does Richness of the Base pertain to moraic structure in an OT analysis of Spanish?

3. Coda rhotics exhibit a good amount of dialectal and stylistic variation, with at least two possible realizations, a trill and a flap. Throughout this book, and unless the topic of discussion is rhotic realization per se (see chapter 4), coda rhotics will be transcribed as [r], abstracting away from the variation.

4. What is the relevance of the notion of harmonic alignment with regard to sonority and syllable types in Spanish?

5. Compare derivational and nonderivational accounts of onset maximization in Spanish.

6. What is the relevance of the notion of sonority for onset clusters in Spanish?

7. How does OT explain neutralization processes in the coda in Spanish? How does OT account for dialectal variation in the treatment of codas?

8. How do nonsyllabic vocoids (i.e., glides) contribute to reducing the number of onsetless syllables?

GOING BACK TO THE SOURCES

Colina 2006c:

> Optimality-theoretic advances in our understanding of Spanish syllabic structure. *Optimality-Theoretic Studies in Spanish Phonology*. Ed. Fernando Martínez-Gil and Sonia Colina. Philadelphia: John Benjamins.

Harris 1983:

> *Syllable Structure and Stress in Spanish*. Cambridge, MA: The MIT Press.

Harris 1989a:

> Sonority and syllabification in Spanish. *Studies in Romance Linguistics*. Ed. Carl Kirschner and Janet DeCesaris. Philadelphia: John Benjamins.

Harris 1989b:

> Our present understanding of Spanish syllable structure. *American Spanish Pronunciation*. Ed. Peter C. Bjarkman and Robert M. Hammond. Washington, DC: Georgetown University Press.

Hualde 1989a:

> Procesos consonánticos y estructuras geométricas en español. *Lingüística* 1:7–44.

Hualde 1991:

> On Spanish syllabification. *Current Studies in Spanish Linguistics*. Ed. Héctor Campos and Fernando Martínez-Gil. Washington, DC: Georgetown University Press.

Hualde 1997:

> Spanish /i/ and related sounds: An exercise in phonemic analysis. *Studies in the Linguistic Sciences* 27:61–79.

Hualde 1999b:

> Patterns in the lexicon: Hiatus with unstressed high vowels in Spanish. *Advances in Hispanic Linguistics. Papers from the Second Hispanic Linguistics Symposium*. Ed. Javier Gutiérrez-Rexach and Fernando Martínez-Gil. 182–97. Somerville, MA: Cascadilla Press.

Martínez-Gil 1997:

> Obstruent vocalization in Chilean Spanish: A serial versus a constraint-based approach." *Probus* 9:165–200.

Martínez-Gil 2001:

> Sonority as a primitive phonological feature: Evidence from Spanish complex onset phonotactics. *Features and Interfaces in Romance: Essays in Honor of Heles Contreras*. Ed. Julia Herschensohn, Enrique Mallén, and Karen Zagona. Philadelphia: John Benjamins.

Piñeros 2001:

> Segment-to-segment alignment and vocalization in Chilean Spanish. *Lingua* 111:163–88.

Piñeros 2006:

> The phonology of nasal consonants in five Spanish dialects. An alignment-based account of coda effects in a Caribbean Spanish dialect. *Optimality-Theoretic Studies in Spanish Phonology*. Ed. Fernando Martínez-Gil and Sonia Colina. 146–71. Philadelphia: John Benjamins.

KEY TOPICS

Spanish Phonology

> onset maximization
>
> onset strengthening
>
> onset clusters
>
> sonority scale
>
> MSD
>
> coda clusters
>
> moraic structure
>
> diphthongs versus hiatuses
>
> glides
>
> parsing of glides
>
> quantity sensitivity
>
> Chilean vocalization
>
> nasal and lateral assimilation
>
> place of articulation
>
>> of obstruents
>>
>> of sonorants
>
> obstruent deletion
>
> coda neutralizations
>
> coda devoicing
>
> voicing assimilation

Phonological Theory/OT

> Richness of the Base
>
> harmonic alignment

positional faithfulness

markedness and faithfulness constraints

identity constraints

factorial typology

TOPICS FOR FURTHER RESEARCH

1. How could one account for the ill-formedness of /s/ + obstruent onset clusters in Spanish (and in many other languages), as well as for its exceptional behavior in word final clusters?

2. How could one account for the coarticulation of nasals followed by an obstruent (velar and assimilated points of articulation), as in [eŋm̩-fermo] 'sick'?

3. Cross-linguistic evidence seems to suggest that rising diphthongs are more marked than falling ones. Why does Spanish allow both rising and falling diphthongs?

4. Is the construct glide really necessary? (Roca 1997)

5. Could the behavior of diphthongs in other Romance languages shed any light on their behavior in Spanish?

6. Is it possible to explain why /f/ is allowed as the first member of an onset cluster without introducing intermediate levels of representation (other than the output) in OT? Would this constitute additional evidence for versions of the theory that argue for more than one level, like Stratal OT or candidate chains? (McCarthy 2007)

NOTES

1. Orthographic <h> is not pronounced in Spanish.

2. Exceptional languages for which it has been claimed that an intervocalic consonant is parsed with the first vowel (VC.V) are Barra Gaelic (Clements 1986) and Arrernte (Breen and Pensalfini 1999).

3. Also referred to in some OT publications as DEP-IO(Seg) and MAX-IO(Seg).

4. Coda rhotics exhibit a good amount of dialectal and stylistic variation, with at least two possible realizations, a trill and a flap. Throughout this book, and unless the topic of discussion is rhotic realization per se (see chapter 4), coda rhotics will be transcribed as [r], abstracting away from the variation.

5. Hualde (1991) uses an X-bar theory of syllabification. Generally, N" corresponds to the onset, N' is the rhyme, and N is the nucleus.

6. For falling diphthongs, *peine* [pei̯.ne] 'comb,' evaluation proceeds in the same fashion, except for the replacement of *NUC/glide (trivially satisfied) with *CODA/glide, *CODA.

7. Weight-by-Position would translate into a violation of DEP-IOμ under the domination of the relevant stress constraint that makes coda segments moraic/heavy in a quantity-sensitive system.

8. Colina (2006c) proposes IDENT(son) instead of IDENT(cons). Although both constraints obtain the desired result, IDENT(cons) captures the feature specifications and restrictions affecting onset glides more adequately, as sonorants, unlike nonconsonantal segments, can be well-formed onsets (see also Roca (2005) for the same constraint).

9. In addition, in most dialects /dl/ and /tl/ are not possible onset clusters. These segments incur OCP violations regarding identical specifications for [coronal], [continuant], and [voice] (in the case of /dl/). Mexican Spanish has /tl/ onset clusters.

10. MSD is referred to as ONSET-SONORITY (ON-SON) in Colina (1995).

11. This account poses a challenge for OT as it imposes a restriction on the form of the underlying representation (contrary to Richness of the Base): It is only at the level of underlying representation that /f/ does not contain a [+continuant] specification ([f] is [+continuant] in the output); furthermore, the generalization applies at a level other than the surface level (i.e., output), contrary to the spirit of OT. The alternative that comes to mind is to continue to consider /f/ exceptional with regard to its sonority classification.

12. Although the nonstop allophones of voiced obstruents have traditionally been considered fricatives (Navarro Tomás 1980; Quilis 1981, 1993; Hualde 1991), recent phonetic and phonological evidence points at their approximant nature. In this chapter, I have adopted the more traditional fricative view for reasons of consistency with the referenced research. Replacing [β, ð, ɣ] with [β, ð̞, ɰ] has no consequences for the analysis presented here.

13. In an alignment format (Piñeros 2001): ALIGN-L(Obstruent, σ) >> ALIGN-L(Nasal, σ) >> ALIGN-L(Liquid, σ) >> ALIGN-L(Glide, σ).

14. Many languages that have voiced sonorants do not have voiceless ones. Those with voiceless sonorants, however, also have voiced ones.

15. An alternative to the voicing analysis is assuming that the feature [+voice] is being parsed through the following onset, thus reducing the number of features appearing in the coda (i.e., the coda fails to license a laryngeal specification). An account in which voicing is the result of trying to improve the sonority of the coda would not work, as it does not explain why sometimes codas are devoiced. Under the current approach, both devoicing and voice assimilation result from markedness restrictions on the coda (markedness over faithfulness).

16. The observation made above regarding example 2.45 and the voice specification of the input (i.e., underlying representation) also applies to the continuancy specification of the output (Richness of the Base).

17. Exceptionally, /-x/, *reloj,* and /-t/, *cénit,* can appear in final codas (Hualde 1999a; contra Harris 1989b and Roca 2007, personal communication).

18. Ranking for dialects with deletion of single coda obstruents (retention requires MAX-IO >> *CODA/stop; see also section 5.1.1).

19. Note that [s] is always retained in a consonant cluster, even when pre-
    ceded by a more sonorous consonant, as in /transporte/ [tɾas.por.te]
    'transport.' This can be attributed to the special status of [s] and the
    ranking of *s/CODA with respect to *COMPLEX CODA. (See chapters 4
    and 5 for the role of *s/CODA in aspiration and initial epenthesis.) An
    alternative account is that the nasal can be partially parsed as nasaliza-
    tion on the vowel, thus avoiding its complete deletion, a strategy not
    available for [s]. This permits satisfaction of *COMPLEX CODA without
    violating MAX-IO.

3

Syllabification across Words

3.1 RESYLLABIFICATION

Chapter 2 provided a general OT account of syllable types and phonotactics. The basic descriptive facts and word syllabification mechanisms of Spanish were accounted for by means of the interaction of universal markedness and faithfulness constraints ranked in language or dialect-specific fashion. The current chapter focuses on syllabification phenomena across words.

Spanish exhibits a well-known phenomenon traditionally known as *resyllabification*, by which a word-final consonant, which would be in a coda position in the word, is parsed as the onset of the following vowel-initial word. OT and its system of minimally violable constraints reveal an important insight into the nature of resyllabification. In lay terms, the principle that the edge of a syllable and a word must coincide (i.e., be aligned) at the beginning of a word can be sacrificed in order to provide an onset for a vowel-initial word, as in example 3.1c. However, when the word already has an onset (i.e., it is consonant-initial), there is no need to resyllabify a second consonant, as in example 3.5; this resyllabification would unnecessarily misalign the syllable and the word. I will return to this insight in detail when the OT analysis is presented.

Example 3.1

a. los [los]   'the'   b. amigos [a.mi.ɣos]   'friends'   c. [lo.sla.mi.ɣos]

   más [mas]   'more'   osos [o.sos]   'bears'   [ma.slo.sos]

   reloj [re.lox] 'watch'   azul [a.sul]   'blue'   [re.lo.xla.sul]

Harris (1983) proposes the rule in example 3.2 that a consonant in the coda becomes an onset consonant when in word-final prevocalic position. Hualde (1991) offers an improved analysis by eliminating a separate resyllabification rule and proposing instead a second, postlexical application of the independently necessary CV

Example 3.2

Resyllabification: [+cons] → [+cons] / ____#V

                 | |

               coda   onset

Rule (Onset Rule) (example 3.3). The postlexical application of the CV rule alters previously built structure, because associating to the onset the segment linked to the coda at the lexical level deassociates the same segment from the coda position (cf. figure 3.2, postlexical level).

Example 3.3

Syllabification	[mas][o.sos]
(including CV rule)	
Postlexical component	[mas.o.sos]
Postlexical application of CV rule	[ma.so.sos]

Nevertheless, one piece of the puzzle is still missing. In Spanish, resyllabification is limited to one consonant. Although consonant clusters are preferred to two heterosyllabic consonants word-internally, this is not so across words. Evidence for the heterosyllabic syllabification of the cluster in example 3.5 can be found in the tendency of word-final obstruents to undergo coda processes such as deletion and neutralization (e.g., [klu] [klup] [kluɸ] 'club'; [pu] [puf] 'pub').

Example 3.4

hablamos   [a.βla.mos]   *[aβ.la.mos] 'we talk'

Example 3.5

club lindo   [kluβ.lin̦.do]   *[klu.βlin̦.do] 'pretty club'

Serial account of resyllabification: why does the Complex Onset Rule apply only lexically?

Hualde accounts for the data in examples 3.4 and 3.5 by proposing that the application of the Complex Onset Rule is limited to the lexical domain. In other words, while the CV Rule applies lexically and postlexically (figures 3.1 and 3.2), the Complex Onset Rule only has a lexical application (figures 3.1–3.3).

Lexical level

1. Node projection: Mark vowels as syllable heads, create N nodes, and project N' and N" nodes.
2. Complex nucleus: Adjoin a prevocalic glide under the N node.
3. CV Rule: Adjoin a consonant to the left of the nucleus under the N" node.
4. Complex Onset: Adjoin a second consonant under the N" node if the result would be a permissible onset cluster (stop or /f/ + liquid, except */dl/ and (*)/tl/).
5. Coda Rule: Adjoin a segment to the right of the nucleus under N'.
6. Complex coda: Adjoin a consonant to the right of a glide under N'.
7. /s/-Adjunction: Adjoin /s/ under N'.

Postlexical level

CV Rule: Adjoin a consonant to the left of the nucleus under the N" node.

Complex Onset: Does not apply.

Figure 3.1 Spanish syllabification rules (Hualde 1991)

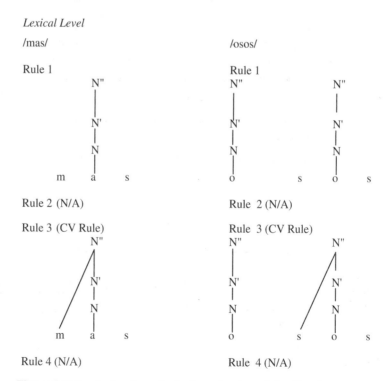

Figure 3.2 Lexical and postlexical application of the CV (Onset) Rule

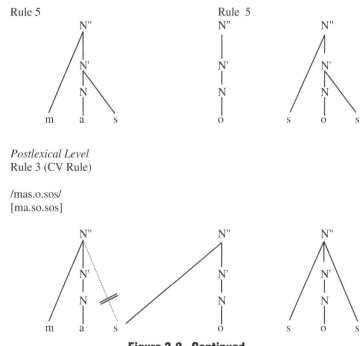

Rule 5   Rule 5

Postlexical Level
Rule 3 (CV Rule)

/mas.o.sos/
[ma.so.sos]

Figure 3.2   Continued

OT account of
resyllabifi-
cation   Although Hualde's solution (1991) is descriptively adequate, its explanatory
value is limited—it does not explain why the Complex Onset Rule is restricted to
the lexical domain. In contrast, an OT analysis (Colina 1995, 1997) easily accounts
for the difference in behavior between single consonants and consonant clusters:
While resyllabification of a single consonant across words is necessary to satisfy
ONSET, this is not the case with the second consonant of a cluster. Resyllabifying
consonants (or vowels) across words incurs a violation of an alignment constraint
that requires the left edge of the stem to be aligned with the left edge of the syllable.

Example 3.6

ALIGN (Stem, L, Syllable, L) (ALIGN-LST): Align the left edge of the stem with
the left edge of the syllable.[1]

[ma.slo.sos], for instance, misaligns the stem (l) and the syllable (.). Misalignment is possible under ONSET domination when it is required to provide an onset
for what would otherwise be an onsetless syllable.

Example 3.7

ONSET >> ALIGN (Stem, L, Syllable, L)

In [kluβ.liṇ.do] ONSET satisfaction is no longer at stake, therefore, ALIGN-LST
selects [kluβ.liṇ.do] over misaligned *[klu.βlliṇ.do]. *CODA must be ranked

below ALIGN-LST given that a coda consonant (*CODA violation) is preferred to misalignment (ALIGN-LST violation).

Example 3.8 /masosos/ [ma.so.sos]

	ONSET	ALIGN-LST
a. ☞ ma.slo.sos		*
b. mas.lo.sos	*!	

Example 3.9

ONSET >> ALIGN (Stem, L, Syllable, L) >> *CODA

Example 3.10 /klublindo/ [kluβ.li̩n.do]

	ONSET	ALIGN-LST	*CODA
a. ☞ kluβ.llin.do			*
b. klu.βllin.do		*!	

Example 3.11 **Resyllabification**

ALIGN-LST also selects the right candidate in prefixed forms like /sublunar/ [suβ.lunar] or /desarmar/ [de.sar.mar] (see chapter 4 for more on prefixes and syllabification).

Example 3.12 /sublunar/ [suβ.lunar]

	ONSET	ALIGN-LST	*CODA
a. ☞ suβ.llu.nar			*
b. su.βllu.nar		*!	

Example 3.13 /desarmar/ [de.sar.mar]

	ONSET	ALIGN-LST	*CODA
a. ☞ de.slar.mar		*	
b. des.lar.mar	*!		*

/ablar/

Rule 1

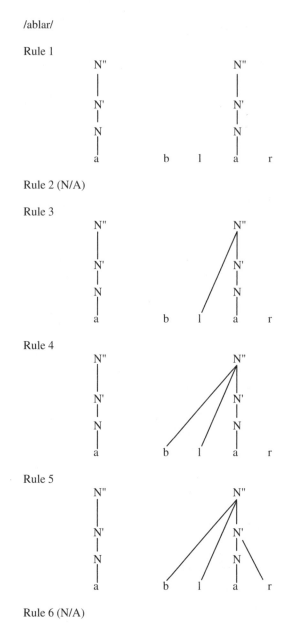

Rule 2 (N/A)

Rule 3

Rule 4

Rule 5

Rule 6 (N/A)

Rule 7 (N/A)

Figure 3.3 Complex Onset Rule applies lexically (within the word)

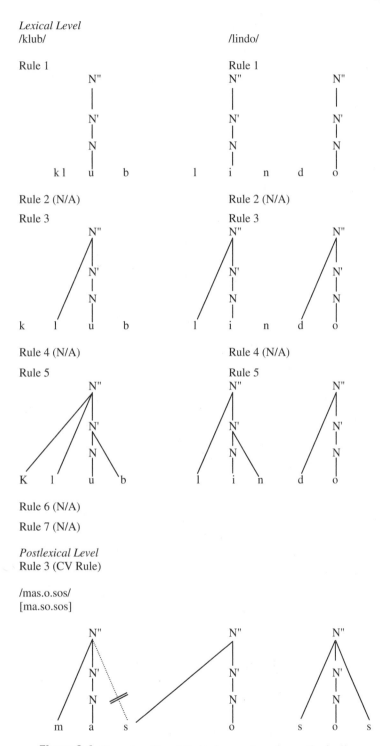

Figure 3.4 Complex Onset Rule does not apply postlexically

3.2 DIPHTHONGIZATION ACROSS WORDS

Diphthongiza-
tion within the
word

In section 2.2.1, diphthongization (also known as syllable merger) was explained as the result of avoiding an ONSET violation within a word through violations of the low-ranked *COMPLEX NUCLEUS, *NUC/glide, and MAX-IOμ. In other words, diphthongization, or parsing a glide in the nucleus and creating a complex nucleus, is preferred over an onsetless syllable. This was shown in examples 2.24 and 2.25, repeated here for convenience as examples 3.14 and 3.15.

Example 3.14   Diphthongization

*ONSET/glide, ONSET >> *COMPLEX NUCLEUS, *NUC/glide, MAX-IOμ

Example 3.15   /pierde/ [piér.ðe] 'he loses'

	*ONSET/glide	ONSET	*COMPLEX NUCLEUS	*NUC/glide	MAX-IOμ
a. ☞ piér.ðe			*	*	*
b. pi.ér.ðe		*!			
c. pjér.ðe	*!				*

In example 3.15, candidate (a) violates *COMPLEX NUCLEUS, *NUC/glide, and MAX-IOμ; however, these are all ranked below ONSET, which (b) violates. Parsing the vocoid as part of the onset (complex onset) as in (c) is not possible either, as *ONSET/glide also dominates COMPLEX NUCLEUS, *NUC/glide, and M-IOμ.

Diphthongiza-
tion across
words

Diphthongization applies across words in Spanish, *mi amigo* [mia.mi.ɣo] 'my friend,' where it is the result of the domination of ONSET over ALIGN-LST and MAX-IOμ.

Example 3.16   /miamigo/ [mia.mi.ɣo]

	ONSET	ALIGN-LST	MAX-IOμ
a. ☞ mila.mi.ɣo		*	*
b. mi.la.mi.ɣo	*!		

As seen in example 3.16, it is preferable to misalign the syllable and the stem and delete a mora, as in (a) (violations of low-ranked ALIGN-LST and MAX-IOμ), than to have an onsetless syllable (ONSET violation, (b)). This common motivation behind diphthongization (avoiding onsetless syllables) is shared across dialects; however, the strategies used to accomplish this goal vary across dialects and styles. In what follows, I present data corresponding to two dialects, Peninsular and Chicano, and show how an optimality-theoretic account explains each one of them. I also point out the advantages of this type of analysis versus a serial one.

Example 3.17 **Diphthongization (across words): basic ranking**

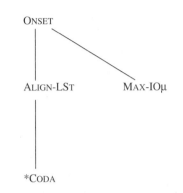

3.2.1 DIPHTHONGIZATION ACROSS WORDS: PENINSULAR SPANISH

Target for
gliding
depends on
sonority

In Peninsular Spanish any group of vowels can be a diphthong, especially if both are unstressed. Which vowel loses its mora has to do with the sonority of the vowels involved and with stress assignment. Speed and style are also factors, as mid vowels will become glides in faster speech, and more commonly in connected speech than in words in isolation (Navarro Tomás 1980; see also Roca 1991 for additional data).

Example 3.18

t[u̯a]buelo	'your grandfather'	m[i̯a]buelo	'my grandfather'
trib[u̯a]siática	'Asian tribe'	mil[i̯a]ntigua	'old military service'
t[u̯o]ruga	'your caterpillar'	m[i̯o]ruga	'my caterpillar'
trib[u̯i]ndígena	'indigenous tribe'	mil[i̯u]rgente	'urgent milt. service'

traig[o̯a]lhajas	'I bring jewels'	t[e̯a]maré	'I will love you'
teng[o̯e]nchufes	'I have plugs'	vend[e̯o]rugas	'he sells caterpillars'
t[eu̯]tiliza	'he uses you'	t[ei̯]mpide	'he prevents you from'
teng[ou̯]sados	'I have used-adj'	tod[oi̯]maginación	'all imagination'
tod[ae̯]spaña	'all Spain'	tod[ai̯]talia	'all Italy'

In example 3.19, identical vowels are reduced to one.

Hualde (1994) proposes a rule by which a vowel next to another vowel loses its mora if it is the higher of the two. He argues that it is not necessary to indicate this condition on the application of the rule as it is automatically obtained through the universal sonority scale that selects the most sonorous element as the nucleus of a

Example 3.19

canta Antonio	cant[a]ntonio	'Antonio sings'
te espero	t[e]spero	'I wait for you'
mi imaginación	m[i]maginación	'my imagination'
otro osado	otr[o]sado	'another daring individual'
espíritu universal	espírit[u]niversal	'universal spirit'

Example 3.20

café amargo	caf[e̯á]margo	'bitter coffee'
cantó Antonio	cant[o̯á]ntonio	'Antonio sang'
menú antiguo	men[u̯á]ntiguo	'old menu'

syllable. Similarly, when the vowel that loses its mora is the stress carrier, stress automatically shifts to the nucleus, the most sonorous component of the diphthong.

Derivational
models cannot
incorporate
sonority in a
direct way

As has probably become clear by now, the problem with a serial account of this type is that it cannot incorporate the universal sonority scale in any direct manner. An OT analysis can elegantly formalize this generalization by means of a constraint hierarchy based on the universal sonority scale. As seen in chapter 2, the constraint hierarchy in example 2.29b (repeated here as example 3.21b) correctly selects the target for mora deletion within the word.

Example 3.21

a. *ONSET/glide, ONSET >> *COMPLEX NUCLEUS, MAX-IOμ

b. low/μ >> mid/μ >> hi/μ

The situation is similar across words, as high vowels are more likely to lose their moras than mid vowels and low vowels because their moraicity incurs a higher constraint violation, and mid vowels are more likely to lose their moras than low vowels. In other words, low vowels make the best vowels (i.e., the worst glides) because they are the most sonorous segments and therefore the best moraic segments (nuclei). Mid vowels make the second best vowels and the second best nuclei (i.e., second worst glides) because they are the most sonorous segments after the low vowels. High vowels are the third choice for nuclear status and therefore the first choice for gliding.

In fast speech and across words, all Spanish vowels except for /a/ can become glides.

How to incorporate rate of speech into an optimality-theoretic account is not entirely clear. Although the topic is beyond the scope of this book (see Topics for Further Research in section 3.3), it is not unreasonable to hypothesize that faithfulness constraints could be demoted at the postlexical level. Fast speech would refer to normal connected speech. This approach argues the need for at least a two-level phonology (lexical and postlexical) even under OT, along the lines of Stratal OT (Bermúdez-Otero, in press). An alternative account resorts to the difference between input-to-output and output-to-output faithfulness, where phrasal outputs are in an OO correspondence relation with the output of prosodic words (the output of the lexical component). In this case MAX-OOμ, the relevant constraint for fast speech, is ranked lower than MAX-IOμ, which is relevant for careful, slow speech and the lexical level. The Stratal OT versus OO correspondence approach to phonology is also pertinent to the topic of stress shift addressed below.

Taking into consideration that the motivation behind diphthongization across words is to avoid an onsetless syllable by underparsing a mora and misaligning the word and syllable (ONSET >> ALIGN-LST, MAX-IOμ), the gliding generalization can then be obtained in a straightforward manner through ranking permutations of ONSET with respect to the hierarchy in example 2.21b, as seen in example 3.22:

Example 3.22   Glide formation and vowel height in Peninsular Spanish: no low glides

low/μ, ONSET >> ALIGN-LST, MAX-IOμ, mid/μ >> hi/μ, *CODA

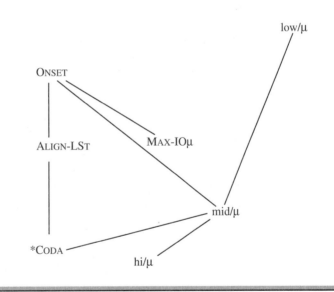

According to example 3.22, the vowel that glides depends on sonority (i.e., high vowels make better glides than mid vowels, and low glides are not possible), rather than on position in the syllable. In other words, a high glide is better than a mid one, regardless of whether it is the first vocoid or the second one in the sequence. Note that gliding of the second vocoid results in a falling diphthong and thus in a *CODA violation, which must therefore be low-ranked. ONSET dominates mid/μ, because, in connected speech, a mid glide is better than an onsetless syllable (hiatus), for instance, teng[o̯e]nchufes 'I have plugs' in example 3.18. As will be shown below in 3.2.2, Chicano Spanish, which does not allow mid glides, exhibits a different ranking of ONSET with respect to the glide sonority hierarchy in example 3.21b, as seen in example 3.23:

Example 3.23   **Glide formation and vowel height in Chicano Spanish: no low or mid glides**

low/μ >> mid/μ

mid/μ, ONSET >> ALIGN-LST, MAX-IOμ, hi/μ

In example 3.24, candidate (c) is ruled out because it violates ONSET. Candidate (b) is also eliminated because of the low glide. As a result, (a) is the optimal candidate and the winner.

Example 3.24   **Diphthongization across words in Peninsular Spanish[2] /miamigo/ [mi̯a.mi.ɣo]**

	low/μ	ONSET	ALIGN-LST	MAX-IOμ	hi/μ
a. ☞ mi̯la.mi.ɣo			*	*	*
b. mila̯.mi.ɣo	*!		*	*	
c. mi.la.mi.ɣo		*!			

In candidate (b) of example 3.25, the first vocoid in the sequence is a glide, so it violates the more highly ranked mid/μ and loses to candidate (a). (c), without a diphthong, incurs an ONSET violation. Thus, *CODA cannot be ranked higher than mid/μ.

Example 3.25   **Sonority over position in the syllable: the second vowel loses its mora if it makes a better glide /teutilisa/ [te̯u.ti.li.θa]**

	low/μ	ONSET	ALIGN-LST	MAX-IOμ	mid/μ	hi/μ	*CODA
a. ☞ te̯u.ti.li.θa			*	*		*	*
b. te̯lu.ti.li.θa			*	*	*!		
c. te.lu.ti.li.θa		*!					

Example 3.26   **Vowels of identical height: the first one loses its mora /miliurxente/ [mi.li̯ur.xen̩.te]**

	low/μ	ONSET	ALIGN-LST	MAX-IOμ	mid/μ	hi/μ	*CODA
a. ☞ mi.li̯lur.xen̩.te			*	*		*	
b. mi.lilu̯r.xen̩.te			*	*		*	*!
c. mi.li.lur.xen̩.te		*!					

Syllable position as a criterion in glide selection

In example 3.26, candidate (a) is preferred over (b) because (b) incurs an additional violation of *CODA. In other words, when sonority is no longer the deciding criterion in the selection of the glide (given that both vocoids are of the same sonority), the decision is passed on to syllable position. As a result, rising diphthongs are preferred to falling ones, due to the violation of *CODA incurred by the latter. *CODA must in turn dominate *COMPLEX N.

Stress shift is the result of an undominated constraint that requires stress bearers to be moraic. Since stress cannot be deleted, MAX-Stress must also be undominated.

Example 3.27

Stress/μ: Stress bearers must be moraic.

IDENT-Stress (ID-Str): Stress is associated to the same stress bearer in the input as it is in the output (no stress shift).

MAX-Stress: Stress present in the input should be present in the output (do not delete stress).

Example 3.28

Stress/μ, MAX-Stress >> ONSET >> ALIGN-LST, MAX-IOμ, IDENT-Stress

Example 3.29   /menú antiguo/ [me.nu̯án̠.ti.ɣu̯o]

	Stress/μ, MAX-Str	ONSET	ALIGN-LST	MAX-IOμ	ID-Str
a. ☞ me.nu̯lán̠.tiɣu̯o			*	*	*
b. me.nú.lan̠.tiɣu̯o		*!			
c. me.nu̯lan̠.tiɣu̯o	*! (MAX-Str)		*	*	
d. me.nú̯lan̠.tiɣu̯o	*! (Stress/μ)		*	*	

In example 3.29, candidates (c) and (d) are eliminated because they violate the highest ranked stress constraints. (b) incurs an ONSET violation, while the winner's highest mark is for ALIGN-LST. Although (a) also violates ID-Str (due to stress shift), this is a low-ranked constraint. The ranking of ID-Str in relation to mid/μ, hi/μ, and *CODA is undetermined at this point. For that reason and for simplicity of presentation, those constraints have been omitted from example 3.29.

Note that the stress faithfulness constraints introduced in example 3.27 do not indicate whether they are IO or OO constraints. This depends on whether stress is considered to be lexically specified or assigned by means of phonological rules or constraints (i.e., /menú/ or [menú]). While generative phonologists would argue for the second position (contrary to examplar models of phonology as in Hualde 1999b or Bybee 2001), even within a generative model instances of lexically specified stress (marked patterns) cannot be ruled out. For this reason, I prefer to leave the matter undecided and refer to these constraints only as MAX-Str and ID-Str.

Roca (1991), Hualde (1994), and Navarro Tomás (1980, 157) note that stress
shift is only possible if the vowel which was originally stressed is the first
one in the sequence. If the second vowel is stressed, it carries phrase stress
and there is normally no diphthongization:

busca una	busc[a.ú]na	'looks for one'
otro hito	otr[o.í]to	'another milestone'
su alma	s[u.á]1.ma	'his soul'

Additional research into the phonology of stress is necessary to determine the
exact nature of the constraint involved here. Yet it is not unreasonable to speculate that the relevant constraint would be a highly ranked positional IDENT-
Stress that requires faithfulness to phrasal stress. Positional faithfulness was
originally proposed with respect to features in prominent syllabic positions like
IDENT^{ONSET}(voice) (Beckman 1997), but it could be extended to other phonological units in prominent positions (cf. IDENT-PROMINENCE[–continuant], in
section 2.2.2.1.1; also see Colina 2006a for an extension regarding morpheme
realization and the focus position). This restriction on stress shift could also be
related to the ranking of IDENT-Stress with respect to *CODA.

Identical vowels

Identical vowels satisfy ONSET through coalescence (violation of UNIFORMITY),
which also satisfies an OCP-type constraint against identical segments, *GEMI-
NATES (*GEM) (NO-LONG in Baković 2006). The label *GEM is used here
because these segments are in fact geminates, not long vowels.[3]

Example 3.30

*GEM, ONSET >> UNIFORMITY

Example 3.31   Identical vowels /te espeɾo/ [tes.pe.ɾo]

	*GEM	ONSET	ALIGN-LST	MAX-IOµ	UNIF.
a. ☞ tes.pe.ɾo			*	*	*
b. teles.pe.ɾo	*!		*	*	
c. teles.pe.ɾo	*!		*	*	
d. te.les.pe.ɾo		*!			

The constraint low/µ has been omitted from the tableau in example 3.31 for reasons
of space; all candidates trivially satisfy this constraint, since none contains a low
vowel. Also not shown is a candidate with raising of the mid vowel [ties.pe.ɾo].
That this is not the optimal candidate indicates that the constraint requiring identity of featural specification for [high] in the input and output is highly ranked.
This will become relevant in the analysis of the Chicano data. The evidence for
OCP effects (*GEM), rather than those of mid/µ (which would also select (a) over
(b) and (c) in example 3.31) lies in the fact that diphthongs with mid glides
(where the other component of the diphthong is not mid) do not show coalescence, but gliding of the mid vowel. Again, mid/µ, hi/µ, and *CODA have been
omitted for ease of presentation.

Example 3.32   Diphthongization in Peninsular Spanish

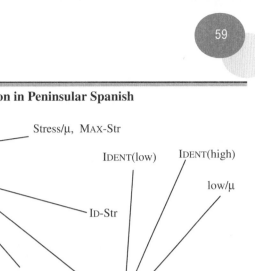

The relevance and rankings of the constraints IDENT(low), IDENT(high), and MAX-V will become apparent in section 3.2.2 in regard to the Chicano Spanish data (see example 3.41a). Although not shown here, in Peninsular Spanish MAX-V dominates ONSET because onset satisfaction is never accomplished through vowel deletion

3.2.2 DIPHTHONGIZATION ACROSS WORDS: CHICANO SPANISH

Chicano Spanish, a variety of Spanish spoken in the southwestern United States, shares some features of diphthongization across words with Peninsular Spanish, but also exhibits some differences in behavior. The data below are from Baković (2006) (see also Martínez-Gil 2000 for additional data).

Example 3.33   Two identical vowels surface as one

lo odio	[loði̯o]	'hate-1SG it/him'
mi hijo	[mixo]	'my son'

Example 3.34   A low vowel is deleted before any word-initial vowel

la iglesia	[liɣlesi̯a]	'the church'
paga Evita	[paɣeβita]	'Evita pays'
casa humilde	[kasumi̯lde]	'humble home'
niña orgullosa	[niɲorɣuyosa]	'proud girl'

Example 3.35 **The first vowel is mid and the second vowel disagrees only in height: only the high vowel surfaces**

se hinca	[siŋka]	'kneels'
como uvitas	[komuβitas]	'like grapes-DIM'

In all remaining cases, when the first vowel is high, as in example 3.36, and when the first vowel is mid and the second vowel differs from it in a feature other than height, as in example 3.37, the first vowel becomes a glide. The second vowel never becomes a glide in Chicano Spanish.

Example 3.36

mi última	[mi̯ultima]	'my last one-FEM'
mi hebra	[mi̯eβra]	'my thread'
mi obra	[mi̯oβra]	'my deed'
mi árbol	[mi̯arβol]	'my tree'
tu hijo	[tu̯ixo]	'your son'
tu época	[tu̯epoka]	'your time'
su Homero	[su̯omero]	'your Homer'
tu alma	[tu̯alma]	'your soul'

Example 3.37

me urge	[mi̯urxe]	'it is urgent to me'
pague ocho	[paɣi̯očo]	'that s/he pay eight'
porque aveces	[porki̯aβeses]	'because sometimes'
tengo hipo	[teŋgu̯ipo]	'I have the hiccups'
como Eva	[komu̯eβa]	'like Eva'
lo habla	[lu̯aβla]	'speaks it'

3.2.2.1 OT ANALYSIS

The constraints and constraint ranking to be presented correspond in general to those proposed by Baković (2006) to account for the Chicano data in examples 3.33–3.37, with a few modifications to allow for comparison with the Peninsular data.[4] The analysis differs from Baković's in that it incorporates sonority constraints that capture the relationship between the sonority of a vocoid and its ability to be parsed as a glide.[5] This is an important factor in trying to explain the strategies resorted to in order to satisfy ONSET. It also serves to account for the difference in resolution strategies across dialects. A few additional minor differences with respect to Baković (2006) are the incorporation of *CODA throughout the analysis to explain the lack of falling diphthongs (cf. Peninsular), and the constraint *COMPLEX N (ONE-TO-ONE in Baković). Although not crucial, these modifications are necessary to show more clearly that an OT analysis can account for cross-dialectal variation with the same set of universal constraints ranked in a dialect-specific manner. This will be essential to demonstrate the superiority of an OT account over a serial one.

Since Chicano Spanish, unlike Peninsular Spanish, does not allow mid glides, ONSET cannot dominate the constraint against mid glides as it does in Peninsular, because this would wrongly predict gliding of mid vowels to avoid an ONSET violation. The ranking is that in example 3.23 above, repeated here as example 3.38.

Example 3.38   **No low or mid glides**

low/µ >> mid/µ

mid/µ, ONSET >> ALIGN-LST, MAX-IOµ, hi/µ

Also, unlike Peninsular, mid vowel raising (i.e., a violation of IDENT(high)) is possible in Chicano in order to avoid a mid vowel glide and an onsetless syllable. IDENT(high) must therefore be dominated by ONSET, as well as by mid/µ.

Example 3.39   **Mid vowel raising**

a. IDENT(high): The [high] specification for the input must be identical to that of the output.

b. mid/µ, ONSET >> IDENT(high), hi/µ

In addition, the data in examples 3.33–3.37 show that glide (or nucleus) selection is not dependent on sonority as in Peninsular Spanish, but on position within the syllable, as it is always the first vocoid that glides and the second that is selected as the nucleus. Such a generalization can be captured by the ranking of *CODA over *COMPLEX N. In example 3.9, on the basis of consonantal resyllabification, it was established that ONSET >> ALIGN-LST >> *CODA, and then, by transitivity, ONSET >> *CODA.

Example 3.40   **The second vowel is never a glide: no falling diphthongs**

ONSET >> *CODA >> *COMPLEX N

When the first vowel is a low vowel (which cannot become a glide due to the high ranking of low/µ), deletion is preferred to gliding of the second vowel, thus the ranking must be *CODA >> MAX-V. Since gliding of a high vowel and mid vowel raising are preferred to deletion of high or mid vowels, then MAX-V must dominate hi/µ, and IDENT(high). Given that these rankings result in a complex nucleus (diphthong), MAX-V also dominates *COMPLEX N.[6] As shown in example 3.41 (b–c), mid/µ is not crucially ranked with respect to *CODA and MAX-V.

Since the only featural change allowed is height, the constraints regulating faithfulness to input specification for the rest of the vowel features (low, back) must also be highly ranked.

In what follows, candidate evaluation is shown for the data above. The relevant rankings are repeated as needed. The tableau in example 3.43 shows candidate evaluation for two identical vowels; identical vowels in the input and their

Example 3.41   Deletion of /a/

a. MAX-V: A vowel present in the input must have a correspondent in the output.

b. low/μ, ONSET >> *CODA >> MAX-V >> IDENT(high), hi/μ, *COMPLEX N

c. mid/μ, ONSET >> IDENT(high), hi/μ

Example 3.42

a. IDENT(low): The [low] specification for the input must be identical to that of the output.

     IDENT(back): The [back] specification for the input must be identical to that of the output.

b. IDENT(low), IDENT(back), ONSET >> *CODA >> MAX-V >> IDENT(high), hi/μ, *COMPLEX N

---

output correspondents are identified through subindices. The crucial ranking is *GEM, ONSET >> MAX-V >> UNIFORMITY. That coalescence is preferred to deletion is reflected in the domination of MAX-V over UNIFORMITY.

     For reasons of ease of presentation, only the crucial constraints are shown in the tableau in example 3.43. Coalescence (UNIFORMITY violation) is resorted to in order to avoid an onsetless syllable, two contiguous identical segments, and vowel deletion. Thus, (a) is the optimal candidate, since it only contains one violation of the lowest ranked UNIFORMITY compared to the violations of top-ranking constraints (*GEM, ONSET) incurred by (b–d). (e) and (f) contain violations of MAX-V due to the deletion of the second and first input vowels, respectively.

Example 3.43   Coalescence under identity
$$/mi_1 \; i_2xo/ \; [mi_{1,2}xo]$$

	*GEM	ONSET	MAX-V	IDENT(high)	hi/μ	UNIF.
a. ☞ mi$_{1,2}$xo						*
b. mi̯i.xo	*!				*	
c. mi̯i.xo	*!				*	
d. mi.i.xo		*!				
e. mi$_1$.xo			*!			
f. mi$_2$.xo			*!			

As seen in example 3.44, candidates with a high glide (b) or a low glide (d) are eliminated because they violate the high-ranking *CODA and low/μ, respectively. (c) contains an ONSET violation. Therefore candidate (a), with low vowel deletion, is the optimal candidate and the winner. The high ranking of *CODA explains the difference with respect to Peninsular Spanish, which would choose (b) as the optimal candidate because of the high ranking of MAX-V (as in example 3.32). For the same input, featural modification of /a/ (to make it into a different vowel and thus avoid violations of *CODA, low/μ) is not a feasible strategy. Therefore, IDENT(low) must be highly ranked, dominating MAX-V. This can be seen in example 3.45.

Example 3.44 **Low vowel deletion**[7]
/la iglesia/ [li.ɣle.sɪ̯a]

low/μ, ONSET >> *CODA >> MAX-V >> IDENT(high), hi/μ

	low/μ	ONSET	*CODA	MAX-V	IDENT(high)	hi/μ
a. ☞ liɣlesɪ̯a				*		
b. laɪ̯.ɣle.sɪ̯a			*!			*
c. la.i.ɣle.sɪ̯a			*!			
d. laɪ̯.ɣle.sɪ̯a	*!					

Example 3.45 **Featural modification of /a/ is not a viable strategy**
/la iglesia/ [li.ɣle.sɪ̯a]

	IDENT(low)	MAX-V	IDENT(high)	hi/μ
a. ☞ li.ɣle.sɪ̯a		*		
b. lei̯.ɣle.sɪ̯a	*!			
c. lii̯.ɣle.sɪ̯a	*!		*	*
d. loi̯.ɣle.sɪ̯a	*!			
e. lui̯.ɣle.sɪ̯a	*!		*	*

Example 3.46 **Gliding: first vowel is high**
/mi ultima/ [mɪ̯ul̯.ti.ma]

	ONSET	*CODA	MAX-V	IDENT(high)	hi/μ	*COMPLEX N
a. ☞ mɪ̯ul̯.ti.ma					*	*
b. miul̯.ti.ma		*!			*	
c. mi.ul̯.ti.ma	*!					
d. mul̯.ti.ma			*!			

In example 3.46, (a) is the optimal candidate because its highest violation is hi/μ. The competing candidates—(b) with gliding of the second vocoid, (c) with no glides, and (d) with deletion of the first vowel—all violate more highly ranked constraints, namely *CODA, ONSET, and MAX-V, respectively.

In example 3.47, candidate (a), in which a high glide corresponds to the mid vowel of the input (raising), is better than competing candidates with a mid glide (b), no glides (c), vowel deletion (d), and a glide corresponding to the second vocoid (e). Candidate (a) only incurs violations of IDENT(high), hi/μ, and *COMPLEX N, which are all ranked below the constraints violated by the other candidates, mid/μ, ONSET, MAX-V, and *CODA.

As example 3.48 shows, candidates with a mid glide (b), two vowels (c), a high glide (d), a falling diphthong (e), and vowel deletion (f) are worse than (a), the candidate with coalescence and a mid vowel in correspondence with a high

Example 3.47 **Gliding: first vowel is mid and the second differs in a feature other than high**
/me urxe/ [mi̯ur.xe]

	mid/μ	ONSET	*CODA	MAX-V	IDENT(hi)	hi/μ	*COMPLEX N
a. ☞ mi̯ur.xe					*	*	*
b. me̯ur.xe	*!						
c. me.ur.xe			*!				
d. mur.xe				*!			
e. me̯ur.xe			*!			*	*

Example 3.48 **Mid vowel does not surface: first vowel is mid and the second disagrees in height only**
/se₁ i₂nka/ [si₁,₂ŋ.ka]

	*GEM	mid/μ	ONSET	*CODA	MAX-V	ID(hi)	hi/μ	*COMP N	UNIF.
a. ☞ si₁,₂ŋ.ka						*			*
b. se̯iŋ.ka		*!						*	
c. se.iŋ.ka			*!						
d. si̯iŋ.ka	*!					*	*	*	
e. se̯iŋka				*!			*		
f. si₂ŋka					*!				

vowel (raising). All the constraints that the other candidates violate (mid/μ, ONSET, *GEM, *CODA, and MAX-V, respectively) are ranked above the constraints, namely, IDENT(high) and UNIFORMITY, violated by (a).

To summarize, some of the main differences in ranking between Peninsular and Chicano are the higher ranking of *CODA in Chicano, which selects the first vowel as the target for gliding (violation of MAX-IOμ), and the low ranking of IDENT(high) in the same dialect, which explains mid vowel raising. The higher ranking of IDENT(high) in Peninsular results in the well-formedness of mid glides, and the high ranking of MAX-V rules out low vowel deletion. Both dialects have a preference for high glides and both reduce identical vowels to one vowel through coalescence. When combined with mid-glide raising and Chicano's dislike for mid glides, this preference for coalescence results in the coalescence of mid-high vowel sequences of the same height in that dialect.

3.2.2.2 COMPARISON WITH A SERIAL ACCOUNT

In order to demonstrate the superiority of an OT analysis of diphthongization across words, I review a recent derivational account of Chicano (Martínez-Gil 2000). Martínez-Gil (2000) explains the Chicano data by means of a series of rules, including a demorification rule in which the first vowel in a diphthong loses its mora (see example 3.49).

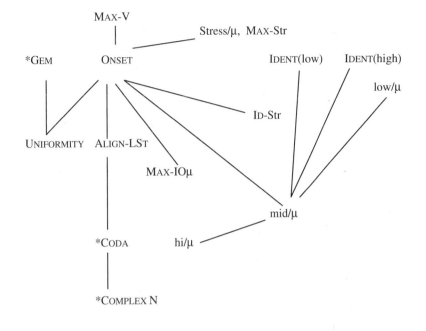

Peninsular Spanish

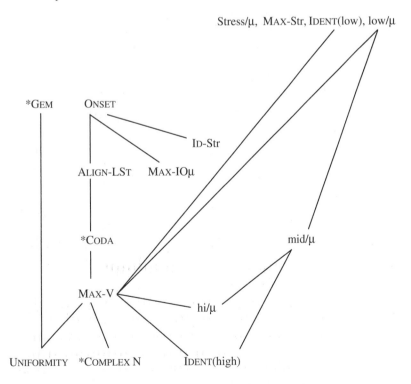

Chicano Spanish

Figure 3.5 Diphthongization in Spanish: Chicano and Peninsular compared

Example 3.49   **Diphthongization in Chicano Spanish**

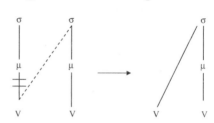

Example 3.50   **Default vowels are high**

σ
|

[−consonant] → [+hi]

Example 3.51   **Deletion of identical vowels**

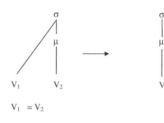

$V_1 = V_2$

Martínez-Gil argues that the universal principle in example 3.50 assigns the feature [+high] to any vowel associated to a non-nuclear position in the syllable, reflecting the fact that high vowels make the best glides (see also Harris 1985) When a high glide is followed by a high vowel with which it agrees in backness, the application of the rule in example 3.50 produces two identical vowels; this serves as the input for a rule that deletes one of two identical vowels, as in example 3.51.

Example 3.52   **Deletion of [+low] [+high] vowel**

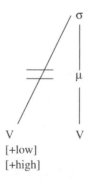

V   V
[+low]
[+high]

When the first vowel in the input to example 3.49 is low, the universal principle in example 3.50 creates a contradiction (+low, +high) that results in the deletion of the vowel specified as [+low] and [+high] (i.e., low vowel deletion) in example 3.52.

Examples 3.53–3.57 contain some sample derivations for the examples presented in the OT account (examples 3.43–3.48).

Martínez-Gil's (2000) analysis argues for the underspecification of mid vowels; thus, when example 3.50 applies to an underspecified mid vowel filling in the feature [+high], as in examples 3.56–3.57, mid vowel raising is obtained as a direct result.

Advantages of an OT account of diphthongization

Although Martínez-Gil's analysis is clearly superior to other serial analyses (see Martínez-Gil 2000 for argumentation and details), it still suffers from several framework-specific deficiencies not faced by a nonderivational account.

Example 3.53   /mi ixo/

[mi̯ixo]   diphthongization (example 3.49)

[mixo]   deletion of identical vowels (example 3.51)

Example 3.54   /la iglesia/

[la̯iɣlesi̯a]   diphthongization (example 3.49)

[li̯ɣlesi̯a]   deletion of [+low] [+high] vowel (example 3.52)

Example 3.55   /mi ultima/

[mi̯uḻtima]   diphthongization (example 3.49)

Example 3.56   /me urxe/

[me̯urxe]   diphthongization (example 3.49)

[mi̯urxe]   default glides are high (example 3.50)

Example 3.57   /se inka/

[se̯iŋka]   diphthongization (example 3.49)

[si̯iŋka]   default glides are high (example 3.50)

[siŋka]   deletion of identical vowels (example 3.51)

For instance, the diphthongization rule in example 3.49 is a language-specific rule that does not provide any insight into why a rule like this should exist. An OT account, on the other hand, reveals the motivation behind diphthongization: the universal tendency (expressed through a universal constraint) to avoid onsetless syllables. It also highlights typological differences with regard to diphthongization: While some languages tolerate onsetless syllables (in order to be faithful to the input), others resort to various strategies to improve upon the syllable type.

Peninsular and Chicano Spanish belong to this last type of language, despite the fact that they make use of different strategies. In doing so, they exhibit variation in the ranking of faithfulness over markedness constraints. Chicano allows modification of input specification for [high], while Peninsular has faithfulness ranked higher than markedness, allowing for the more marked mid glide, rather than being unfaithful to the input by making it high. Peninsular does not permit vowel deletion, again because of the higher ranking of faithfulness constraints. Chicano, on the other hand, values unmarked syllable structure more than faithfulness, and will delete a vowel rather than create a syllable with a coda. Another problem of derivational accounts is that they do not provide a true explanation of the fact that Peninsular Spanish allows mid glides, while Chicano does not; similarly, derivational accounts offer no real insight into why mid vowels become high glides in Chicano, but not in Peninsular. Since the explanation for the raising of mid vowels in Chicano in a derivational account like Martínez-Gil's (2000) is connected to the underspecification of the default vowel [e], one would have to assume that [e] is not underspecified in Peninsular. However, this difference of behavior remains without justification, since [e] is the default, epenthetic vowel in both dialects.

The real problem is that a derivational account cannot capture the connection between the raising of mid vowels and the need to avoid a mid glide in Chicano, nor can it capture the connection between the gliding of mid vowels and the need to preserve the featural specification of the vowel in Peninsular. An OT account can incorporate these facts directly into the analysis through the hierarchy of constraints because they result from the tension between faithfulness to the underlying representation (a mid vowel) and markedness (mid glides are more marked than high glides according to sonority).

An additional deficiency of a derivational account of Chicano diphthongization is its need for extrinsic rule ordering: In order for the rules to produce the correct output, example 3.50 must apply before example 3.51 (degemination). Finally, Martínez-Gil (2000) uses rule simplification to explain why the second vowel in the sequence is never the target of diphthongization and deletion. A rule like the one existing in Peninsular can apply to both vowels (rule and mirror image application); in Chicano, however, the rule has lost its mirror image. While this works, it does not provide a true explanation of why it should be so. In an OT analysis, that only the first vocoid is affected by diphthongization, deletion, coalescence, or raising shows the effect of a universal *CODA constraint, the effects of which can also be seen in its more strict restrictions on coda consonants in this dialect (compared to Standard Peninsular, see section 2.2.2.1.1).

3.3 SUMMARY

This chapter has reviewed syllabification across words, focusing on consonant resyllabification and diphthongization. A derivational account of resyllabification was summarized and compared to an optimality-theoretic account. The superiority of the OT account was demonstrated by showing that OT and its system of minimally violable constraints bring forth an important insight regarding resyllabification, namely that alignment of the syllable with the word can be sacrificed in order to provide an onset for a vowel-initial word; however, when the word already has an onset (i.e., it is consonant initial), there is no need to resyllabify a second consonant, since this resyllabification would unnecessarily misalign the syllable and the word. A serial account (in which a Complex Onset Rule applies only at the lexical level and an Onset Rule applies lexically and postlexically) cannot capture the true motivation of the phenomenon.

OT analyses of diphthongization in Peninsular and Chicano were presented and shown to be able to incorporate dialectal differences (e.g., gliding of mid vowels versus raising of mid vowels; gliding of only the first vowel in the sequence versus gliding of the least sonorous vowel) in a direct way not available to derivational analyses. A derivational analysis of Chicano diphthongization was compared to the OT account and shown to be a less adequate explanation than the latter.

STUDY QUESTIONS

1. How does an OT account shed light on resyllabification in Spanish?
2. How does an OT account formalize glide selection in syllable merger across words in Peninsular Spanish?
3. What are the major descriptive differences between syllable merger in Peninsular and Chicano Spanish? What are the crucial rankings that account for them in an OT account?
4. In addition to its account of dialectal variation, what are some other advantages of an OT analysis of syllable merger?

GOING BACK TO THE SOURCES

Baković 2006:

> Hiatus Resolution and Incomplete Identity. *Optimality-Theoretic Studies in Spanish Phonology.* Ed. Fernando Martínez-Gil and Sonia Colina. Philadelphia: John Benjamins.

Hualde 1994:

> La contracción silábica en español. *Gramática del español.* Ed. Violeta Demonte. México: El Colegio de México (Nueva Revista de Filología Hispánica VI).

Martínez-Gil 2000:

> La estructura prosódica y la especificación vocálica en español: el problema de la sinalefa en ciertas variedades de la lengua coloquial contemporánea. *Panorama de la fonología española actual.* Ed. Juana Gil Fernández. Madrid: Arco Libros.

Martínez-Gil 2004:

> Hiatus resolution in Chicano Spanish. Paper presented at the 34th Linguistics Symposium on Romance Languages, University of Utah, Salt Lake City.

KEY TOPICS

SPANISH PHONOLOGY

   resyllabification

   onset maximization

syllabification rules

dipthongization (syllable merger)

glide formation

hiatus resolution

sonority scale

mid vowel raising

vowel deletion

degemination

coalescense

stress preservation

stress shift

postlexical (phrasal) environment

PHONOLOGICAL THEORY/OT

input-output versus output-to-output constraints

Stratal OT

TOPICS FOR FURTHER RESEARCH

1. Can speech rate be formalized in OT?
2. Can OT account for stress preservation and stress shifts across the word?
3. Can across-the-word phenomena provide evidence for a word level even in a nonderivational model of phonology?

NOTES

1. The stem is chosen here because it obviates the issue of discriminating between the morphological and the prosodic word (see Roca 2005, 204).
2. Violations incurred by segments not pertinent to the discussion are not included.
3. I thank Iggy Roca (personal communication) for this observation.
4. For an alternative OT analysis of the Chicano data, see Martínez-Gil 2004. Martínez-Gil (2004), however, does not incorporate the account of the Peninsular data.
5. Note, for instance, that Baković does not include candidates with mid or low glides (e.g., [a̯ e̯ o̯]) in his tableaux.
6. As Iggy Roca (personal communication) points out, Chicano Spanish does have falling diphthongs, for example, *jaula* [xau̯la] 'cage.' Baković explains this as the result of a preference for a high glide. This explanation, however, does not account for /a/ deletion in [liɣlesi̯a]. I argue that falling diphthongs exist word-internally as the result of the

domination of Morph-CONTIGUITY (no deletion or insertion morpheme-internally) over MAX-V.

7. Being one-dimensional, tableaux and linear constraint rankings have some representational limitations: Some constraints may appear to dominate others, when in fact they are not crucially ranked. For instance, in Chicano low/μ appears to dominate *CODA. Yet, low/μ is not crucially ranked with respect to *CODA (see Hasse diagrams). The same can be said with respect to mid/μ and *CODA and *MAX-V in examples 3.47 and 3.48, and with respect to *GEM and all constraints but UNIFORMITY in examples 3.43 and 3.48. Hasse diagrams offer a more accurate representation of ranking relations. The reader is urged to consult these.

4

The Syllable and Morphological Constituents

4.1 DOMAIN OF SYLLABIFICATION IN DERIVATIONAL MODELS

In a derivational model of phonology, rules apply sequentially and within certain domains; thus, rule-based models of syllabification need to specify the domain of syllabification, in addition to the order of application of syllabification rules with respect to phonological rules and to morphological operations such as suffixation, prefixation, and compounding. On the basis of resyllabification, aspiration, and onset strengthening data, Hualde (1989b, 1991) convincingly argues that the domain of syllabification in Spanish is a unit smaller than the word. In what follows I will summarize Hualde's proposal and then compare it with an optimality-theoretic account. In an OT analysis domain and rule ordering, facts can be obtained directly from general mechanisms, such as universal constraints that capture the interaction between morphology and syllabification/phonology. The data and analysis to be presented below are important not only with regard to syllabification and its interaction with morphology, but also in terms of shedding light onto certain phonological phenomena, namely /s/-aspiration, /n/-velarization, /r/-strengthening, and onset strengthening, and their role in the controversy regarding serialism and strata in OT.

As was mentioned above, Hualde (1989b, 1991) argues that the domain of syllabification in Spanish is a unit smaller than the word, as syllabification seems to apply before the adjunction of prefixes and before compounding, but after suffixation. In particular, productive prefixes are separated from the rest of the word for syllabification purposes; members of a compound also constitute separate domains. The main piece of evidence in support of this proposal is that processes, such as /s/-aspiration, /n/-velarization, onset strengthening, and /r/-strengthening

73

make reference to syllabic components (coda and onset) that do not correspond to those occupied by the relevant segments in the surface. Thus, the rules must have applied while the segments were in the relevant positions, before the adjunction of prefixes and before compounding, but after suffixation. A subsequent application of resyllabification would then move the segments to their surface positions.

Example 4.1

	'months'	'undone'	'god-heroes'
	[[mes]es]	[des[[eč]o]	[[dios]es][[eroe]s]
Level 1			
Suffixes	[meses]	[des[ečo]]	[[dioses][eroes]]
Syllab.	[me.ses]	[des.[e.čo]]	[[di̯o.ses][e.ro.es]]
Aspiration	h	h	h h
Level 2			
Prefix/Comp.	———	[deh.e.čo]	[di̯o.seh.e.ro.eh]
Resyllab.	———	[de.he.čo]	[di̯o.se.he.ro.eh]
Postlexical level			

/s/-aspiration

/s/-aspiration says that /s/ is realized as [h] in a coda. In example 4.1, at level 1, suffixation is followed by syllabification and aspiration, which explains why stem-final /s/ is not aspirated; aspiration then applies to prefix-final (and word-final) /s/ before prefixes are incorporated into the stem. At level 2, prefix incorporation and compounding take place, followed by syllabification, which will move coda [h] to the onset position. In some dialects (referred to as Caribbean II by Kaisse (1997, 1998)) aspiration applies after prefixation and resyllabification, but before compounding.

/n/-velarization

Some dialects of Spanish also have /n/-velarization, by which /n/ is realized as [ŋ] in a coda. The process is similar to that of /s/-aspiration: In example 4.2, at level 1, suffixation is followed by syllabification and velarization, which explains stem final [n] in the plural; velarization then applies to prefix-final (and word-final) /n/ before prefixes are incorporated into the stem. At level 2, prefix incorporation and compounding take place, followed by resyllabification, which will move coda [ŋ] to the onset position.

Onset strengthening

Two processes affect onset segments: onset strengthening and /r/-strengthening, in which a high vocoid /i/ becomes a palatal fricative or affricate, and a rhotic is realized as a trill at the beginning of a word, respectively. In example 4.3, at level 1, suffixation is followed by syllabification and onset strengthening, explaining the contrast between [des.[i̯e.lo]] and [de.si̯er.to]. Since at this point the prefix [des] has not been incorporated and is therefore not visible, [s] fails to resyllabify to the onset in [des.[i̯e.lo]]. Given that the prefix [des] is not available for syllabification, [i̯] in [i̯elo] will be in the onset at the time that onset strengthening applies, resulting in [des.ye.lo]. At level 2, prefix incorporation and compounding take place, followed by syllabification. Similarly to the previous processes, syllabification must have applied before prefixation and compounding (because the vocoid needs to be in the onset to undergo strengthening); syllabification thus applies in a domain smaller than the word, before the adjunction of prefixes and compounds.

Example 4.2

	'goods'	'well-being'	'inhumane'
	[bi̯en][[bi̯en]es]	[[bi̯en][[est]ar]]	[in[[uman]o]]
Level 1			
Suffixes	[bi̯enes]	[[bi̯en] [estar]]	[in[umano]]
Syllab.	[bi̯en][bi̯e.nes]	[[bi̯en] [es.tar]]	[in[u.ma.no]]
Velariz.	ŋ _____	ŋ	ŋ
Level 2			
Prefix/Comp.		[bi̯eŋ.es.tar]	[iŋ.u.ma.no]
Resyllab.		[bi̯e.ŋes.tar]	[i.ŋu.ma.no]
	[bi̯eŋ][bi̯e.nes]	[bi̯e.ŋes.tar]	[i.ŋu.ma.no]

Example 4.3

	'thawing'	'desert'	'disarmament'
	[des[[i̯el]o]]	[[desi̯ert]o]	[des[[arm]e]]
Level 1			
Suffixes	[des[i̯elo]]	[desi̯erto]	[des[arme]]
Syllab.	[des.[i̯e.lo]]	[de.si̯er.to]	[des.[ar.me]]
Ons. strengt.	y	_____	_____
Level 2			
Prefix/Comp.	[des.ye.lo]	[de.si̯er.to]	[des.ar.me]
Resyllab.	_____	_____	[de.sar.me]
Other rules	[dez.ye.lo]	_____	_____

/r/-
strengthening

In example 4.4, /r/-strengthening must apply before prefixation and compounding; otherwise, incorrect forms such as *[ultɾaɾepublikano], *[aɾinkonado], *[mataɾatas] would occur, since /r/ is no longer in word-initial position after prefixation and compounding. The flap allophone of /r/ appears in onset clusters, in the coda, and optionally in word-final position (see section 4.2.4).

Thus, Hualde (1989b, 1991) concludes that syllabification applies in a domain that is smaller than the word, before the adjunction of prefixes and suffixes, as demonstrated by the application of rules that have syllabic information in their structural description. The interaction between morphology and phonology is seen as resulting from the extrinsic ordering of phonological rules (including syllabification) and morphological operations, and the domain of syllabification.

Example 4.4

	'ultra-republican'	'cornered'	'rat poison'
	[ultra[[[republik]an]o]]	[a[[[rinkon]ad]o]]	[[mata][[[rat]a]s]]

Level 1

Suffixes	[ultra[republikano]]	[a[rinkonado]]	[[mata][ratas]]
/r/-strengt.	r	r	r

Level 2

Prefix/Comp.	[ultrarepublikano]	[arinkonado]	[mataratas]

Example 4.5

	Morphosyntax	Phonology
Level 1	suffixation	syllabification
		/s/-aspiration /n/-velarization onset strengthening /r/-strengthening
Level 2	prefixation and compounding	resyllabification
Postlexical level		resyllabification

4.2 DOMAIN OF SYLLABIFICATION IN AN OT ACCOUNT

In an OT analysis the issues of the domain of syllabification and phonological levels can be obtained directly from the general mechanisms that capture the interaction between morphology and phonology (syllabification). More specifically, this type of interaction is formalized through alignment constraints that refer to morphological and prosodic constituents (Kager 1999, 117–120) provides the general format of alignment constraints). In Spanish two main constraints are responsible for word-level syllabification (before affixation and compounding). One of them is ALIGN-LST (example 4.6), as seen in chapter 3.

Example 4.6

ALIGN (Stem, L, Syllable, L) (ALIGN-LST): Align the left edge of the syllable with the left edge of the stem.

That syllabification applies after suffixation shows the effects of ALIGN-R (example 4.7).

Example 4.7

ALIGN (Word, R, Syllable, R) (ALIGN-R): The right edge of a morphological word coincides with the right edge of a syllable.

Wiltshire (2006) proposes ALIGN-L(PW, σ) and ALIGN-R(PW, σ): The left/right edge of the word and syllable coincide. Formally, for every prosodic word (PW) there must be some syllable such that the left/right edge of the PW and left/right edge of the syllable are aligned.

In what follows it is shown that ALIGN-LST (in combination with the constraints responsible for onset strengthening, /r/-strengthening, /s/-aspiration, and nasal velarization, and those seen for resyllabification in chapter 3) is sufficient to account for the relevant forms. No extrinsic ordering of phonological rules and morphological operations is necessary. There is also no need to refer to a domain of syllabification or to levels or strata. An optimality-theoretic analysis of each of these processes is proposed in sections 4.2.1–4.2.4

4.2.1 /S/-ASPIRATION

/s/-aspiration and nasal velarization differ from /r/-strengthening and onset strengthening in that they affect coda positions; in word- or prefix-final prevocalic positions they constitute examples of opacity, in other words, the relevant segments appear in contexts that do not meet the structural description of their rules. Resyllabification of the word- or prefix-final consonant to the onset should prevent /s/-aspiration and /n/-velarization from applying, since the segments are no longer in coda position; however, the rule seems to have applied nonetheless. Colina (2002) explains this behavior of /s/-aspiration in an optimality-theoretic framework through the effects of output-to-output identity constraints on the form of the Prosodic Word. In an alternative account, Wiltshire (2006) resorts to WEAK constraints.

Some dialects of Spanish (e.g., Granada Spanish, and the dialects referred to as Caribbean I by Kaisse (1997, 1998)) aspirate in prefixal and phrasal contexts as well as in compounds (example 4.8).

Example 4.8

mes	[meh]	'month'
mes-es	[me.seh]	'months'
des-hecho	[de.he.čo]	'undone'
dioses-héroes	[dio.se.he.ro.eh]	'god-heroes'
mes azul	[me.ha.sul]	'blue month'

Colina (2002) proposes that /s/-aspiration in Caribbean I dialects results from the domination of the markedness constraint *CODA/s (no [s] in coda position) over MAX-IO(SL) (example 4.10). Faithfulness constraints (F) (e.g., DEP-IO, MAX-IO,

Example 4.9

*CODA/s: No [s] in coda position

MAX-IO(SL): All supralaryngeal nodes present in the input must be present in the output.

Example 4.10

F, *CODA/s >> MAX-IO(SL)

Example 4.11   /mes + es/ [me.seh]

	F, *CODA/s	MAX-IO(SL)
a. ☞ me.seh		(*)
b. me.heh		(*)*!

IDENT-IO) also outrank MAX-IO(SL), since no other modification of the input segment /s/ is preferred to SL node deletion

Example 4.11 shows evaluation of suffixed forms. In example 4.11 both candidates satisfy *CODA/s: (a) contains no violations of *CODA/s because intervocalic [s] is no longer in coda position. In addition, (a) and (b) share a common violation of MAX-IO(SL), indicated in parentheses, due to aspiration of final /s/. Since (b) has a second violation mark not present in (a), (a) is selected as the winner.

An antiallomorphy constraint is responsible for /s/-aspiration in prevocalic, word-final position

For phrases, an output-to-output antiallomorphy constraint affecting prosodic words becomes relevant (IDENTITY-PrWd). This constraint requires that prosodic words have only one output form in all contexts (antiallomorphy); domination of IDENTITY-PrWd (IDENT-PrWd) by other phonological constraints results in word allomorphy. The relevant ranking appears in example 4.12.

Example 4.12

IDENT-PrWd(SL) >> MAX-IO(SL)

F, *CODA/s >> MAX-IO(SL)

The hierarchy in example 4.12 correctly predicts that the /s/ in *mes azul* will surface as [h]. It also identifies the output prosodic word that stands in correspondence with the output.

In example 4.13, (&) identifies the form in correspondence with output candidates. (a) is a better candidate than (b) because, although (b) is closer to the underlying form /mes/, it is preferable to be faithful to the output of [meh] than to the underlying representation; in other words, (a) violates MAX-IO(SL), which is outranked by IDENT-PrWd(SL) violated by (b). Candidates (c–e) contain faithfulness violations, in addition to violations of IDENT-PrWd(SL). A candidate without resyllabification, [mes.eh], is worse than (a) because in addition to IDENT-PrWd(SL) it also violates *CODA/s and ONSET.

Example 4.13 /mes + asul/ [me.ha.sul]
            &[meh]

	F	*CODA/s	IDENT-PrWd(SL)	MAX-IO (SL)
a. ☞ me.ha.sul				*
b. me.sa.sul			*!	
c. mes.ta.sul	*!(DEP-IO)		*	
d. me.a.sul	*!(MAX-IO)		*	*
e. me.la.sul	*!(IDENT-IO)		*	

> It is important to note that in plural forms such as /mes + es/ [me.seh], the output prosodic word that enters into output-to-output correspondence relations is that of the plural form [me.seh] or alternative candidates; the winning candidate is [me.seh] because it incurs no IDENT-PrWd(SL) violations. Candidates such as [meh] or [mes] would incur additional faithfulness violations. For the singular the relevant prosodic word is the uninflected singular output; potential output candidates such as [meheh] or [meseh] would incur additional faithfulness violations due to the presence of [e] and [h].

In prefixed forms of Caribbean I dialects, the last consonant of the prefix is resyllabified in the onset while still undergoing aspiration. The data for these dialects show that prefixes behave like isolated words with regard to syllabification (rather than like suffixes). Following Peperkamp (1996), Colina (2002) and Wiltshire (2006) argue that this behavior is the result of their prosodic representation; prefixes are adjoined to the prosodic word by violating its recursivity, as in example 4.14.

Example 4.14 **PrWd-adjunction of prefixes**

PrWd

prefix   PrWd

> There is more than sufficient evidence in favor of this proposal. Prefixes have been shown to behave like units typically incorporated at the postlexical level (e.g., prosodic words, clitics) (cf. Booij and Rubach 1984 for Polish; Face 1998 for Spanish). In some languages, like German and Dutch, prefixes can also constitute separate words and, in some cases, they are historically related to independent words; Spanish prefixes, for instance, come from Latin prefixes which were in a close relationship with the prepositions, *in* 'in', *dis* (*de* + *ex*) 'of, from', *inter* 'between' (Penny 1991). In addition, it is reasonable to assume that, as part of the derivational morphology, prefixes may exhibit behavior similar to that of separate words

(not unlike the members of a compound) and contrary to that of suffixes (inflectional morphology). This is confirmed by the fact that the dialectal variation studied in this paper affects prefixes, compounds, and phrases (the morphological levels where we can find prosodic words), but not suffixed forms (always unaspirated). Finally, some languages have two types of prefixes: one that forms a prosodic word with the stem and one that constitutes an independent word (Nespor 1999; see Nespor and Vogel 1986, Peperkamp 1994 for examples in Italian). As seen here, this is the situation found in Spanish cross-dialectally, where some dialects will have one type of prefix and some will have the other.

Wiltshire (2006) shows that the prosodic structure in example 4.14 can be obtained through constraint interaction, in particular through the constraints ALIGN-L(Lex, W) (align the left edge of every lexical word with the left edge of some prosodic word), ALIGN-L/R(PW, σ) (align the left/right edge of every prosodic word with the left/right edge of some syllable), and NONREC (forbids recursive prosodic structure like that in example 4.14), and their ranking: ALIGN-L(Lex, PW) >> ALIGN-L/R(PW, σ) >> NONREC.

Antiallomorphy constraint applies to prefixes in CI dialects

In the Caribbean I dialect type, prefixes are adjoined to prosodic words and therefore IDENT-PrWd(SL) becomes relevant. Consequently, onset [h] before a vowel initial stem results from the domination of IDENT-PrWd(SL) over MAX-IO(SL).[1]

Example 4.15' explains how IDENT-PrWd(SL) violations are computed for candidates (a) and (b) in example 4.16 below ((a) and (b) in example 4.15' here). (&) is the form which stands in correspondence relation with the output forms; correspondents have been identified with subindices. (a), the candidate with aspiration, satisfies IDENT-PrWd(SL), because $h_3 = h_3$; (b) incurs one IDENT-PrWd(SL) violation due to the presence of [s] ($h_3 \neq s_3$). The internal PrWds in (a) and (b), [X]/[e.čo], stand in correspondence with [e.čo], as in $[ma.1[e.čo]_{PrWd}]_{PrWd}$, but not with [ta.par], which would enter into a correspondence relation with forms of the type $[mal.[ta.par]_{PrWd}]_{PrWd}$.

Example 4.15

IDENT-PrWd(SL) >> MAX-IO(SL)

Example 4.15'

IDENT-PrWd(SL)

& $[d_1e_2h_3.[X]_{PrWd}]_{PrWd}$, e.g., $[deh.[ta.par]_{PrWd}]_{PrWd}$

(a) $[d_1e_2h_3.[X]_{PrWd}]_{PrWd}$, e.g., $[de.h[e.čo]_{PrWd}]_{PrWd}$

(b) $[d_1e_2s_3.[X]_{PrWd}]_{PrWd}$, e.g., $*[de.s[e.čo]_{PrWd}]_{PrWd}$

       where X = stem + suffixes

Example 4.16 shows evaluation and candidate selection for Caribbean I dialects.

Allomorph selection, the selection of the allomorph that serves as the correspondent (&) for the output candidates, is a direct consequence of the constraints and constraint ranking. Since all aspirating dialects have [h] in preconsonantal position, regardless of allomorph identity, *CODA/s must dominate IDENT-PrWd(SL).

Example 4.16   /des + eco/ [de.he.čo]
             &[deh]

	F	*CODA/s	IDENT-PrWd(SL)	MAX-IO(SL)
a. ☞ de.he.čo				*
b. de.se.čo			*!	
c. des.te.čo	*! (DEP-IO)	*	*	
d. de.e.čo	*! (MAX-IO)		*	*

Given that ranking, as well as the previously established ones, candidate evaluation chooses output [de.he.čo] in correspondence with the allomorph &[deh] as the optimal candidate. The presence of a [des] allomorph, which would make the correspon-

Example 4.17   /des + tapar/ [deh.ta.par]
             &[deh]

	F	*CODA/s	IDENT-PrWd(SL)	MAX-IO(SL)
a. ☞ deh.ta.par				*
b. des.ta.par		*!	*	
c. des.tra.par	*! (DEP-IO)	*	*	
d. de.ta.par	*! (MAX-IO)		*	*
e. del.ta.par	*! (IDENT-IO)		*	

Example 4.18   /des + tapar/ [deh.ta.par]
             &[des]

	F	*CODA/s	IDENT-PrWd(SL)	MAX-IO(SL)
a. ☞ deh.ta.par			*	*
b. des.ta.par		*!		
c. des.tra.par	*! (DEP-IO)	*		
d. de.ta.par	*! (MAX-IO)		*	*
e. del.ta.par	*! (IDENT-IO)		*	

dence with &[des] possible, is ruled out because preconsonantal [s] violates highly ranked *CODA/s in forms such as *destapar* 'uncover.'

   Replacing &[deh] with &[des] results in the violations seen in example 4.18. Candidate (a) in example 4.17 has fewer violations than (a) in example 4.18, and therefore, correspondent &[deh] in example 4.17 is selected over &[des] in example 4.18 by the constraints and constraint ranking.

   Constraint evaluation for compounds, *dioses heroes* [di̯o.se.he.ro.eh], proceeds similarly to example 4.16. IDENT-PrWd(SL) becomes relevant since compounds have been shown to sometimes consist of prosodic words. [di̯o.se.he.ro.eh] is selected as the optimal candidate because it only incurs a violation of MAX-IO(SL); alternative candidates—[di̯o.se.se.ro.eh], [di̯o.seh.e.ro.eh]—are ruled out on account of IDENT-PrWd(SL) and ONSET violations.

Wiltshire (2006) proposes WEAK constraints as an alternative to output-to-output IDENT-PrWd(SL). WEAK is a cover term for a family of markedness constraints reducing contrasts in weak positions, such as coda or word final. Given the prosodic structure of prefixes, and the constraints ALIGN-L(Lex, PW) and ALIGN-L/R(PW, σ) that have the effect of inserting word boundaries between a prefix and the following word, prefixes are always followed by word boundaries. Word-internal coda /s/ is followed by a syllable boundary. The constraint WEAK/PW (*s/PW), which bans strong segments before a word boundary, and its domination over MAX-IO are responsible for the Caribbean I data (see figure 4.1).

Accounting for dialectal variation in /s/-aspiration

Dialectal variation data in /s/-aspiration offer a useful way to compare analyses. Aspirating dialects of Spanish show cross-dialectal variation affecting coda /s/ across morphemes. In particular, variation affects prefixes, compounds, and phrases. As seen in example 4.8, Caribbean I and Granada Spanish aspirate in prefixal and phrasal contexts, as well as in compounds. Other dialects, like Río Negro Argentinian and the Antillean dialects (Caribbean II in Kaisse 1997, 1998), have no aspiration of a prefix-final /s/ before a vowel-initial stem but aspirate compound- and word-final /s/ before a vowel-initial word (example 4.19). Finally, Chinato (cf. Hualde 1991) and Buenos Aires Argentinian (Kaisse 1997, 1998) retain prevocalic underlying /s/ in both phrasal and prefixal contexts (example 4.20).

Example 4.19

mes	[meh]	'month'
mes-es	[me.seh]	'months'
des-hecho	[de.se.čo]	'undone'
dioses-héroes	[dio.se.he.ɾo.eh]	'god-heroes'
mes azul	[me.ha.sul]	'blue month'

Example 4.20

mes	[meh]	'month'
mes-es	[me.seh]	'months'
des-hecho	[de.se.čo]	'undone'
dioses-héroes	[dio.se.se.ɾo.eh]	'god-heroes'
mes azul	[me.sa.sul]	'blue month'

The account of variation as an advantage of the OT analysis of /s/-aspiration

Under a serial analysis, this pattern of variation has been explained by means of ordered rules (Hualde 1989b; Kaisse 1997, 1998): Some dialects order aspiration before prefixation or compounding and others afterwards. Thus in Hualde (1989b, 1991), Caribbean I would have the rule ordering seen in example 4.1, but in Caribbean II, aspiration would be ordered after prefixation and before compounding. Buenos Aires Argentinian orders aspiration after prefixation and compounding. The problem with this type of account is that it offers no true explanation as to why rules are ordered differently across dialects with regard to prefixing and compounding, but not with regard to suffixation, which has only one attested order (/s/-aspiration always after suffixation). In other words, why is it that variation affects prefixes and words, but not suffixation? In Hualde (1989b, 1991) the correct results are obtained by stipulating that the domain of syllabification is a unit smaller than the word, which excludes prefixes but includes suffixes; as a result, rules with syllabic information in their descriptions cannot apply to units such as the stem (without suffixes), to which syllabification has not applied yet. Yet, this solution introduces an additional difficulty since syllabification is said to apply in a domain that is not coextensive with a known morphological constituent—it is neither the root, nor the derivational stem, nor the word. In other words, Hualde's analysis requires a unit for which there is no independent motivation. Furthermore, that the Caribbean II data are explained by ordering aspiration after prefixation raises the question of why no dialect orders aspiration after compounding and before the phrasal level, thus exhibiting prevocalic aspiration only in the phrasal context (not in compounds). One possible solution is to argue that Caribbean II dialects have a different domain of syllabification (the morphological word, including prefixes) and aspiration is ordered after prefixation. Yet, this does not explain the illformedness of *[de.sie.lo] in those dialects.

In OT analyses, such as those presented by Colina (2002) and Wiltshire (2006), the above facts are explained in a direct manner through the interaction of resyllabification constraints, the special prosodic structure of prefixes and IDENT constraints (WEAK constraints in Wiltshire). As I show below, variation in the behavior of prefixes is not the result of extrinsic rule ordering, but of the unstable, variable nature of prefixes as to their prosodic word status (Colina 2002).

Dialects which fail to aspirate before a vowel in both phrasal and prefixal contexts (Chinato and Buenos Aires Argentinian) reflect, of course, the domination of MAX-IO(SL) over IDENT-PrWd(SL), the opposite ranking of that proposed above for Caribbean I (example 4.21).

Example 4.21   /mes + asul/ [me.sa.sul]
                   &[meh]

	F	*CODA/s	MAX-IO(SL)	IDENT-PrWd(SL)
a. me.ha.sul			*!	
b. ☞ me.sa.sul				*
c. mes.a.sul		*!		*
d. mes.ta.sul	*!(DEP-IO)	*		*
e. me.a.sul	*!(MAX-IO)		*	*

In Caribbean II, prefixes are not prosodic words; the antiallomorphy constraint is vacuously satisfied

The observed dialectal variation in /s/-aspiration in prefixes (Caribbean I, Granada Spanish (example 4.8) versus Río Negro Argentinian and Caribbean II (example 4.19)) is a consequence of variation in the prosodic representation of prefixes in the dialects under consideration. In Río Negro Argentinian and Caribbean II, prefixes are not adjoined to the prosodic word (instead they are incorporated into it as shown in the prosodic structure represented in example 4.22); therefore, prefixes in these dialects are not affected by IDENT-PrWd; in other words, no correspondence relation exists between the output form of the prefix, [deh], and its realization when attached to the base, [de.se.čo]$_{PrWd}$. Candidate evaluation is shown in example 4.23.

Example 4.22   Adjunction of prefixes

PrWd
/ \
prefix   stem + suffixes

Example 4.23   /des + ečo/ [de.se.čo]
&[de.se.čo]

	F	*Coda/s	Ident-PrWd(SL)	Max-IO(SL)
a. de.he.čo			*!	*
b. ☞ de.se.čo				
c. des.te.čo	*! (Dep-IO)	*	*	
d. de.e.čo	*! (Max-IO)		*	*
e. de.le.čo	*! (Ident-IO)		*	

In example 4.23, (b) is the optimal candidate because it does not incur any constraint violations; the prefix is not adjoined to a prosodic word, so there is no output-to-output correspondence relation and Ident-PrWd is vacuously satisfied. Candidate (a) violates Max-IO(SL) and Ident-PrWd(SL); (c–e) contain F and Ident-PrWd violations (considering the derived form as the relevant prosodic word entering into a correspondence relation here), in addition to one *Coda/s violation for (c) and one Max-IO(SL) violation for (d).

Wiltshire (2006) accounts for variation through reranking of the constraints in figure 4.1. She argues that the prosodic structures remain the same in the dialects whose contexts for aspiration differ; only the constraint ranking relevant to the realization of the allophones differs. Thus, Weak|$_{PW}$ and Weak|$_σ$ over Max-IO(SL) account for the pattern of aspiration in Caribbean I; Weak|$_{PW}$ below Max-IO(SL) gives a variety that aspirates only in codas (Argentinian); and Max-IO(SL) above both Weak constraints gives a dialect with no aspiration at all. However, this leaves Caribbean II, with prevocalic word-final aspiration only (no prevocalic prefix-final aspiration), unexplained. It seems that, whether one resorts to Ident constraints or to Weak constraints, it is not possible to explain the differences in the behavior of prefixes in the two Caribbean dialects without referring to different prosodic structures: in Caribbean I, prefixes behave like words (they have PrWd status or project a word boundary), while in Caribbean II, they do not (no PrWd status and no projection of a word boundary).

In sum, an OT analysis of aspiration and its interaction with morphology brings to the foreground the idea that the source of variation in aspiration has to do with the prosodic status of prefixes. While the insight itself is not framework-specific, OT can capture PrWd effects in a direct manner through output-to-output identity constraints that apply to prefixes that have prosodic word status (or through constraints that require the insertion of a word boundary as in Wiltshire 2006). That suffixes are never adjoined to the prosodic word explains the lack of variation with

Structures & Input	Candidate Outputs	WEAK|$_{PW}$	WEAK|$_\sigma$	MAX-IO(SL)
[internal]$_{PW}$	[dis.ko]		*!	
/disko/	☞ [dih.ko]			*
/asul/	☞ [a.sul]			
	[a.hul]			*!
[morph - suf]$_{PW}$	[djes.mo]		*!	
/dies-mo/	☞ [djeh.mo]			*
/dies-es/	☞ [dje.seh]			*
	[dje.heh]			**!
[pre[morph]$_{PW}$]$_{PW}$	[des.[kremaða]]	*!	*!	
/des + kremada/	☞ [deh.[kremaða]]			*
/des + igual/	[de.s[igwal]	*!		
	☞ [de.h[igwal]			*
[word]$_{PW}$[word]$_{PW}$	[bitʃos].[raroh]	*!	*!	*
/bitʃos/ /raros/	☞ [bitʃos].[ra.roh]			**
/bitʃos/ /estraɲos/	[bitʃo.s][eh.traɲoh]	*!		**
	☞ [bitʃo.h][eh.traɲoh]			***

Figure 4.1 Caribbean Spanish I aspiration (Wiltshire 2006)

regard to suffixation. Furthermore, it is worth noting that, although it would be possible to order aspiration after both prefixation and compounding (before phrasal concatenation), no dialect seems to present this pattern. In an OT account with output-to-output constraints (PrWd), this has a straightforward explanation: the members of a compound always have prosodic-word status in Spanish.

The Spanish data and analyses just presented are of relevance to the ongoing debate on the derivational residue within OT. While a Lexical Phonology model (Kiparsky 1982, 1985; Mohanan 1986), in which phonological rules apply sequentially, interwoven among morphological operations, is in principle incompatible with parallel candidate evaluation as proposed by OT, some OT practitioners have argued for strata within OT (Booij 1997; Rubach 1997; Bermúdez-Otero 1999, 2003, in press; Itô and Mester 2003). For Spanish aspiration in particular, Roca (2005) presents an analysis of /s/-aspiration in Río Negro Argentinian in which the output of the word level serves as input for the phrase level. He contends that the output of the word level ve[h]luno 'thou seest one' enters the phrase-bounded evaluation and the output ve.hlu.no is correctly selected on the basis of the constraints and contraint ranking. The constraints Roca proposes are those responsible for resyllabification (in his proposal ALIGN (Wd, σ)-L replaces the current ALIGN-LST), the markedness constraint against coda [s], and IDENT constraints. Roca points out that an output-to-output account that resorts to Base Identity constraints is bound to fail, but he does not discuss the possibility of an antiallomorphy constraint along the lines of IDENT-PrWd. Roca does not address dialectal variation.

This section has shown that the cross-dialectal aspiration data can in fact be accounted for in a parallel fashion along the lines of Colina (2002) and Wiltshire (2006) through OO constraints and, therefore, the aspiration data alone do not present sufficient evidence for a stratal version of OT. Nonetheless, the issues of strata and opacity within OT remain undecided and in much need of further exploration.

> For evidence in favor of Stratal OT, see Bermúdez-Otero (2006) for arguments based on Spanish denominal derivation. McCarthy (2007) argues against Stratal OT, claiming that it cannot explain within-strata opacity. OT with candidate chains (OT-CC) is presented as the alternative to existing proposals for dealing with opacity in OT. OO faithfulness is retained to explain phrasal and cyclic phenomena, as OT-CC does not insist on a connection between opacity and cyclicity (McCarthy 2007).

4.2.2 VELARIZATION OF CODA NASALS

An account similar to that of /s/-aspiration can be offered for the velarization of coda nasals in Caribbean dialects of Spanish. The data in example 4.2 are repeated in example 4.24 for convenience. The relevant constraints and ranking are in examples 4.25 and 4.26.

Example 4.24

bien	[bi̯eŋ]	'good'
bien-es	[bi̯e.nes]	'goods'
in-humano	[i.ŋu.ma.no]	'inhumane'
bienestar	[bi̯e.ŋes.tar]	'well-being'
con uno	[ko.ŋu.no]	'with one'

Example 4.25

*PA/coda: No point of articulation (PA) in coda position.

MAX-IO(PA): All PA nodes present in the UR must be in the output.

Example 4.26

F, *PA/coda >> MAX-IO(PA)

The true nature of velar nasals is not uncontroversial (Ohala and Ohala 1993). Among other proposals, it has been argued that velar nasals have no point of articulation (Trigo 1988), and that velar nasals share the dorsal point of articulation of the preceding vowel (Piñeros 2006). Under either assumption a velar nasal in the coda satisfies *PA/coda by not parsing a PA in the coda.

Note that it could be argued that the nasal has no underlying point of articulation. Under that assumption, (a) in example 4.27 would have no violations of MAX-IO(PA) and would still be selected as the winner. Example 4.28 shows evaluation of suffixed forms.[2]

The hierarchy in example 4.29 correctly predicts that the /n/ of *bien estar* will surface as [ŋ]. In example 4.30, (&) identifies the output form that stands in correspondence with the output.

With regard to prefixes, the data available at this point behave like aspiration in Caribbean II, as seen in example 4.31.[3]

Example 4.27 /bien/ [bieŋ]

	F, *PA/coda	Max-IO(PA)
a. ☞ bieŋ		*
b. bien	*!	
c. bie	*!	

Example 4.28 /bien + es/ [b.ie.nes]

	F, *PA/coda	Max-IO(PA)
a. ☞ bie.nes		
b. bieŋes		*

Example 4.29

Ident-PrWd(PA) >> Max-IO(PA)

*PA/coda >> Max-IO(PA)

Example 4.30 /bien + estar/ [bie.ŋes.tar]
　　　　　　　&[bieŋ]

	*PA/coda	Ident-PrWd(PA)	Max-IO(PA)
a. ☞ bie.ŋes.tar			*
b. bie.nes.tar		*!	

Example 4.31 /in + umano/ [i.ŋu.ma.no]
　　　　　　　&[iŋ]

	*PA/coda	Ident-PrWd(PA)	Max-IO(PA)
a. ☞ i.ŋu.ma.no			*
b. i.nu.ma.no		*!	

4.2.3 ONSET STRENGTHENING

Nasal velarization and /s/-aspiration affect coda positions, and, in word- or pre-fix-final prevocalic positions, they exhibit opacity effects. Onset strengthening and /r/-strengthening differ in that they are relevant in the onset, which is a strong position. As seen in chapter 2, onset strengthening is the result of the constraints and rankings in example 4.32.

A candidate like [de.slie.lo] ((b) in examples 4.33 and 4.34), which avoids onset strengthening through resyllabification of the final consonant of the prefix as an onset, is not possible because it would misalign the syllable and the stem (Align-LST violation).

Example 4.32

Onset strengthening:

*ONSET/glide, ONSET >> MAX-IOμ, IDENT(cons)

Resyllabification:

ONSET >> ALIGN-LST

It is preferable to create an acceptable onset by underparsing a mora and changing the specification of the feature consonant (MAX-IOμ and IDENT(cons) violations), as in (a) in example 4.34. This indicates that ALIGN-LST dominates IDENT(cons) (the ranking of ALIGN-LST with respect to MAX-IOμ is undetermined, despite the appearance of the tableau in example 4.34). (c) is ruled out because it parses a glide in the onset, thus violating the highly ranked constraint *ONSET/glide.[4]

Example 4.33   /des + ielo/ [dez.yelo][5]

	ALIGN-LST
a. ☞ dez.lye.lo	
b. de.slie.lo	*!

Example 4.34   /des + ielo/ [dez.ye.lo]

	*ONSET/glide	ONSET	ALIGN-LST	MAX-IOμ	IDENT(cons)
a. ☞ dez.lyelo				*	*
b. de.slie.lo			*!	*	
c. des.ljelo	*!			*	

In example 4.35, evaluation is shown for the phrase level (across words). In this case, the realization of the word-final glide is retained after resyllabification to the onset, which indicates that faithfulness to the PrWd is more important than the constraint on onset glides and that ONSET actually dominates *ONSET/glide.[6]

Example 4.35   / lei/ + /alguna/ [le.jal.ɣu.na]
              &[lei]

	IDENT-PrWd (cons)	*ONSET	*ONSET/glide	ALIGN-LST	MAX-IOμ	IDENT(cons)
a. le.ylal.ɣu.na	*!			*	*	*
b. lei.lal.ɣu.na		*!			*	
c. ☞ le.jlal.ɣu.na			*	*	*	

Wiltshire (2006) also offers an alternative analysis of the data. As in her aspiration analysis, IDENT-PrWd is replaced by WEAK constraints.

4.2.4 /R/-STRENGTHENING

The main purpose of this section is to account for the interaction between /r/-strengthening, morphological processes, and resyllabification (the data in example 4.4); however, in order to do that, a summary analysis of the basic distributional facts of rhotics in Spanish needs to be presented first. Spanish has two nonlateral liquids, a trill and a flap. Phonemic in intervocalic position (/karo/ 'car' versus /kaɾo/ 'expensive'), they are in complementary distribution in other contexts: the trill appears in word-initial position [rosa], after a heterosyllabic consonant [enrike], and in some dialects in coda position [mar]; the flap surfaces as the second element of a consonant cluster [bɾaso] and in coda position [maɾ] in some dialects. The analysis of the trill and flap in Spanish is not uncontroversial. Extant proposals vary with regard to the following issues: which one of the two realizations is considered underlying; the nature of the trill (geminate versus one single segment); the feature that contrasts the flap and the trill; and rhotic specification with respect to the feature [continuant].

> Bonet and Mascaró (1997) provide quite possibly the best known analysis proposing an underlying trill. Most others argue for an underlying flap (Harris 1983; Roca 2005).

At this point, for the purposes of this analysis, I will make the following assumptions: The trill is a single segment: It cannot be considered a geminate because it is syllabified in the onset (Hualde 2004, 18; cf. Italian *car.ro* versus Spanish *ca.rro*); it is also [–continuant] and less sonorous than the flap.

An advantage of an OT account is that, with the exception of a few dialects (see below), it does not need to take a stand with regard to the form of the underlying representation, because under Richness of the Base, it is the constraints and constraint ranking, independent of underlying representation, which select the optimal candidate. The analysis proposed below shows this to be true and therefore obviates the need to decide which allophone is underlying.

Trills in word-initial position   I propose that the phenomenon often referred to as /r/-strengthening in derivational terms is in fact related to onset preference for less sonorous segments (obstruents and [–continuant] segments). More specifically, /r/-strengthening is the result of the high ranking of a constraint against nontrilled [ɾ] in stem-initial position, *|[ɾ]. The fact that Spanish allows for a contrast in word-internal position between trilled and nontrilled [ɾ] indicates that the relevant identity constraint dominates the constraints that ban [ɾ] and [r] in onset position, *[ɾ]/onset, *[r]/onset. That only the trill is possible in stem-initial position means that the constraint against the nontrill in stem-initial position dominates identity. As was mentioned above, deciding what feature is responsible for the contrast between the flap and the trill in Spanish is not an easy matter. Because of this, I will refer to this constraint as IDENT /R/, using /R/ as a cover term for the feature that contrasts [r] and *[ɾ]. IDENT /R/ is dominated by *|[ɾ], since any potential [ɾ] in stem-initial position will be replaced by a trill.

> *|[ɾ] is not an alignment constraint in the sense of the ALIGN family, since these constraints are not usually formulated in the negative. *|[ɾ] has a close connection with constraints of the type *[ɾ]/onset that relate the phonetic

inventory of a language to syllabic positions; *I[ɾ] plays a similar role with respect to the edges of morphological constituents, in this case, the stem.

Example 4.36

*I[ɾ]: no [ɾ] in stem-initial position

*[ɾ]/onset: no [ɾ] in onset position

*[r]/onset: no [r] in onset position

*[r]/coda: no [r] in coda position

IDENT /R/: A trill in the input must correspond with a trill in the output; a flap in the input must correspond with a flap in the output.

Example 4.37

*I[ɾ] >> IDENT /R/ >> *[ɾ] /onset, *[r]/onset

Example 4.38   /Iɾatas/ [ra.tas]

	*I[ɾ]	IDENT /R/	*[ɾ]/onset	*[r]/onset
a. ☞ Iɾa.tas		*		*
b. Iɾa.tas	*!		*	

Example 4.39   /Iratas/ [ra.tas]

	*I[ɾ]	IDENT /R/	*[ɾ]/onset	*[r]/onset
a. ☞ ɾa.tas				*
b. Iɾa.tas	*!	*	*	

Assuming an underlying representation with a flap (nontrill), candidate (a) in example 4.38 is optimal because, despite the violation of IDENT /R/, it satisfies the more highly ranked constraint that bans flaps from stem-initial position, *I[ɾ]. If a trill was posed for the underlying representation (example 4.39), the results of evaluation would be the same: In addition to the constraints violated by (b) in example 4.38, (b) in example 4.39 violates IDENT /R/; (a) in example 4.39 only incurs a mark for *[r]/onset.

Flaps in syllable-final position

In syllable-final (including word-final) position, many dialects have a flap, with an optional trill under emphasis (Harris 1983). This seems to indicate that the trill is banned in the coda (highly ranked *[r]/coda). The variation facts seem to be a bit more complicated, but I will put this aside for now.

Examples 4.40 and 4.41 show evaluation for a coda rhotic assuming an underlying flap and an underlying trill, respectively. The tableaux demonstrate that the same output is selected ((b) in examples 4.40 and 4.41), regardless of underlying representation, due to the domination of *[r]/coda over IDENT /R/ and in accordance with the postulate of Richness of the Base.

Example 4.40 /Imaɾ/ [maɾ]

	*I[ɾ]	*[r]/coda	IDENT /R/	*[ɾ]/onset	*[r]/onset
a. Imar		*!	*		
b. ☞ Imaɾ					

Example 4.41 /Imar/ [maɾ]

	*I[ɾ]	*[r]/coda	IDENT /R/	*[ɾ]/onset	*[r]/onset
a. Imar		*!			
b. ☞ Imaɾ			*		

Trills preceded by a heterosyllabic consonant

When preceded by a heterosyllabic consonant, the trill surfaces in all varieties. Such an outcome (as well as the absence of cross-dialectal variation) can be accounted for if one assumes a fortition process similar to that of affrication of the palatal fricative or fortition of a voiced obstruent when preceded by a nasal with which it agrees in point of articulation, as in *conyuge* [koɲɟuxe] 'spouse' (Padgett 1994; Baković 1994). That a rhotic that shares its point of articulation with a preceding consonant also shares its stricture (continuancy) features is a natural consequence of a feature geometry model, such as the one proposed by Padgett (1994), in which place dominates stricture (see Hualde 1989a for an analysis of continuancy assimilation in voiced obstruents in Spanish that also requires a shared PA node). I will refer to the constraint that requires that shared PA nodes also share stricture nodes with the shorthand notice AGREEPA(–continuant). Note, however, that the relevant constraint(s) here are in fact those responsible for assimilation of point of articulation. As seen in (b) in example 4.42, a candidate with a flap is ruled out because of a violation of the highly ranked AGREEPA(–cont).[7] The heterosyllabic consonants that precede /r/ are alveolar /n/, /l/, /s/, thus sharing point of articulation and requiring a [–continuant] trill. Additional evidence for this account can be found in the fact that /s/ assimilates to /r/ and then is deleted when followed by /r/, /israel/ [i.ra.el].[8]

Example 4.42 /lenɾike/ [en.ri.ke]

	AGREEPA (–cont)	*I[ɾ]	*[r]/coda	IDENT /R/	*[ɾ]/onset	*[r]/onset
a. ☞ lenrike				*		*
b. lenɾike	*!				*	

Trill/flap contrast in intervocalic position

In the intervocalic position, the flap and the trill are contrastive in Spanish. As seen in candidate (a) in examples 4.43 and 4.44, the form that matches the underlying representation is the winner because it does not violate IDENT /R/. The winner is determined by the underlying representation along with the ranking of the relevant faithfulness constraint, IDENT /R/, over markedness, *[ɾ]/onset and *[r]/onset. Faithfulness over markedness is the ranking that accounts for preservation of contrast (versus neutralization) in OT.

Example 4.43   /kaɾo/ [ka.ɾo]

	AGREEPA (−cont)	*l[ɾ]	*[r]/coda	IDENT /R/	*[ɾ]/onset	*[r]/onset
a. ☞ ka.ɾo					*	
b. ka.ro				*!		*

Example 4.44   /karo/ [ka.ro]

	AGREEPA(−cont)	*l[ɾ]	*[r]/coda	IDENT /R/	*[ɾ]/onset	*[r]/onset
a. ☞ ka.ro						*
b. ka.ɾo				*!	*	

Rhotics in morphologically derived environments: compounds and prefixed forms

The proposed set of constraints and their ranking explain the data in example 4.4, and the fact that prefix-final or word-final [ɾ] is unaltered even if it surfaces in word-initial position as the result of resyllabification.

In example 4.45, assuming an underlying representation with a flap (non-trill), candidate (a) is optimal because, despite the violation of IDENT /R/, it satisfies the more highly ranked constraint that bans flaps from stem initial position, *l[ɾ]. If a trill were proposed for the underlying representation, as in example 4.46, the results of evaluation would be the same, as (b) would violate the same constraints as (b) in example 4.45, plus IDENT /R/; (a) in example 4.46 only incurs a mark for *[r]/onset.

Example 4.45   /mata + lɾatas/ [ma.ta.ra.tas]

	AGREEPA (−cont)	*l[ɾ]	*[r]/coda	IDENT /R/	*[ɾ]/onset	*[r]/onset
a. ☞ ma.ta.lra.tas				*		*
b. ma.ta.lɾa.tas		*!			*	

Example 4.46   /mata + lra.tas/ [ma.ta.ra.tas]

	AGREEPA (−cont)	*l[ɾ]	*[r]/coda	IDENT/R/	*[ɾ]/onset	*[r]/onset
a. ☞ ma.ta.lra.tas						*
b. ma.ta.lɾa.tas		*!		*	*	

The lack of a stem boundary explains a flap in nonproductive compounding, for example, e[ɾ]upción 'eruption.'

Trills in a phrasal context

Moving on to the phrasal context, as seen in examples 4.47 and 4.50, the allophone of /R/ that appears across words is identical to the one that occurs within the word: word-final /R/ is a flap, even when resyllabified in word-initial position (example 4.47), and word-initial /R/ is a trill at the beginning of a word, when preceded by another word (example 4.50). Given that the stem boundary is unaffected by resyllabification, and since *l[ɾ] is the highest ranking constraint, this is to be expected.

Example 4.47   /beɾlosas/ [be.ɾlo.sas] 'to see female bears'
&[beɾ]

	AGREEPA (−cont)	*l[ɾ]	*[r]/coda	IDENT-PrWd(R)	IDENT /R/	*[ɾ]/onset	*[r]/onset
a. be.rlo.sas				*!	*		*
b. ☞ be.ɾlo.sas						*	

In example 4.47, (a) is ruled out on the basis of a violation of IDENT-PrWd(R). The same outcome is obtained if one assumes an underlying representation with a trill, as in example 4.48. The correspondent &[beɾ] is guaranteed on the basis of *[r]/coda >> IDENT /R/. *[r]/coda must also dominate IDENT-PrWd(R) given that the ban on coda trills is more important than avoiding allomorphy; in other words, the hypothetical [ber] correspondent is ruled out by this ranking, as shown in example 4.49.

Example 4.48   /berlosas/ [be.ɾlo.sas] 'to see female bears'
&[beɾ]

	AGREEPA (−cont)	*l[ɾ]	*[r] /coda	IDENT-PrWd(R)	IDENT /R/	*[ɾ] /onset	*[r] /onset
a. be.rlo.sas				*!			*
b. ☞ be.ɾlo.sas					*	*	

Example 4.49   /ber/ [beɾ] 'to see'
&[ber]

	*[r]/coda	IDENT-PrWd(R)	IDENT /R/
a. ber	*!		
b. ☞ beɾ		*	*

In examples 4.50 and 4.51, a flap incurs a violation of *l[ɾ] independently of whether the underlying representation contains a trill or a flap.

Example 4.50   /belrosas/ [be.lro.sas] 'he/she sees roses'

	AGREEPA (−cont)	*l[ɾ]	*[r]/coda	IDENT /R/	*[ɾ]/onset	*[r]/onset
a. be.lɾo.sas		*!		*	*	
b. ☞ be.lro.sas						*

Example 4.51   /belɾosas/ [be.ro.sas] 'he/she sees roses'

	AGREEPA (−cont)	*|[ɾ]	*[r]/coda	IDENT /R/	*[ɾ]/onset	*[r]/onset
a. be.lɾo.sas		*!			*	
b. ☞ be.ro.sas				*		*

Roca (2005) also proposes an OT analysis of /r/-strengthening. In addition to the markedness constraint against word-initial flaps, he includes a constraint banning trills from complex onset *Cr̄ which selects [bɾa.so] over *[bra.so] 'arm.' Note, however, that this constraint may be unnecessary under the assumption that the sonority of the trill is lower than that of a flap (similar to that of an obstruent). A candidate like *[bra.so] would therefore be ruled out on the basis of an MSD violation. Roca presents data from some dialects that ban the flap from word-final position, [amor] *[amoɾ], requiring a constraint against word-final flap.

Rhotics and dialectal and stylistic variation

As mentioned above, there is dialectal variation regarding coda /R/. Some dialects are reported to have a trill in coda position (Bonet and Mascaró 1997; Roca 2005), [mar] 'sea.' Bonet and Mascaró (1997) argue that this strengthening must be a postlexical process because it is bled by resyllabification. Additional data are required to better understand the conditions under which coda strengthening takes place. Yet, under the assumption that in these dialects all coda rhotics are trills, except for when they are resyllabified in prevocalic position, one could argue for the high ranking of a constraint that bans flaps when not followed by a vowel (this includes consonants and absolute final position when no other segment follows). This constraint could be motivated on the basis of assimilation regarding degree of aperture, since flaps can be considered approximants and thus have a degree of aperture that is closer to vowels than to consonants. Given this, one could ask what rules out outputs such as *[ma.res] 'seas' or *[ma.rles] 'sea is' in these dialects, since the restriction on coda flaps no longer applies and these forms preserve identity (to the base in the plural form and to other forms of the prosodic word in the phrasal example). As mentioned earlier, much more work is needed in these dialects; yet, one possible explanation may have to do with the fact that one output *[ma.res] would correspond to two UR: a hypothetical monomorphemic /mares/ and /maɾ/+/es/.

The stylistic variation reported in Harris (1983), in which a coda trill surfaces under emphasis in dialects that otherwise have coda flaps, can be explained as the result of a preference for less sonorous segments in prominent positions, already seen in chapter 2 (section 2.2.2.1.2, IDENT-PROMINENCE[−cont] >> *r/coda) with regard to the selection of coda stops over fricatives under emphasis. That trills appear under emphasis offers additional evidence for the proposal that trills behave like stops, being less sonorous than flaps and possibly [−continuant].

Although the focus of this analysis is not rhotics per se, nor the comparison with other analyses, a word is needed regarding other accounts. Recent accounts of rhotics in Spanish do not explain the data that are the focus of the analysis here (example 4.4) (Bonet and Mascaró 1997; Bradley 2006). One important objective of these analyses is to explain why the contrast is limited to intervocalic position; Bonet and Mascaró (1997) attribute the intervocalic contrast to sonority considerations related to the demisyllable. Bradley (2006), within a Dispersion Theory model, explains that the contrast occurs only in intervocalic position because this is the position that allows for the greatest perceptual distance. I argue that the restriction of the contrast to intervocalic position is not the result of perceptual distinctiveness or sonority, but of the contextual distribution of the original Latin geminates. The Latin geminate flap evolved into the modern day trill through reranking of *GEM to a dominant position, which resulted in the ban against geminates. A candidate with deletion of one half of the Latin geminate is ruled out, since the resulting flap would merge with the singleton (*MERGE). As a result, a trill is preferred (instead of a flap—a violation of IDENT /R/). Lexicon Optimization (LO) dictates that the learner faced with no geminates in the output will eventually opt for the underlying representation that most closely resembles the output, that is, a trill. This results in the subsequent restructuring of the underlying representation, from Latin /karro/ to Modern Spanish /karo/.[9]

4.3 SUMMARY

In a derivational model of phonology, rules apply sequentially and within certain domains; thus, rule-based models of syllabification need to specify the domain of syllabification and the order of syllabification rules with respect to other phonological rules, and to morphological operations, such as suffixation, prefixation, and compounding. On the basis of resyllabification, aspiration, and onset strengthening data, Hualde (1989b, 1991) convincingly argues that the domain of syllabification in Spanish is a unit smaller than the word, as syllabification seems to apply before the adjunction of prefixes and before compounding, but after suffixation. It is also necessary to establish rule ordering with respect to morphological operations.

An OT account obviates the need to define domain of syllabification through the use of general mechanisms, namely universal constraints and language-specific ranking previously motivated for the language. No extrinsic ordering of phonological rules and morphological operations rules is necessary either. An important family of constraints, capturing the interaction between morphology and phonology, is the ALIGN family that requires alignment of the edges (right or left) of morphological units (root, stem, word, suffix, prefix) with the edges (right or left) of phonological components (segment, onset, coda, syllable, prosodic word). In Spanish, ALIGN-LST is the ALIGN constraint relevant to the interaction of morphological phenomena, such as suffixation, prefixation, and compounding, with phonological phenomena, such as /s/-aspiration, /n/-velarization, /r/-strengthening, and onset strengthening. ALIGN-LST, in combination with constraints relevant to each of these processes, serves to account for the /s/-aspiration, /n/-velarization, /r/-strengthening, and onset strengthening data. It is argued that the OT analyses of these phonological phenomena provide for a better understanding of the data and of dialectal variation, particularly in the case of aspiration and velarization. These phenomena constitute examples of opacity and overapplication of rules, thus presenting a challenge for an entirely parallel model of evaluation. In this regard, the Spanish data are of crucial importance to the debate on the derivational component in OT; more specifically, they speak to the matter of whether some versions of the theory like Stratal OT and OT-CC are necessary or desirable. The analyses proposed here show that it is possible to account for the present data without resorting to levels of constraints, by using identity constraints or WEAK constraints.

STUDY QUESTIONS

1. What are the key components of a derivational account of /s/-aspiration in Spanish?

2. What are some of the difficulties faced by a rule-based account of /s/-aspiration such as Hualde's (1989b, 1991)?

3. In what way do aspiration data in Spanish constitute a challenge for OT? What is the role played by output-to-output constraints? What is another key element in the explanation of the dialectal variation found in /s/-aspiration?

4. What role do markedness and faithfulness play in /s/-aspiration and nasal velarization?

5. What are the main points that need to be considered by an analysis of Spanish rhotics that also takes into account the role of the morphology?

6. In an OT account of onset strengthening, what explains the failure of the vocoid to become a fricative in a phrasal context?

GOING BACK TO THE SOURCES

Colina 2002:

Interdialectal variation in Spanish /s/ aspiration. *Structure, Meaning and Acquisition in Spanish*. Ed. James Lee, Kimberly Geeslin, and Clancy Clements. Somerville, MA: Cascadilla Press.

Hualde 1989b:

Silabeo y estructura morfémica en español. *Hispania* 72:821–31.

Hualde 1991:

On Spanish syllabification. *Current Studies in Spanish Linguistics*. Ed. Héctor Campos and Fernando Martínez-Gil. Washington, DC: Georgetown University Press.

Kaisse 1997:

Aspiration and resyllabification in Argentinian Spanish. *University of Washington Working Papers in Linguistics* 15:199–209.

Kaisse 1998:

Resyllabification: Evidence from Argentinian Spanish. *Formal Perspectives on Romance Linguistics*. Ed. J. Marc Authier, Barbara E. Bullock, and Lisa A. Reed. Philadelphia: John Benjamins.

Roca 2005:

> Strata, yes; structure preservation, no. Evidence from Spanish. *Romance Languages and Linguistic Theory 2003*. Ed. Twan Geerts, Ivo van Ginneken, and Haike Jacobs. Philadelphia: John Benjamins.

Wiltshire 2006:

> Prefix boundaries in Spanish varieties: A non-derivational OT account. *Optimality-Theoretic Studies in Spanish Phonology*. Ed. Fernando Martínez-Gil and Sonia Colina. Philadelphia: John Benjamins.

KEY TOPICS

SPANISH PHONOLOGY

> aspiration
>
> velarization
>
> onset strengthening
>
> /r/-strengthening
>
>> see also fortition, tensing
>
> resyllabification
>
> suffixes
>
> prefixes
>
> compounds
>
> phrases
>
> prosodic word
>
> coda processes
>
> dialectal variation
>
> Argentinian Spanish
>
> Caribbean Spanish
>
> Granada (Andalucian) Spanish
>
> Peninsular Spanish

PHONOLOGICAL THEORY/OT

> opacity
>
> overapplication of rules
>
> lexical phonology
>
> derivations and OT
>
> morphology-phonology interface
>
> Stratal OT
>
> identity constraints
>
> output-to-output constraints
>
> OT with candidate chains
>
> alignment constraints

TOPICS FOR FURTHER RESEARCH

1. Contrary to Bradley's (2006) nonderivational proposal, Colina (in press) argues that an OT analysis of /s/-voicing in Ecuadoran Spanish does not require strata or levels. What is the significance of the Ecuadoran data (Lipski 1989; Robinson 1979) in the debate regarding the need for levels (or lack thereof) in OT? Does the phonology of Spanish have anything else (new data, new analyses) to contribute to the discussion?

2. Investigate cross-dialectal variation regarding nasal velarization and prefixation/compounding. Do the data show the same patterns exhibited by /s/-aspiration?

3. The phonetic nature of the flap and the trill: What is the feature that contrasts them?

4. Trills in coda position: How widespread are they in the Spanish-speaking world? What are the exact conditions under which they surface? How could one account for them under an OT analysis? Could they offer any insights regarding the debate on the need for derivations/strata within OT?

5. How could one account for variable rhotic realizations in coda position?

6. In phrases like *salír rápido,* Harris (1983) claims that there is neutralization to a single trill; yet, there exists some experimental evidence (Hualde 2004) indicating that this does not always happen. How could an OT model account for this type of variation?

NOTES

1. Note that the structure in example 4.14 should not be understood to mean that the prefix constitutes its own separate prosodic word (rather, it is adjoined to the prosodic word, thus forming another prosodic word). See example 4.15 for the relevant correspondence relations.

2. Under the proposal in which the point of articulation of the nasal is not specified underlyingly, a velar nasal in the plural would be ruled out by a highly ranked constraint against velar nasals in the onset.

3. No data are available on the other dialects.

4. As pointed out in chapter 2, interested readers should refer to Roca (2005) for a similar analysis of onset strengthening.

5. Candidates with coda /s/ followed by a voiced consonant surface with [z] due to a process of voice assimilation not considered in the tableaux.

6. The evidence for this ranking only becomes apparent in the across-the-word environment.

7. Posing an underlying representation with a trill means that the loser, candidate (b), incurs one additional violation (IDENT /R/).

8. Note that /sr/ sequences are the only ones that do not involve a [–continuant] segment as the first member of the cluster. They are extremely rare word-internally, with 'Israel' being the only case mentioned in the literature. Bradley (2006) proposes that the constraint *[stri-

dent][vibrant] and the ranking *sɾ >> *sr are responsible for the lack of [s.ɾ] sequences in the output.

9. Harris (1969, 1983, 2002) argues that there is only one phoneme—a flap—and that the contrast is between a geminate and a nongeminate flap (not between a flap and a trill). The arguments against the one-phoneme analysis presented by much recent work (Bonet and Mascaró 1997; Bradley 2006) are that Spanish has no underlying geminates, and the underlying geminate that corresponds to the surface trill never appears in the output.

5

Repair Mechanisms and Structure Improvement: Epenthesis and Deletion

5.1 EPENTHESIS

This section reviews various types of epenthesis. Of these, only initial epenthesis is unquestionably a purely phonological repair mechanism. Other well-known epenthetic phenomena, such as plural epenthesis and epenthesis in diminutive formation, are morphophonological. Thus, an important task for any analysis is to disentangle the role played by each component of the grammar, while also explaining their interaction. In morphophonological epenthesis, the traditional notion of *repair*, as understood in derivational phonology, is unable to capture the reality of the phenomenon, which becomes clear under the optimality-theoretic notion of the *emergence of the unmarked*. In other words, epenthesis in the plural and diminutives is not guided by the exclusive need to repair ill-formed structure, but by the attempt to make surface structure as unmarked as possible under the new conditions created by the morphology. Word-final epenthesis, as it has been known in the literature since Harris (1969), is shown not to be an active phenomenon in the phonology and morphology of Spanish.

5.1.1 WORD-FINAL EPENTHESIS?

In recent years, a renewed interest in final epenthesis has surfaced in Spanish phonology (Morin 1999; Colina 2003a, 2003b; Bonet 2006). The need to evaluate optimality-theoretic accounts of phenomena such as plural epenthesis, diminutive formation, and syllabification, which are dependent on the status of final *–e*, has led researchers to re-examine the status of word-final *-e* and, subsequently, to question its validity, with several recent studies arguing against it. In what follows I go over the arguments to help the reader first understand why recent OT approaches argue for the underlying status of -*e*, and ultimately comprehend the relevance of this issue for Spanish morphophonology and for a model of phonology such as OT, which, due to its parallel nature, cannot put aside controversial areas of the phonology, but must deal with them alongside better understood processes.

Arguments for word-final epenthesis

Traditionally, the final vowel of Spanish words like *parte* 'part' and *nube* 'cloud' has been analyzed as the result of word-final epenthesis (Harris 1986a, 1986b, 1991a, 1991b, 1999). It has often been observed that, whereas -*a*, -*o* can be preceded by any consonant or consonant cluster, -*e* has a somewhat different distribution. Specifically, -*e* follows consonants and consonant clusters not permitted in word-final position, as seen in (c) in example 5.1, and it is less common after the set of consonants allowed in word-final position [d l n r s θ]. As a result, Harris (1986a, 113) concludes that "this highly skewed distribution" of -*e* must be the result of an epenthesis rule that inserts a mid vowel to allow the parsing of otherwise unsyllabifiable coda consonants; -*e* after syllabifiable coda consonants is part of the underlying representation. The same analysis is adopted by Harris (1991a, 1991b, 1999), Colina (1995), and many others. The main argument in favor of this proposal is that final epenthesis captures an important generalization regarding the syllable structure of Spanish: namely, that /č x p t k b g f/ are not syllabifiable word-finally.

No final epenthesis

Recent analyses (Colina 2003a; Bonet 2006), however, argue against word-final epenthesis. They propose that, at one point in the history of the language, there probably was an active rule of final epenthesis, but that currently there is no such process, and that final -*e* has been restructured as underlying and reinterpreted as a word marker, or terminal element (TE).[1] It is argued that the current repair mechanism for parsing unsyllabifiable word-final consonants or consonant clusters is deletion or neutralization of various coda features (see sections 2.2.2.1.2 and 2.2.2.1.3).

Example 5.1

a. -*o#*		b. -*a#*	
himno	'hymn'	columna	'column'
parto	'childbirth'	carta	'letter'
canto	'chant'	santa	'female saint'

c. -*e#*		d. -*CC#*	
solemne	'solemn'	*	
parte	'part'	*	
guante	'glove'	*	
traste	'guitar fret'	*	
nube	'cloud'	*	

Example 5.2

a. *-o#*

dedo	'finger'			
polo	'polo'
cono	'cone'
cero	'zero'
caso	'case'
cazo	'ladle'

b. *-a#*

seda	'silk'
cola	'tail'
luna	'moon'
cera	'wax'
casa	'house'
caza	'hunting'

c. *-e#*

sede	'site'
prole	'offspring'
pene	'penis'
ere	'letter 'r''
fase	'phase'
cruce	'intersection'

d. *-C#*

sed	'thirst'
sol	'sun'
atún	'tuna'
mujer	'woman'
as	'ace'
cruz	'cross'

Arguments for no final epenthesis

Several arguments exist in favor of the no-epenthesis proposal. Given the exceptions to the generalization regarding final *-e* for which *-e* needs to be underlyingly specified ((c) in example 5.2), it can be argued that the presence of *-e* is not truly predictable and the robustness of the generalization is weakened. Furthermore, that the analyst can draw a descriptive generalization on the data does not necessarily imply that such generalization is part of the knowledge of the native speaker, as it could be the result of a historical process or gap (see section 2.2.1, "Is Spanish quantity sensitive?", for a similar situation regarding stress). One way to test whether the process is active synchronically would be to ask native speakers to pronounce nonce words that end in illegal consonants. Although I know of no experiment that does this, the treatment of borrowings comes close to replicating this situation. As shown in example 5.3 (see Bonet 2006 for additional examples), illegal consonants and consonant clusters in borrowings are repaired through deletion and various types of neutralization, rather than epenthesis (Colina 2003a). In other words, final epenthesis is no longer productive as a repair strategy.

Example 5.3

club	[klú]	*[klube]	'club'
chalet	[čalé]	*[čaléte]	'chalet'
carnet	[karné]	*[karnéte]	'ID'
bistec	[bisté]	*[bistéke]	'steak'

An additional argument against final epenthesis is that final epenthesis, with numerous exceptions, behaves differently from exceptionless initial epenthesis (example 5.4).

Example 5.4

esfera	'sphere'	hemisferio	'hemisphere'
escribir	'write'	inscribir	'inscribe'
eslavo	'Slav'	yugoslavo	'Yugoslavian'
estrés	'stress'		
stop	[estop]		

> A possible way to retain final epenthesis alongside final deletion is to argue that final epenthesis is a lexical process, while deletion and coda neutralization have a postlexical application. In addition to the controversial status of level phonology in OT (see chapter 4), Colina (2003a) shows that the assumption that final epenthesis is a lexical process cannot explain the differences with respect to initial epenthesis, as initial epenthesis must also be lexical. Furthermore, the lexical or postlexical status of word-final epenthesis is not uncontroversial itself, as evidenced by proposals (Crowhurst 1992) in which word-final epenthesis is argued to be postlexical.

In sum, a comparison of two possible analyses of final -e, namely, -e is an underlying word marker or -e is epenthetic, reveals little evidence in support of final epenthesis. The burden of proof therefore rests on the analyst arguing for final epenthesis.

OT account of word-final -e   An OT analysis does not need any additional constraints to account for the behavior of final -e. According to Richness of the Base, which states that no restrictions are allowed on the input, one must allow for inputs without underlying -e, in addition to those with it. Given the constraints and constraint ranking in example 5.5 (see also sections 2.2.2.1 and 2.2.2.3, and example 2.60), an underlying word-final cluster results in deletion in the output, as seen in example 5.6, and output [e] corresponds to input /e/; that is, /e/ must be present in the input in order to obtain the correct output (example 5.7). A potential underlying representation with a word-final obstruent in the input would surface with either deletion or featural neutralization depending on the ranking of MAX-IO and *CODA/obstruent for the particular dialect, shown here as undetermined to allow for both possibilities. (See examples 2.60 and 5.76 for the ranking for a dialect that deletes coda stops in clusters as well as their singleton counterparts; retention of singleton coda stops reflects the opposite ranking, i.e., MAX-IO >> *CODA/stop.)

Example 5.5

*COMPLEX CODA, DEP-IO >> MAX-IO, *CODA/obstruent >> *CODA/nasal >> *CODA/liquid >> *CODA/glide

Example 5.6   **Final cluster deletion**
/mart/ [mar]

	*COMPLEX CODA	DEP-IO	MAX-IO	*CODA/ obstruent	*CODA/ nasal	*CODA/ liquid
a. ☞ mar			*			*
b. mart	*!			*		*
c. marte		*!				*

Example 5.7   **Word-final -*e***
/marte/ [marte] 'Mars'

	*COMPLEX CODA	DEP-IO	MAX-IO	*CODA/ obstruent	*CODA/ nasal	*CODA/ liquid
a. mar			*!*			*
b. ☞ marte						*
c. mart	*!		*	*		*

5.1.2 PLURAL EPENTHESIS

Standard plural formation in Spanish consists of adding *s* [s] to nonverbs ending in unstressed vowels ((a) in example 5.8) and *es* [es] to those ending in consonants. Words ending in a stressed vowel take [es] or [s] except for those ending in –*é*, which only take [s] ((c) in example 5.8).[2] There is an additional group of words, often treated as exceptional, whose singular ends in a stressless vowel + [s] and remains invariant in the plural, *crisi*[s], *crisi*[s] 'crisis, crises' (versus regular *lapi*[s], *lapi*[s]*es* 'pencil, pencils'). (See also the standard sources (Foley 1967; Saltarelli 1970; Contreras 1977; Harris 1980), and, for a more recent description, Roca 1996.)

Plural allomorphy responds to syllable well-formedness conditions

The Spanish data in example 5.8 and the two allomorphs of the plural have been traditionally attributed to syllabification requirements. They have been accounted for as the result of epenthesis (Saltarelli 1970; Contreras 1977; Harris 1980, 1991a, 1999; Colina 1995; Moyna and Wiltshire 2000) or deletion (i.e., apocope) (Foley 1967; Harris 1970; Roca 1996). In the epenthesis proposal the plural morpheme /s/ is realized as [es]; [e] is inserted in contexts in which plural morpheme attachment would result in an ill-formed consonant cluster, like **mujers* (example 5.9).

Apocope analyses argue for an account in which the plural morpheme is underlyingly /s/; the singular of those forms that take [es] in the plural ends in an underlying /e/, which is subsequently deleted (example 5.10).

Among optimality-theoretic accounts of pluralization, Roca (1996) presents an apocope account. Moyna and Wiltshire (2000) offer an epenthesis analysis based on the ill-formedness of the consonant cluster resulting from the attachment of /s/ to a consonant-final base. It will be argued below that phonological repair of an ill-formed cluster cannot be the true motivation behind plural epenthesis. Bonet (2006) proposes that the plural allomorph is subcategorized by the base and thus underlyingly specified as /s/ or /es/ for each word class.

Example 5.8

	Singular	Plural	Gloss
a.	libro	libros	'book(s)'
	caso	casos	'case(s)'
	niña	niñas	'girl(s)'
	prole	proles	'offspring(s)'
	bote	botes	'boat(s)' / 'container(s)'
b.	mujer	mujeres	'woman, women'
	mal	males	'evil(s)'
	papel	papeles	'paper(s)'
	árbol	árboles	'tree(s)'
	pared	paredes	'wall(s)'
	césped	céspedes	'lawn(s)'
c.	tisú	tisúes ~ tisús	'tissue(s)'
	rubí	rubíes ~ rubís	'ruby, rubies'
	puré	purés *purees	'puree(s)'

Example 5.9

mujer	mujeres (*mujers)	'woman, women'
mal	males (*mals)	'evil(s)'
papel	papeles (*papels)	'paper(s)'
árbol	árboles (*árbols)	'tree(s)'

Example 5.10

mujer /muxeɾe/	mujeres	'woman, women'
mal /male/	males	'evil(s)'
papel /papele/	papeles	'paper(s)'
árbol /árbole/	árboles	'tree(s)'

Plural epenthesis preferred to apocope

The bulk of the literature favors epenthesis proposals on the grounds that the rule of singular -*e* deletion presented by the apocope analysis is unnatural in Spanish and unnecessarily burdens the lexicon. Colina (2006b) argues that epenthesis proposals, however, do not provide a satisfactory explanation of why some clusters like *ls* undergo plural epenthesis (e.g., *sol-es* 'suns'), despite being well formed, as demonstrated by the singular forms, *vals* 'waltz,' *solsticio* 'solstice.' While it could be argued that a form like *vals* is not part of the core, native lexicon, the same cannot be said of forms like *seis* [séi̯s] 'six' that also have epenthesis in the plural, *ley* [léi̯] 'law,' *[lei̯s] [le.yes] 'laws.'

Plural
epenthesis as
emergence of
the unmarked

Based on the distinction between input and output faithfulness proposed by
optimality-theoretic Correspondence Theory (Benua 1995; McCarthy and Prince
1995), Colina (2006b) proposes that epenthesis of [e] in the plural reflects the
emergence of the unmarked (McCarthy and Prince 1994) with respect to the constraint against coda consonants (*CODA). The relevant correspondence relation
for the singular is an input-to-output correspondence relation. *CODA is usually
violated in the singular, because of the domination of DEP-IO (input-to-output
faithfulness) over *CODA (markedness). In the plural, however, the relevant correspondence relation is of the output-to-output type, DEP-IO is trivially satisfied,
and domination of *CODA over DEP-OO results in epenthesis.

The output of
the plural is in
a correspon-
dence relation
with the output
of the singular

Several arguments demonstrate the existence of an output-to-output correspondence relation in plural formation. First, the plural morpheme, unlike other
Spanish suffixes, is attached to the morphological word after all derivational and
inflectional morphemes, including terminal elements, for example, *cas-a*, *cas-a-s*,
'house(s)' versus *cas-er-o* 'housekeeper.' Second, forms with underlying final
obstruents, such as *boicot* /boikót/ [boi̯kó] 'boycott' (see *boicotear* [bojkotear] 'to
boycott'), often have plurals of the type [boi̯kós], where the underlying /t/ does
not surface, indicating that the plural is modeled on the output of the singular,
[boi̯kós] *[boi̯kotes]. Singulars ending in an obstruent + *e*, such as *bote*, select
the [s] allomorph, because they are formed on the vowel-final output of the singular, [bote] [bote-s].

> For additional evidence of output-to-output effects between singular and
> plural, such as depalatalization (e.g., *desdén*, *desdenes*, *desdeñes*, 'disdain,
> n. sing,' 'disdains, n. pl,' 'you disdain, subjunctive'), see Lloret and Mas-
> caró's (2006) analysis. Lloret and Mascaró use the constraint IDENTITY-
> BASE (PLACE) to account for over-application of depalatalization in the
> plural. Their account, however, raises the question of why there is not over-
> application of nasal velarization or aspiration in the plural of the relevant
> dialects.

Example 5.11 contains the constraints and ranking; examples 5.12 and 5.13 show
candidate evaluation for the singular and the plural forms, respectively.

As seen in example 5.12, candidates (b) and (c), with epenthesis and deletion, are ruled out because of the high ranking of MAX-IO and DEP-IO. Candidate (a) is the winning candidate because it only violates *CODA, the lowest-
ranked constraint.

Plurals of
consonant-
final singulars

Since the plural form is in an output-to-output relation to the singular in
example 5.13, the relevant faithfulness constraints are not DEP-IO and MAX-IO,
which regulate correspondence between the input and the output and are therefore
trivially satisfied, but DEP-OO and MAX-OO, which pertain to output-to-output
correspondence relations. The domination of *CODA over DEP-OO explains plural
epenthesis. The strings in correspondence are [muxer] [muxeɾes]. Although both
(a) and (b) in example 5.13 incur *CODA violations on account of the plural morpheme /s/, (b) has one more *CODA violation and is thus eliminated. The winner,
(a), has one violation of DEP-OO, but this is the lowest-ranked constraint.

> At this point it is important to clarify how *CODA violations are being
> assessed. In the OT literature, more than one segment in the coda is normally
> counted as a violation of the constraint against complex codas (*COMPLEX
> CODA), rather than a *CODA violation (Kager 1999). The current analysis

argues that, in addition to a *COMPLEX CODA violation, these segments also incur *CODA violations. One of the arguments for this position is that for sonorant + /s/ clusters, an analysis in which the ranking *COMPLEX CODA >> MAX-IO is the reason for deletion makes the wrong predictions. For example, such an analysis predicts that the plural of [sol] 'sun' should be the ill-formed *[sos]. In contrast, the output-to-output account proposed here straightforwardly accounts for why nonplural clusters undergo deletion while plural ones prefer epenthesis through the following rankings:

(i) DEP-IO >> *CODA >> MAX-IO (singular)

(ii) MAX-OO >> *CODA >> DEP-OO (plural)

Example 5.11

a. *Constraints I* (Benua 1995; McCarthy and Prince 1995)

MAX-IO: Every segment present in the input must have a correspondent in the output.

DEP-IO: Every segment present in the output must have a correspondent in the input.

*CODA: No coda segments.

DEP-OO: Every segment present in the output of the plural must have a correspondent in the output of the singular.

MAX-OO: Every segment present in the output of the singular must have a correspondent in the output of the plural.

b. *Ranking*

MAX-IO, DEP-IO >> *CODA

*CODA >> DEP-OO

Example 5.12   **Evaluation of singular forms**
                       /muxer/ [muxer]

	MAX-IO	DEP-IO	*CODA
a. ☞ muxer			*
b. muxere		*!	
c. muxe	*!		

Example 5.13   **Evaluation of plurals of consonant-final singulars I**
                       /muxer/ [muxer] + /s/ [muxeres]

	MAX-IO	DEP-IO	*CODA	DEP-OO
a. ☞ muxeres			*(s)	*
b. muxers			*(s) *(r)!	

In sum, epenthesis in the plural cannot be due to the need to satisfy *COM-PLEX CODA rather than *CODA (contra Colina 1995; Moyna and Wiltshire 2000). A second argument in favor of assessing individual *CODA violations, as well as *COMPLEX CODA violations, is that the correct plural outputs can be obtained through class-specific *CODA constraints (e.g., *CODA/stop, *CODA/sonorant), which are independently needed in Spanish to account for coda stop deletion versus retention of coda sonorants (e.g., /eklipse/ [eklise] 'eclipse' versus /bolber/ [bolβer]). In addition, contrasts such as the follow-ing indicate that deletion is driven by the coda type (obstruent versus sono-rant) and not by the complexity of the cluster.

(i) /ekspresidente/ [es.pre.si.ðeṇ.te] 'ex-president' (deletion) versus /pers-pektiba/ [pers.pe.ti.βa] 'perspective' (no deletion)

(ii) /biseps/ [bi.ses] 'biceps' (deletion) versus /bals/ [bals] 'waltz,' /seis/ [seịs] 'six,' Sáinz [saịns] 'Sáinz, last name' (no deletion)

Codas with more than one segment also contain *COMPLEX CODA viola-tions, not shown here for reasons of space. Also for reasons of economy, coda-specific constraints (*CODA/stop, *CODA/fricative, *CODA/sonorant) are lumped together under the label *CODA (see chapter 2 for these con-straints). For each violation, the offending segment is shown in parentheses, thus indicating the nature of the coda violation involved.

To complete the evaluation of the plurals of consonant-final singulars, two additional candidates need to be considered: (c) and (d) in example 5.15. The constraints shown in example 5.14 are necessary to rule out these candidates.

Example 5.14   Constraints II

REALIZE MORPHEME (RM): All morphemes must be realized. A morpheme is realized if its input has a correspondent in the output (Samek-Lodovici 1993; McCarthy 2002, 124; Kurisu 2001).

ALIGN (Pl, R, Wd, R) (ALIGN-PL): The right edge of the plural morpheme must be aligned with the right edge of the word.

Example 5.15   Evaluation of plurals of consonant-final singulars II
/muxer/ [muxer] + /s/ [muxeɾes]

	MAX-IO	DEP-IO	RM	ALIGN-PL	*CODA	DEP-OO
a. ☞ muxeɾes					*(s)	*
b. muxers					*(s) *(r)!	
c. muxerse				*!	*(r)	*
d. muxeɾe			*!			*

RM and ALIGN-PL must dominate *CODA because the plural of vowel-final
(unstressed) singulars is formed by attaching [s] to the right of the vowel
(example 5.16).

Example 5.16 **Evaluation of plurals of vowel-final singulars**
/niɲa/ [niɲa] + /s/ [niɲas]

	MAX-IO	DEP-IO	RM	ALIGN-PL	*CODA	DEP-OO
a. ☞ niɲas					*(s)	
b. niɲase				*!		*
c. niɲa			*!			

Plural
epenthesis
with CC
clusters that
are well-
formed in the
singular

The account in Colina (2006b) also explains plural epenthesis in clusters that
appear to be well-formed in the singular. Since the relevant faithfulness constraint in the plural (DEP-OO) is dominated by markedness (*CODA), *CODA
effects become visible by demanding open syllables. In other words, -e is
inserted in plurals to allow a coda consonant to be parsed as an onset to the
epenthetic vowel. Thus, while DEP-IO >> *CODA selects [bals] 'waltz' over
*[balse] or *[bales] in the singular (example 5.17), in the plural the ranking of
markedness over output faithfulness, *CODA >> DEP-OO, chooses [soles] over
*[sols] (example 5.18).

Examples 5.19 and 5.20 show competing candidates for a form with a high
glide + /s/ cluster. Evaluation proceeds as in examples 5.17 and 5.18.[3]
Singulars that are e-final form their plural like other vowel-final words, since I
have argued that -e is underlying. Crucially, however, in an output-to-output
account of the plural, whether final -e is underlying or epenthetic in the singular
has no bearing on the analysis, since the output of the singular, in correspondence
with the plural, will always contain a final -e, regardless of whether it is epenthetic and thus absent from the input (DEP-IO violation), or underlying (no DEP-
IO violation).

Example 5.17 /bals/ [bals]

	MAX-IO	DEP-IO	RM	ALIGN-PL	*CODA	DEP-OO
a. ☞ bals					*(l)*(s)	
b. balse		*!			*(l)	
c. bal	*!				*(l)	
d. bales		*!			*(s)	

Example 5.18 /sol/ [sol] + /s/ [soles]

	MAX-IO	DEP-IO	RM	ALIGN-PL	*CODA	DEP-OO
a. ☞ soles					*(s)	*
b. solse				*!	*(l)	*
c. sol			*!		*(l)	
d. sols					*(s)*(l)!	

Example 5.19   /seis/ [se̯is]

	Max-IO	Dep-IO	RM	Align-Pl	*Coda	Dep-OO
a.☞ se̯is					*(i̯)*(s)	
b. se̯ise		*!			*(i̯)	
c. se̯i	*!				*(i̯)	
d. seyes		*!			*(s)	

Example 5.20   /lei/ [le̯i] + /s/ [leyes]

	Max-IO	Dep-IO	RM	Align-Pl	*Coda	Dep-OO
a. ☞ leyes					*(s)	*
b. le̯ise				*!	*(i̯)	*
c. le̯i			*!		*(i̯)	
d. le̯is					*(s)*(i̯)!	

Plurals of singulars ending in unstressed vowels

Colina (2006b) explains variation in the plurals of forms ending in stressed vowels (*rubí, rubies ~ rubís,* 'ruby, rubies'; example 5.8c) through conflicting demands on the output, which are nonexistent in (unstressed) vowel- and consonant-final bases. Attachment of the [es] allomorph to consonant-final bases brings about unmarked structure: syllabic (by opening the final VC syllable), morphological (by conforming to the preferred structure for the morphological word consisting of a stem and an unstressed vocalic terminal element, *cas + a* 'house,' *hotel, hotel + es* 'hotel(s)'), and metrical (iambic feet become trochaic). This is not the case, however, for forms like *rubí* 'ruby.' The [es] allomorph (*rubi.es*) creates an unmarked trochaic foot (satisfies FtForm (Troch)), but it also introduces an onsetless syllable (Onset violation). The [s] form of the plural (*ru.bís*), on the other hand, results in a syllable onset (satisfies Onset) but creates an iambic foot (FtForm (Troch) violation). Under these conflicting demands, Onset and FtForm (Troch) remain unranked, resulting in variation and in the production of two alternative outputs (example 5.22).

Example 5.21   Constraints III

Onset: Syllables have onsets.

FtForm (Troch): The preferred foot type is a (syllabic) trochee.

Stress-Ident (OO): Preserve stress.

Example 5.22   /rubí/ [rubí] + /s/
            [rubíes] ~ [rubís]

	Dep-IO	Max-IO	Stress-Ident	FtForm (Troch)	Onset
a. ☞ rubíes					*
b. ☞ rubís				*	
c. rúbis			*!		

In addition, STRESS-IDENT, requiring the preservation of stress, must dominate ONSET and FTFORM (TROCH), because stress shift cannot be resorted to
in order to avoid ONSET or FTFORM (TROCH) violations. As seen in the tableau in example 5.22, candidate (c), with stress shift, is ruled out because it
violates the more highly ranked STRESS-IDENT, despite containing no violations of ONSET or FTFORM (TROCH).

Forms that are *é* final (*café, cafés *cafees*, 'coffee') without variation are
accounted for by means of an OCP-type constraint that bans identical con-
secutive segments and dominates FTFORM (TROCH).

It is important to note that it has been argued (Roca, personal communication, among others) that the [es] allomorph in forms that end in a stressed
vowel is prescriptive, originating in the norms of the Royal Academy. Under
this assumption, the current analysis makes the right prediction, as epenthesis is obviated by the absence of *CODA violations.

It was mentioned earlier in this section that plural formation in Spanish is a morphophonological process. Recent work under various theoretical frameworks has
convincingly shown that morphology plays a role in plural formation (Harris
1999; Colina 2003a; Bonet 2006; Bermúdez-Otero 2007), in contrast with earlier,
purely phonological accounts (Foley 1967; Saltarelli 1970; Contreras 1977). The
output-to-output analysis presented here (see also Colina 2006b) expresses the
generalization that the plural allomorph [es] is the result of trying to improve on
the phonological and morphological form of the output: phonologically, by
replacing CVC with CV, and morphologically, by providing the terminal element
preferred by the unmarked form of the morphological word in Spanish. This generalization is captured through the output-to-output correspondence relation
established between the output of the singular (morphological word) and the output of the plural (also a morphological word). It is argued that if a form is not recognized as a morphological word of Spanish (e.g., xenonym, unassimilated loan),
the correspondence relation does not apply and therefore epenthesis fails to
apply; in other words, epenthesis occurs only in a morphological domain.

Colina (2003a) proposes the constraint MWD (morphological words end in
terminal elements) in combination with an output-to-output constraint
DEP-Bsf (every element of a suffixed form has a correspondent on the
base). The disadvantage of this account is that MWD does not appear to be
a likely constraint in a model of phonology in which constraints are universal. Bermúdez-Otero's analysis (2007) adopts a model of organization of
the Spanish nonverbal lexicon into morphological classes similar to those
of Harris (1999): *e*-stem nominals (Class III in Harris 1999) have Ø or *-e* as
terminal elements (stem formatives in Bermúdez-Otero's terminology). In
addition, Bermúdez-Otero proposes a language-specific rule by which *e*-
stem nominals take the non-null allomorph before the plural suffix. This
account therefore requires two allomorphs for *-e* final and consonant-final
nominals (*e*-stems), a rule for the selection of the correct allomorph of the
plural, and an additional morphological class for *-e* nominals that surface
with an *-e* despite the well-formedness of the previous coda consonant
(Class IV in Harris 1999; e.g., *clase* 'class'). In contrast, the current proposal only requires the use of independently motivated universal con-

straints such as *CODA and the notion of output-to-output (morphological word). The output-to-output account finds additional motivation in the analysis of the Dominican data below (see section 5.1.3).

OT account of pluralization versus serial accounts

To sum up, an OT account of the plural is clearly superior to derivational accounts for the following reasons:

a. It explains plural epenthesis with clusters that appear to be well-formed in the singular, (e.g., *vals* *vales, *valse 'waltz'; *solsticio* *solesticio 'solstice' versus *sol-es* *sols 'suns') through the emergence of OO constraints (DEP-OO).

b. It highlights the difference between plural epenthesis (exceptional) and initial epenthesis (unexceptional). Plural epenthesis is morphological (morphology-dependent constraints), and initial epenthesis is phonological (purely phonological constraints).

c. It relies on constraints that are independently motivated for Spanish and other languages (universal).

d. As will be shown in section 5.1.3, an output-to-output account of pluralization and a set of universal constraints also explain apparently odd types of pluralization, such as the so-called double plural of Dominican Spanish, without having to resort to separate rules or special mechanisms.

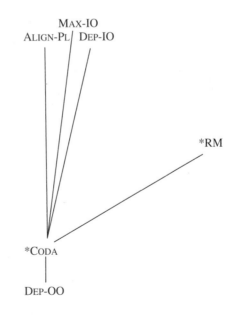

Figure 5.1 Constraint ranking for Spanish plural formation (standard dialects)

5.1.3 EPENTHESIS IN DOMINICAN DOUBLE PLURALS

In addition to standard methods of pluralization, Dominican Spanish has an alternative plural formation mechanism, normally referred to as the "double plural," in which '(e)se' [(e)se] is adjoined to the base, *libro > librose* 'book, books,'

Example 5.23

Base	Double plural	Gloss[4]
gallina	gallinase	'hens'
lata	latase	'cans'
pintura	pinturase	'paints'
esto	estose	'these'
eso	esose	'those'
muchacho	muchachose	'boys'
arriba	arribase	'ups'
mujer	mujerese	'women'
pan	panese	'breads'
papel	papelese	'papers'
vudú	vuduse	'voodoos'
ají	ajise	'peppers'

---

mujer > *mujerese* 'woman, women' (Jiménez Sabater 1975; Núñez-Cedeño 1980, 2003; Harris 1980; Terrell 1986).

Núñez-Cedeño (2003) shows that double plural selection is governed by pragmatic factors. The double plural is realized only on the lexical head of an NP in intonationally prominent focus position, indicated here by the use of capitals, for example, la AMARÍLLASE versus *lase AMARÍLLASE (double plural on the entire NP). Example 5.24 illustrates the use of double plurals in context (the corresponding nonfocus forms are marked by the use of italics).

Core proposal for Dominican pluralization Optimality-theoretic accounts, such as Colina (2006a), explain the double plural facts, both its form and the criteria governing its selection, in a direct way through general mechanisms of syllabification and pluralization. More specifically, Colina (2006a) proposes an optimality-theoretic analysis that builds on the output-to-output account of pluralization in standard dialects (Colina 2006b), and demonstrates that there is no double plural in Dominican, in the sense that the double plural is based on the regular plural. There is only one plural morpheme, the traditional /s/. The apparently redundant attachment of the plural morpheme results from the restrictions on coda obstruents found in Dominican (/s/-deletion and -aspiration) in combination with the need for overt realization of morphemes in prominent positions.

The difference between the regular plural and the double plural (focused) is that in the latter, a highly ranked constraint requires that the plural in focused positions have morphological exponence. In more general terms, [se] is the output realization of plural /s/ followed by epenthetic [e] in intonationally prominent (focus) positions. Thus, the Dominican data can be explained mostly through the syllabification constraints proposed for pluralization in the standard dialects (section 5.1.2), coda constraints and their language-specific ranking in Dominican, and a morpheme realization constraint for focused positions. Because they are universal, morpheme realization constraints in focused posi-

Example 5.24 (Ramón, male, age 28) (Núñez-Cedeño 2003, 74–76)

Researcher: Ramón, bueno ¿y qué va a hacer con esas pinturas?
'Well, Ramón, what are you going to do with those paints?'

Ramón: Pue la AMARÍLLASE la subo pa la azotea. No la BLÁNCASE; ÉSASE se quedan aquí porque hay que pintal toa la PARÉDESE, y usar la pintura. Si yo le digo que doña Remi na má me da a mi pa comprar lata de PINTÚRASE y fíjese lo grande que son la parede, eso no se pinta con tan chin pintura.
'I am bringing the yellow ones up to the roof. Not the white ones; those will stay here because I got to paint all walls and use the paints. I tell you, doña Remi just gives me enough to buy two cans of paint and look how big these walls are, they cannot be painted with so little paint.'

Researcher: Me imagino que se comen la poca grama que queda, esta muy seco, pero tambien hay *gallina*.
'I think they are eating up the little there is, it is dry but there are some hens as well.'

Don Otilio: No, GALLÍNASE no, esa son PALÓMASE.
'No, they're not hens, those are pigeons.'

---

tions also exist in the standard dialects; the lack of /s/-deletion in these dialects, however, renders them inactive.

Despite the non-overt realization of the plural morpheme in regular plurals, deletion is still the preferred mechanism, as the plural meaning can be recovered either from [e] in consonant-final bases or through other marks (verb agreement, article allomorph, etc.). A phonological zero, however, is not always the preferred outcome for plural [s]. Since focus position is a prominent, strong position, deletion is no longer the best strategy for the realization of the plural morpheme on focused NP heads; as a result, coda [s] is avoided through epenthesis, [se]. Consideration of the pragmatics and semantics of double plural selection thus reveals the presence of the alternation [Ø] ~ [s].

In contrast with the nonderivational proposal sketched above in which all plural realizations [Ø] ~ [e] ~ [se] ~ [ese] correspond to one underlying /s/, most derivational analyses postulate a separate plural morpheme for Dominican double plurals, /(e)se/. In fact, given the serialist nature of the framework, it is difficult to imagine a proposal without a separate morpheme. A rule-based account cannot obtain both the simple and double plural outputs from a unique plural morpheme /s/. In such a model, trying to derive both [oɾeha] and [oɾehase] from /oɾeha + s/ requires a rule of epenthesis and another of deletion. No matter the order of application of the rules, it is impossible to obtain both output forms (example 5.25).

> Serial accounts of Dominican plurals need a separate form for the double plural

An alternative analysis that needs to be ruled out is one that assumes, as most of the literature does, that there is no underlying /s/ in plain Dominican plurals and that [se] is inserted in plurals in focus position (/(e)/ ~ /se/). Evidence for /s/ in the regular plurals (as opposed to no morphological pluralization) lies in the presence of the alternation [Ø] ~ [s]. Example 5.26 demonstrates the existence of this alternation: as explained above, plural /s/ surfaces as zero in regular pluralization and as [s] when followed by epenthetic [e] in focused positions. The plural allomorph

---

Example 5.25

UR	/oreha + s/		/oreha + s/
deletion	[oreha]	epenthesis	[orehase]
epenthesis	————	deletion	————
output	[oreha]		[orehase]

Example 5.26   **Plural allomorph output forms in Dominican**

	Standard plural [Ø] [e]	Plural in focus position [se] [ese]
casa	casa	casase
mujer	mujere	mujerese

---

is often zero because /s/ will normally be in coda position and will therefore be deleted like other coda obstruents; yet, when deletion is no longer acceptable, and epenthesis is preferred, [e] allows [s] to be syllabified in an onset position and thus be realized as [s].

Another argument against the zero-plural-morpheme account is that it needs to specify an additional morpheme for focused plurals /se/ along with nonfocused /e/ for consonant-final words. On the other hand, the /s/-plus-epenthesis proposal can account for the facts through a single plural morpheme /s/ and general mechanisms of syllabification already existing in the language; it also captures the connection between the plural and [e] as the default epenthetic vowel in Spanish (*yugoslavo* versus *eslavo*) and with the realizations of the plural in standard dialects.

In what follows I go over some of the essentials of the optimality-theoretic account of pluralization in Dominican (Colina 2006a).

As was mentioned above, Dominican Spanish has greater restrictions on coda segments than the Peninsular dialects described in section 2.2.2.1. It does not normally allow coda obstruents in word-internal or word-final positions (Jiménez Sabater 1975), which are often realized as zero (*usted, ustedes* [u.te] [u.te.ðe] 'you-polite, sg. and pl.'). (Aspiration of /s/ is also possible, although less common in popular speech.[5])

Example 5.27

mosca	[móka]	'fly'
basta	[báta]	'enough'
asno	[áno]	'donkey'
gas	[ga]	'gas'
virus	[bí.ru]	'virus'
usted	[u.té]	'you-polite'

OT account of
/s/-deletion in
Dominican

The relevant constraints were presented in section 2.2.2.1 (example 2.33), but they are repeated in example 5.28 for convenience. Coda obstruents are deleted as the result of the domination of *CODA/obstruent over MAX-IO. As seen in example 5.29, candidate (c), with two violations of MAX-IO (two obstruents deleted) but no coda obstruents (the higher ranking *CODA/obstruent is satisfied), is the winner. A candidate with epenthesis (a violation of DEP-IO), (a), is ruled out, since DEP-IO is highly ranked; (b) incurs a violation of high ranking *CODA/obstruent.

Example 5.28

*CODA/obstruent: No obstruents in coda position (McCarthy 2002, 106).

MAX-IO: Every segment present in the input must have a correspondent in the output (Benua 1995; McCarthy and Prince 1995).

DEP-IO: Every segment present in the output must have a correspondent in the input (Benua 1995; McCarthy and Prince 1995).

*CODA/obstruent, DEP-IO >> MAX-IO

Example 5.29 Lexical (nonplural) coda obstruents in Dominican /usted/ [ute]

	*CODA/obstruent	DEP-IO	MAX-IO
a. utede		*!	(*)
b. uted	*!		(*)
c. ☞ ute			(*)*

In accordance with the ill-formedness of coda [s], plural /s/ is realized as zero in popular speech, thus surfacing as zero [Ø] in vowel-final forms (example 5.30) and [e] in consonant-final ones (example 5.31). Examples 5.30 and 5.31 also contain the corresponding double plurals.

As demonstrated in section 5.1.2 for pluralization in the standard dialects, the plural is an output-to-output relation to the singular; thus, OO faithfulness constraints, which evaluate correspondence relations between two output forms, become relevant in the evaluation of plural outputs. In addition, under

Example 5.30 Bases ending in unstressed vowels

Singular	Plural	Double plural	Gloss
gallina	gallina[Ø]	gallinase	'hens'
lata	lata[Ø]	latase	'cans'
pintura	pintura[Ø]	pinturase	'paints'
e(s)to	e(s)to[Ø]	e(s)tose	'these'
eso	eso[Ø]	esose	'those'
muchacho	muchacho[Ø]	muchachose	'boys'
arriba	arriba[Ø]	arribase	'ups'

Example 5.31   **Bases ending in consonants or stressed vowels**

Singular	Plural	Double plural	Gloss
mujer	mujere[Ø]	mujerese	'women'
pan	pane[Ø]	panese	'breads'
papel	papele[Ø]	papelese	'papers'
vudú	vudu[Ø]	vuduse	'voodoos'
ají	aji[Ø]	panese	'peppers'

OO correspondence, [s] and [e] in the plural outputs violate DEP-OO (see examples 5.33–5.35), since [s] and [e] are not present in the output of the singular. [e] does not incur a DEP-IO violation given that the relevant correspondence relation is output-to-output (the plural is formed on the output of the singular). DEP-IO is vacuously satisfied. Domination of *CODA over DEP-OO makes plural epenthesis possible, while word-final epenthesis is ruled out by DEP-IO >> *CODA (see section 5.1.2).

In example 5.33, the domination of *CODA/obstruent and ALIGN-PL over RM selects (c), with no plural [s] and a violation of RM, as the winning candidate because (b) and (a) incur violations of *CODA/obstruent and ALIGN-PL due to a coda [s] and a misaligned plural, respectively.

Example 5.32

*CODA/obstruent >> ALIGN-PL >> RM

Example 5.33   **Plural of vowel-final singulars[6]**
                   /oɾeha + s / [oɾeha]
                   &[oɾeha]

	*CODA/obstruent	ALIGN-PL	RM	DEP-OO
a. oɾehase		*!		*(s)*(e)
b. oɾehas	*!			*(s)
c. ☞ oɾeha			*	

Similarly, in example 5.34, (a) and (b) are eliminated because of *CODA/obstruent and ALIGN-PL violations; (c), with no plural morpheme realization (RM violation), is the winner due to the lower ranking of RM. Note, however, that an additional candidate (d) [muher] must be considered and ruled out in example 5.35.

*CODA and its domination over DEP-OO (as demonstrated for standard plurals) suffice to obtain the correct output. Thus, while sonorant codas are not repaired by deletion or epenthesis in the singular (*muher* *muhe *muhere 'woman'), indicating that DEP-IO, MAX-IO >> *CODA, this is not the case for plural forms where the constraint ranking is *CODA >> DEP-OO. In example 5.36, (c) and (d) are therefore tied with respect to RM, passing the decision onto *CODA, which correctly chooses (c) [muhere]. *CODA is not crucially ranked with respect to RM. These results are to be expected under the optimality-theoretic analysis of the plural presented in section

Example 5.34   **Plural of consonant-final singulars**
/muher + s/ [muhere]
&[muher]

	*CODA/obstruent	ALIGN-PL	RM	DEP-OO
a. muherse		*!		*(s)*(e)
b. muheres	*!			*(s)*(e)
c. ☞ muhere			*	*(e)

Example 5.35   **/muher + s/ [muhere] (preliminary)[7]**
&[muher]

	*CODA/obstruent	ALIGN-PL	RM	DEP-OO
a. muherse		*!		*(s)*(e)
b. muheres	*!			*(s)*(e)
c. muhere			*	*(e)!
d. ☞ muher			*	

Example 5.36   **/muher + s/ [muhere] (final)**
&[muher]

	*CODA/obstruent	ALIGN-PL	RM	*CODA	DEP-OO
c. ☞ muhere			*		*
d. muher			*	*!	

5.1.2, thus providing further evidence for an output-to-output analysis of plural formation in Spanish.

As mentioned earlier, the use of the double plural (versus [Ø] or [e]) is governed by pragmatic factors (Núñez-Cedeño 2003). The double plural is realized only on the lexical head of an NP in focus position, indicated here by the use of capitals (la AMARÍLLASE versus *lase AMARÍLLASE).

In addition to a general RM constraint, a second RM constraint—RM/FOC (example 5.37)—is needed. It requires morphemes to be realized overtly in prosodically emphatic, prominent positions, such as focus. RM/FOC accounts for plural realization (double plurals) in focus position in Dominican.

Evaluation for focused forms of vowel-final singulars proceeds as in example 5.38. Candidate (c) is eliminated on account of RM/FOC violations, while (b) violates the highly ranked *CODA/obstruent. The highest constraint violated by (a) is ALIGN-PL, so (a) is the winner, despite the misalignment of the plural morpheme.

Plurals of focused forms: epenthesis needed for plural realization in focus position

Example 5.37

RM/FOC: All morphemes must be realized overtly in focus position (intonationally or otherwise strong position).

Example 5.38 **/OREHA + s/ [OREHASE]**
                &[oreha]

	RM/FOC	*CODA/obstruent	ALIGN-PL	RM	DEP-OO
a. ☞ OREHASE			*		*(s)*(e)
b. OREHAS		*!			*(s)
c. OREHA	*!			*	

Evaluation of the focused forms of consonant-final singulars proceeds as in example 5.39. Candidates (c) and (d) are eliminated on account of RM/FOC violations, while (b) violates the highly ranked *CODA/obstruent. Despite the tie with regard to ALIGN-PL, (e), MUHERESE, is better than (a), MUHERSE, because of the additional *CODA violation incurred by the latter. (e) is thus selected as the optimal candidate.[8] An additional candidate MUHESE (not shown in the tableau) is also ruled out, indicating that the antideletion constraint MAX-OO dominates *CODA.

Example 5.39 **/MUHER + s/ [MUHERESE]**
                &[muher]

	RM/FOC	*CODA/ obstruent	ALIGN-PL	RM	*CODA	DEP-OO
a. MUHERSE			*		*!	*(s) *(e)
b. MUHERES		*!			*	*(s)*(e)
c. MUHERE	*!			*		*(e)
d. MUHER	*!			*	*	
e. ☞ MUHERESE			*			*(s) *(e) *(e)

Serial analyses
fail to capture
the connection
between
double plurals
and
syllabification
in Dominican
In sum, serial analyses fail to capture the connection between double plurals and syllabification mechanisms in Dominican Spanish, as the presence of [e] after [s] is related to the ill-formedness of coda /s/. They also need to specify separate underlying morphemes for the regular plurals and the double plurals. In contrast, optimality-theoretic accounts (Colina 2006a) can explain the double plural facts in a direct way through general mechanisms of syllabification and pluralization, thus highlighting the superiority of a correspondence-theoretic account.

An OO account reveals the natural and universal aspects of Dominican plural formation generally obscured by derivational formalisms, and the relevance of OO constraints in plural formation in Spanish, not only in standard dialects, but also in dialects with more unusual plurals. The OT analysis brings to the foreground the pluralization mechanisms shared by all dialects, and explains the so-called double plurals of Dominican as simply the result of the same pluralization mechanisms in interaction with morpheme realization constraints and the dialect-specific ranking of syllabification constraints (crucially, a high-ranking *CODA/obstruent constraint). In addition, an OT analysis offers a new insight with regard to plural epenthesis, seen now as the result of favoring CV structure (or in morphological terms, words are vowel-final in Spanish) in a morphologically derived, word-level context (output-to-output). In other words, epenthesis of [e] in the plural reflects the emergence of the unmarked (McCarthy and Prince 1994): *CODA effects are seen in the OO phonology of the plural, but not in the language as a whole, an effect of the ranking DEP-IO >> *CODA >> DEP-OO.

The issue of the morphological versus phonological status of plural epenthesis in Spanish appears much clearer now. While plural epenthesis may still be considered phonological, it does not belong to the input-to-output phonology, but to the OO phonology. This accounts for plural epenthesis after codas that would be well-formed in nonplural outputs. At the same time, the connection with the morphological structure of Spanish becomes obvious as the morphology reveals a bias toward CV structure evidenced by the preference for vowel-final words (TEs). Finally, the difference in behavior with regard to exceptionless word-initial epenthesis receives a straightforward explanation, given the morphological dependency of plural epenthesis and the purely phonological motivation of initial epenthesis, as shown below (section 5.1.4).

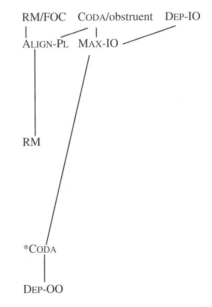

Figure 5.2 Constraint ranking for Dominican Spanish plural formation

5.1.4 WORD-INITIAL EPENTHESIS

Spanish has a well-known process of initial epenthesis in which [e] is inserted before a word-initial [s] cluster. This process applies without exception to native words and borrowings, (a) and (b) in example 5.40. Although less common, Spanish also has examples of deletion of the first member of an ill-formed word-initial cluster.

Since there are no alternations (the initial stop never surfaces), it could be argued that the underlying representation does not contain a cluster. However, under Richness of the Base, which does not allow restrictions on the form of the underlying representation, it is important to offer an account that would prevent a potential /pn/ or /ps/ cluster from surfacing in word-initial position. The following analysis takes this into consideration.

Example 5.40

a. esfera   'sphere' *versus*   hemisferio   'hemisphere'

   escribir   'write'   inscribir   'inscribe'

   eslavo   'Slav'   yugoslavo   'yugoslavian'

b. estrés   'stress'

   stop [estop]   'stop'

Example 5.41

pneumatico   [neumátiko]   'tire'

psicología   [sikoloxía]   'psychology'

OT account of word-initial epenthesis and deletion

As seen in section 2.2.1, the constraint MSD (Maximum Sonority Distance), which requires that there exists the maximum sonority distance between possible onset segments, is in part responsible for this phenomenon. MSD is a highly ranked constraint. It could be argued that it dominates the faithfulness constraint against epenthesis, DEP-IO, given that [ezlaβo] is preferred to [slaβo] as the output of /slabo/.[9] Note, however, that for an underlying representation with an obstruent initial cluster, /psikoloxía/, as in example 5.42, the repair strategy resorted to is not epenthesis (as predicted by the ranking), but deletion, [sikoloxía].[10] Thus, a candidate with epenthesis, *[epsikoloxía], must incur a more serious violation than those incurred by [ezlaβo] (or perhaps epenthesis, [ezlaβo], is better than deletion, [laβo]).

Deletion in [sikoloxía] could be explained as trying to avoid a coda stop. This can be easily justified, as coda stops in Spanish are often deleted or show neutralization in voice or continuancy (see section 2.2.2.1), whereas [s] is an acceptable segment in nonaspirating dialects. Thus, the constraint *CODA/obstruent is divided into a highly ranked *CODA/stop and less highly ranked *CODA/s. However, such an account leaves epenthesis in /s/ + C clusters unexplained: While [s] in the coda is well-formed in many dialects of Spanish, coda [s] is still worse than no coda at all (deletion). Furthermore, since deletion, (c) in example 5.42, is preferred to epenthesis, (a), DEP-IO must be more highly ranked than MAX-IO. This, in combination with the ranking *CODA/stop >> *CODA/s, would make a candidate with deletion, such as (c) in example 5.43, always better than the actual winner, (a) [ezlaβo] (see also examples 5.76–5.77 below). One must conclude that there is an additional, highly ranked constraint that prevents deletion of [s] in word-initial clusters. Such a constraint (referred to below as MAX-IO #s) is not without justification, as /s/ + C clusters are preserved in many languages, such as English, despite their highly marked sonority contour. One could speculate that MAX-IO #s is a phonetically grounded constraint related to the sibilant nature (higher noise) of /s/. In Spanish, MAX-IO #s dominates DEP-IO, as seen in example 5.43, in which the candidate with epenthesis, (a), is the winner because (b) is ruled out by a violation of MSD and (c) deletes word-initial /s/.[11]

Example 5.42   /psikoloxía/ [sikoloxía]

	Msd	Dep-IO	*Coda/stop	Max-IO	*Coda/s
a. epsikoloxía		*!	*		
b. psikoloxía	*!				
c. ☞ sikoloxía				*	

Example 5.43   /slabo/ [ezlaβo]

	Msd	Max-IO #s	Dep-IO	*Coda/stop	Max-IO	*Coda/s
a. ☞ ezlaβo			*			*
b. slaβo	*!					
c. laβo		*!			*	

Additional candidates with word-internal epenthesis—[pesikoloxía], [selaβo]—are ruled out by the high ranking of CONTIGUITY, a constraint banning epenthesis morpheme internally. CONTIGUITY appears to be undominated in Spanish, as epenthesis only occurs word initially and word finally (before the plural suffix, or after it in the double plurals of Dominican).

The tableaux and constraint rankings in examples 5.42 and 5.43 clearly reveal the advantages of an OT account; the same universal constraints and rankings (already presented in section 2.2), in combination with some new ones, account for both epenthesis and deletion in word-initial position. An OT analysis shows how constraint interaction (relevant for some forms and not others) can produce what are apparently very different solutions for similar inputs. Further support for the constraints and constraint rankings proposed for particular phenomena is obtained when additional data can be explained with the same constraints and rankings.

In addition to word-initial epenthesis and plural epenthesis (standard and Dominican), Spanish also has a process often referred to as "medial epenthesis" (Harris 1983; Eddington 1992).

Example 5.44

abr-ir 'open' *versus* aber-tura (*abrtura) 'opening'

Word-medial epenthesis?

I argue that cases like example 5.44 are more adequately treated as lexicalized forms, rather than the result of epenthesis in word-medial position. It has been shown that the active process in Spanish is one of deletion of a consonant in an ill-formed consonant cluster (section 5.1). In addition, as seen in word-initial epenthesis and plural epenthesis, Spanish does not allow epenthesis within morphemes (high ranking of CONTIGUITY). Finally, deletion is also found in cases similar to example 5.44, like example 5.45.

Example 5.45

esculp-ir 'to sculpt' *versus* escul-tura (*esculpetura) 'sculpture'

5.1.5 EPENTHESIS IN DIMINUTIVES

An account of epenthesis in Spanish needs to address diminutive formation, since monosyllabic words exhibit an epenthetic *-e* in their diminutives—*pan*, *pane-cito* 'bread'—as do disyllabic bases that end in a diphthong, *tapia*, *tapie-cita* [tapiesita] 'wall.' Depending on the analysis, epenthesis may also be present in *e*-final disyllabic bases, *madre*, *madre-cita* 'mother.' As will be shown here, an OT account is particularly well-suited to explain the complex nature of epenthesis in diminutivization, a phenomenon that is the result of various interacting factors.

In what follows, I present Colina's OT account of epenthesis in diminutives (2003b) and compare it, when relevant, to serial analyses such as Crowhurst's (1992).[12] Basic aspects of the overall analysis of diminutivization are presented as necessary for the explanation of the epenthesis data. The reader interested in the details of the analysis of diminutive formation per se is referred to Colina's analysis.

OT proposal for Spanish diminutive formation

Colina's basic proposal (2003b) is as follows. The Spanish diminutive selects between two allomorphs according to the morphological class and morphological structure of the base. *-it-* attaches to word classes with a TE *(-a, -o,* and *-e; cas-a, cas-it-a* 'house'; *pel-o, pel-it-o* 'hair'; *envas-e, envas-it-o* 'container') and *-citV* to words with no TE *(canción, cancion-cita* 'song'). The basic allomorphy results from the preference of the diminutive for word-level attachment, as well as from the tendency of Spanish words to end in TEs, combined with a general prohibition against TEs in nonfinal positions. When word-level attachment is not possible due to the presence of a TE (TEs can never appear in nonfinal position), *-it-* (the allomorph that can be attached word-internally) is selected. The preference for words with TEs in the Spanish lexicon makes *-it-* the most commonly selected allomorph. In addition, the default pattern just described can be altered by high-ranking phonological markedness constraints on the shape of the prosodic word. In other words, an unexpected allomorph may be selected when the resulting output will have better prosodic form than that obtained through selection of the expected allomorph; for instance, for *clas-e* 'class' most dialects have the diminutive *clase-cita*, rather than the expected *clas-it-a*. Colina argues that this is because *-cita* selection results in two binary feet with all syllables parsed *(clàse)-(cíta)*, whereas selection of *-it-a* would result in either non-binary feet or unparsed syllables, **(cla) (síta)*, **cla(síta)*. Segmental identity of the final vowel and the default epenthetic vowel [e] is crucial and explains the difference in behavior observed in disyllables ending in *-a* and *-o*: *cas-a, ca(s-íta)* versus **(càs-e-) (cíta)*.

Most (if not all) existing analyses (Prieto 1992; Miranda 1999) derive the two forms of the diminutive (*-it-* and *-citV*) from a single underlying allomorph (e.g., *-citV* in Crowhurst 1992) on the basis of mostly phonological criteria. Colina (2003b), however, proposes two underlying allomorphs, selected according to the word class of the base. I start by presenting the arguments in favor of two allomorphs.

Arguments for two underlying diminutive allomorphs

Consider, for instance, pairs like those mentioned by Harris (1994): *corona, coronita* 'crown' versus *llorona, lloroncita* 'crybaby.' It is clear that speakers need to refer to morphological information in order to select the right allomorph. The difference between *coronita* and *lloroncita* is that each is derived from a base belonging to a different word class. *Lloroncita* is derived from consonant-final *llorón*, whereas *coronita* results from vowel-final *corona*. The forms of the diminutives are then as predicted: *-citV* after a base with no TE, and *-it-* with a TE base.

Evidence from proper nouns can be used in support of this proposal, namely that *llorón* is the base for both the feminine and masculine of the diminutive. Some dialects of Spanish have *Juan-cito* as a possible diminutive for *Juan*; in these dialects, however, the feminine diminutive is not **Juan-cita*, but *Juan-it-a*. Such an outcome can only be accounted for by assuming that the masculine and the feminine are derived from separate bases, a reasonable assumption considering that these are proper names and therefore separate entities. Thus, *Juan*, with no TE, takes the *-citV* allomorph, *Juan-cito*; whereas *Juan-a*, with TE *-a*, takes the *-it-* form of the diminutive, *Juan-it-a*. The same applies to the contrast between *Lloron-a/Lloron-it-a* (a female character in Mexican folklore) and *lloron-a/lloron-cita* (common noun) (Harris 1994). Since *Llorona* is a proper noun for which there is no masculine (**Llorón*), *Lloronita* can only have TE-final *Llorona* as its base, resulting in the diminutive *Lloronita* (**Lloroncita*). In sum, it is not the internal structure of the base that is responsible for the *lloroncita/coronita* contrast (as Harris (1994) claims), but the morphological class of the form that serves as the base for diminutivization.

Patterns of diminutivization

The basic patterns of diminutivization are shown below in examples 5.46–5.51 for Peninsular Spanish (Colina 2003b). Only those patterns also seen in Mexican Spanish are presented here in order to facilitate the comparison with Crowhurst (1992), which serves as an example of a derivational account. Although I will not review it here, Colina's OT analysis (2003b) accounts for dialectal differences between Peninsular, Mexican (Crowhurst 1992), Paraguayan (Jaeggli 1978), and Nicaraguan (Miranda 1999) through constraint reranking.

Words with a TE select *-it-* (example 5.46).The vowel after *-it-* corresponds to the TE of the base, except for *-e*, when V is realized as *-a* if the gender of the base is feminine and *-o* if masculine. That the final vowel is not part of the suffix (*-itV*) is demonstrated by contrasts such as *map-a* (masc), *map-it-a*, **map-it-o* versus *model-o* (fem) *model-it-o *model-it-a*.

Example 5.46

Base	*Diminutive*	
map-a	map-it-a	'map-MASC'
cas-a	cas-it-a	'house-FEM'
libr-a	libr-it-a	'pound-FEM'
man-o	man-it-o	'hand-FEM'
plan-o	plan-it-o	'map-MASC'
libr-o	libr-it-o	'book-MASC'
coron-a	coron-it-a	'crown-FEM'
problem-a	problem-it-a	'problem-MASC'
pregunt-a	pregunt-it-a	'question-FEM'
zapat-o	zapat-it-o	'shoe-MASC'
model-o	model-it-o	'model-FEM'

Words with no TE select *–citV* (example 5.47). The final vowel in *-citV* matches the gender of the base, *-a* for feminine and *-o* for masculine.

Example 5.47

Base	Diminutive	
virgen	virgen-cita	'virgin-FEM'
canción	cancion-cita	'song-FEM'
pintor	pintor-cito	'painter-MASC'
escritor	escritor-cito	'writer-MASC'
ademán	ademan-cito	'gesture-MASC'
espray	espray-cito	'spray-MASC'
convoy	convoy-cito	'convoy-MASC'
café	cafe-cito	'coffee-MASC'
canapé	canape-cito	'canape-MASC'

Monosyllabic words exhibit epenthesis and select –citV (example 5.48).

Example 5.48

Base	Diminutive	
sol	sol-e-cito	'sun-MASC'
piel	piel-e-cita	'skin-FEM'
pan	pan-e-cito	'bread-MASC'
flor	flor-e-cita	'flower-FEM'
mes	mes-e-cito	'month-MASC'
red	red-e-cita	'net-FEM'
rey	rey-e-cito	'king-MASC'

Disyllabic words with TE -e take the -citV allomorph (example 5.49).

Example 5.49

Base	Diminutive	
clas-e	clas-e-cita	'class-FEM'
fas-e	fas-e-cita	'phase-FEM'
coch-e	coch-e-cito	'car-MASC'
madr-e	madr-e-cita	'mother-FEM'
padr-e	padr-e-cito	'father-MASC'
mont-e	mont-e-cito	'mount,-MASC'
part-e	part-e-cita	'part-FEM'

Trisyllabic and longer -*e* forms prefer the -*it*- diminutive in Peninsular Spanish (examples 5.50 and 5.51).

Example 5.50

Base	*Diminutive*	
estuch-e	estuch-it-o	'case-MASC'
envas-e	envas-it-o	'container-MASC'
elegant-e	elegant-it-o	'elegant-MASC'

Example 5.51

Base	*Diminutive*	
chocolat-e	chocolat-it-o	'chocolate-MASC'
pirámid-e	piramid-it-a	'pyramid-FEM'
aguacat-e	aguacat-it-o	'avocado-MASC'

Diminutives of TE-final bases and bases with no TE

Epenthesis is found in both vowel- (TE) and consonant-final bases. The following constraints are needed to account for these two basic types:

Example 5.52

*TE-: No terminal elements in positions other than word final. In an alignment format: The right edge of a terminal element must be aligned with the right edge of a word.

-*citV* to PrWd: The left edge of the suffix -*citV* must be aligned with the right edge of the prosodic word (PrWd).

DIM to PrWd: The left edge of the diminutive affix (DIM) must be aligned with the right edge of the prosodic word.

-it- to V_{TE}: The right edge of the -*it*- allomorph must be aligned with the left edge of a [+syllabic] TE of the base.

An important distinction is drawn between the behavior of the two allomorphs. -*citV* attaches to the prosodic word (-citV to PrWd), thus invoking output-to-output constraints. The -*it*- allomorph, however, is attached to the stem (without terminal elements, -it- to V_{TE}), rendering output-to-output constraints inoperative. Overall, diminutive affixation prefers word-level attachment when not in conflict with more important constraints.

Words with TEs must violate DIM to PrWd in order for the TE to appear in word-final position; thus, the ranking must be *TE-, -citV to PrWd >> DIM to PrWd.

In example 5.53, (c) violates *TE- because it has a TE in word-internal position; in the other two candidates, however, the diminutive suffix is not aligned with the right edge of the word, thus violating DIM to PrWd. (b) is worse than (a), because it misaligns the -*citV* allomorph, violating -citV to PrWd in addition to DIM to PrWd.

Example 5.53　　**TE-final bases**
　　　　　　　　　　cas-a + DIM　　cas-it-a

	*TE-	-citV to PrWd	DIM to PrWd
a. ☞ cas-it-a			*
b. cas-cita		*!	*
c. cas-a]-cita	*!		

In example 5.54, (b) violates -it- to V_{TE}, the constraint that requires the right edge of the suffix -it- to be aligned with the left edge of a TE (in other words, it requires -it- to be an infix). This makes (a), the candidate with the -citV allomorph, the winner.

Example 5.54　　**Bases with no TE**
　　　　　　　　　　ademán + DIM　　ademán-cito

	*TE-	-it- to V_{TE}	-citV to PrWd	DIM to PrWd
a. ☞ ademán]-cito				
b. ademán]-it-		*!		

Monosyllabic bases

Epenthesis in monosyllabic bases (example 5.48) requires the additional constraints in example 5.55. As mentioned above, these are output-to-output constraints, given word-level attachment of the -citV affix.[13] The relevant rankings are in example 5.56.

In example 5.57, (b) is the optimal candidate because, although (a) is a word, it is not a minimal word, thus violating PrWd-MinWd. (b) manages to satisfy PrWd-MinWd through a violation of the lowest-ranked constraint, DEP-Bsf (having a segment not present in the base). An additional candidate *pan-it-o* (not shown in the tableau) violates undominated -it- to V_{TE} because *pan* lacks a TE and the right edge of the -it- allomorph is not aligned with the left edge of a vocalic TE of the base (V, *o*, or *a*).

> An additional constraint against the insertion of a mora not present in the input rules out a form that would satisfy PrWd-MinWd by making the final consonant moraic. The ranking responsible is DEPμ-Bsf >> DEP-Bsf. Other dialects of Spanish, such as Nicaraguan, actually do this by selecting *pancito* as the optimal form, indicating that the ranking is DEP-Bsf >> DEPμ-Bsf.

Disyllabic e-final bases: emergence of the unmarked prosodic word

An additional case of epenthesis is that of *e*-final disyllabic bases (example 5.49). Colina (2003b) argues that forms like *clase-cita* can surface with -*e* in nonfinal position because -*e* is reinterpreted as epenthetic. This is possible given that the segmental content of the TE happens to be identical to that of the default epenthetic vowel. Reinterpretation allows for the preferred pattern of diminutivization to emerge: the diminutive suffix attaches to the word, and in this case, to the unmarked minimal word. In other words, although unstressed final -*e* usually functions as a TE, the preference of diminutivization for word-level attachment, the unmarked status of the disyllabic foot as the minimal word, and the fact that

Example 5.55

Prosodic Word-Minimal Word (PrWd-MinWd): Cover term for the combined effects of prosodic constraints that require that all prosodic words be disyllabic (Colina 2003b, 59; see for details).

DEP-Bsf: Every element of the suffixed form (Sf) has a correspondent in the base (B).

Example 5.56

PrWd-MinWd >> DEP-Bsf

-citV to PrWd >> DEP-Bsf

Example 5.57   Monosyllabic bases
pan + DIM   pan-e-cito

	PrWd-MinWd	-citV to PrWd	DIM to PrWd	DEP-Bsf
a. pan]-cito	*!			
b. ☞ pan-e]-cito				*

[e] is also the epenthetic vowel in Spanish, favor the reinterpretation of -e as epenthetic and the selection of the -citV allomorph in disyllabic bases ending in -e.

Evidence for the reanalysis proposal lies in its ability to account for the generalization that -citV selection with TE -e generally affects only disyllabic forms. The crucial difference between disyllabic and longer -e forms is that the disyllabic bases are the only ones subject to epenthesis (to avoid a subminimal base), while this is not the case with longer forms (e.g., *chocolat-it-o* *chocolat-e-cito*). Disyllabic bases with TEs other than -e cannot be reinterpreted as epenthetic because of featural disparity (versus *casa-cita*) (violation of IDENT.Seg B-Sf). The presentation here abstracts away from the technical details and formalization of the reinterpretation of -e (involving coalescence, i.e., a violation of UNIFORMITY). The interested reader is referred to Colina's analysis (2003b). In the tableaux, epenthetic segments are recognized because they contain a violation of DEP-Bsf, whereas underlying -e is a TE element and therefore incurs a *TE- violation.

Example 5.58

IDENT.Seg B-Sf: A segment in B is identical to its correspondent in Sf.

In candidate (d) of example 5.59, -e is interpreted as a TE and therefore violates *TE-. -e in (e) is interpreted as epenthetic, thus violating DEP-Bsf only. (c) has the TE -a in word-internal position, incurring a *TE- violation; (a) and (b) misalign the diminutive with respect to the PrWd, and (b), in addition, misaligns -citV. Since DEP-Bsf is the lowest ranked constraint, (e) is the optimal candidate.

The high ranking of IDENT.Seg B-Sf explains the ill-formedness of (d) in example 5.60, *case-cita*, a candidate in which the epenthetic vowel is not identical to the word final vowel.

Example 5.59   Disyllabic *e*-final bases
clas-e + DIM   clas-e-cita

	*TE-	PrWd-MinWd	-citV to PrWd	DIM to PrWd	DEP-Bsf
a. clas-it-a				*!	
b. clas-cita			*!	*	
c. clas-a]-cita	*!				
d. clas-e]-cita	*!				
e. ☞ clas-e]-cita					*

Example 5.60   Disyllabic *-a/-o* bases
cas-a + DIM   cas-it-a

	*TE-	IDENT.Seg B-Sf	PrWd-MinWd	-citV to PrWd	DIM to PrWd	DEP-Bsf
a. ☞ cas-it-a					*	
b. cas-cita				*!	*	
c. [casa]-cita	*!					
d. [case]-cita		*!				*

In the case of longer-than-disyllabic forms, reinterpretation of *-e* as epenthetic in (c) in example 5.61 does not help satisfy PrWd-MinWd (through the creation of a minimal word); therefore *-e* is treated as a TE, selecting the *-it-* allomorph.

Example 5.61   Longer than disyllabic *e*-final bases
estuch-e + DIM   estuch-it-o

	*TE-	IDENT.Seg PrWd	PrWd-MinWd	-citV to PrWd	DIM to PrWd	DEP-Bsf
a. ☞ estuch-it-o					*	
b. estuch-e]-cito	*!		*			
c. estuch-e]-cito			*!			*

Bases ending in diphthongs

Finally, it is important to consider epenthesis in bases with diphthongs in their final syllables. Despite ending in *-o* and *-a*, these forms behave like *e*-final bases. Disyllabic bases take *-citV* and epenthesize *-e*; longer-than-disyllabic bases take *-it-*.

Example 5.62

Base	*Diminutive*	
tapi-a	tapi-e-cita	'wall-FEM'
radi-o	radi-e-cita	'radio-FEM'
farmaci-a	farmac-it-a	'pharmacy-FEM'
escritori-o	escritor-it-o	'desk-MASC'

Note that the stem-final glide, if it were followed by the *-it-* allomorph, would result in glide deletion (since two high vocoids are not permitted in a rhyme in Spanish) with subsequent misalignment and encroachment of the *-it-* allomorph with respect to the stem (stem = *tapi-*; *-it-* is aligned to *tap-* in *tap-it-a*). In order to avoid this undesirable result, the *-citV* allomorph is selected. Misaligned candidates violate ALIGN it-R, (a) in example 5.64. Candidates that do not preserve a diphthong incur violations of IDENTμ B-Sf, (b).

Example 5.63

ALIGN -it-, Left, Stem Right (ALIGN-it-R): The left edge of the diminutive allomorph *-it-* must be aligned with the right edge of the stem.

IDENTμ B-Sf: A moraic segment in the base (B) will have as its correspondent a moraic segment in the corresponding suffixed form (Sf), and a nonmoraic segment will correspond to a nonmoraic one.

Since *-citV* is a word-level allomorph, output-to-output, prosodic identity constraints become active. The data indicate that *-citV* is possible for disyllabic bases only (which satisfy PrWd-MinWd). When PrWd-MinWd is not at stake (longer-than-disyllabic bases), misalignment is the preferred output. IDENTμ B-Sf dominates IDENT.Seg B-Sf, since *tapiecita* is preferred over *tapicita*. IDENT.Seg B-Sf must be ranked below ALIGN-it-R, given that *tapiecita* is better than *tapita*. Finally, *TE- dominates IDENT.Seg B-Sf because *tapiecita* is preferred over *tapiacita*.

As seen in example 5.64, (a) is eliminated on the basis of the misalignment of suffix and stem [i], incurring a violation of ALIGN-it-R; (b) is ruled out because it does not preserve the diphthong of the base (IDENTμ B-Sf violation). (c), *tapiacita*, is worse than (d), *tapiecita*, because it contains a TE that is not in word-final

Example 5.64   Disyllabic, diphthong-final bases

tapi-a + DIM   tapi-e-cita
  | | | |
   μ   μ

	*TE-	PrWd-MinW	IDENTμ B-Sf	ALIGN -it-R	IDENT. Seg B-Sf	-citV to PrWd	DIM to PrWd	DEP B-Sf

a. tapi-t-a
  |
  μ
				*!			*	

b. tapi-cita
  |
  μ
			*!			*	*	

c. tapi-acita
  | |
   μ
	*!							

d. ☞
tapi-e]-cita
  | |
   μ
					*			*

position. -*e* in (d) does not violate *TE-, because it is reinterpreted as epenthetic (not a TE), thus only obtaining marks for IDENT.Seg B-Sf and DEPB-Sf, both ranked lower than the constraints violated by its competitors.

Words with three (or more) syllables and a final diphthong do not preserve the diphthong, *sandalia, sandal-it-a*. As seen in example 5.65, this is predicted by the constraints and constraint ranking proposed.

Example 5.65   **sandali-a + DIM   sandal-it-a**

	*TE-	PrWd- MinWd	IDENTμ B-Sf	ALIGN -it-R	IDENT. Seg B-Sf	-citV to PrWd	DIM to PrWd	DEP B-Sf
a. ☞ sandal-it-a				*			*	
b. [sandali-e-] cita)		*!			*			*
c. [sandali-a-] cita)	*!	*						

In example 5.65, (a) is the optimal candidate because (b) and (c) violate PrWd-MinWd and *TE-. Both constraints are more highly ranked than ALIGN-it-R, the highest ranked constraint violated by (a). (a) does not incur violations of PrWd-MinWd, IDENTμ B-Sf, or IDENT.Seg B-Sf because the diminutive allomorph selected (-*it*-) does not attach to the prosodic word, but to the stem. Thus, PrWd-MinWd, IDENTμ B-Sf, and IDENT.Seg B-Sf are vacuously satisfied.

OT versus derivational accounts of diminutivization

In sum, an OT model of phonology that relies on constraint interaction is particularly well-suited to account for epenthesis in diminutive formation, as it responds to a complex interaction of morphological and phonological factors. That such a model was not available to phonologists until the advent of OT may have been in part responsible for the almost completely phonological basis of existing accounts of diminutivization and, consequently, for the lack of success in accounting for instances of epenthesis, which reflect both morphological and phonological factors.

Although allomorph selection is generally dependent on the morphological class of the base (TE-final or not), the preference of diminutive suffixes in Spanish for word-level attachment introduces phonological principles of markedness, relative to the prosodic word, which could determine the selection of the alternative allomorph. The notion of output-to-output correspondence in OT directly captures identity requirements between the prosodic word of the base and the diminutive form, as well as the emergence of unmarked forms (the disyllabic prosodic word) in the context of diminutivization. Previous analyses were not able to capture these generalizations in a straightforward manner. For instance, Crowhurst (1992) correctly notes that the suffix -*citV* has a preference for word-level attachment (also mentioned in Harris 1983). Yet, she is forced to specify a disyllabic template associated with the suffix; an optimality-theoretic account, however, can obtain this generalization from universal constraints on the shape of the minimal word. The effects of the minimality requirement can be seen in disyllabic bases (e.g., *clase*) that allow for reinterpretation of -*e* as epenthetic when attachment to the minimal, unmarked prosodic word is possible. Crowhurst

(1992) also argues that *-e* is epenthetic in disyllabic bases, but in a serial account she must resort to a number of complex mechanisms, such as level ordering, directionality of syllabification, and extraprosodicity, to account for the epenthesis site (*madre* versus **mader*).

> Word-initial epenthesis, *escribir*, and onset maximization, /a.blar/ **/ab.lar/, indicate that the directionality of syllabification in Spanish must be right to left; however, right-to-left syllabification would derive **mader* instead of *madre*. Crowhurst argues that word-initial epenthesis is lexical and that at the lexical level directionality of syllabification is right to left. At this point in the derivation, the second consonant in the final cluster is extraprosodic and therefore invisible to the syllabification mechanisms. Extraprosodicity is revoked postlexically, at which level syllabification is from left to right, thus correctly inserting *-e* after /r/, *madre*. Diminutivization is argued to be a postlexical process that eliminates the extraprosodic status of /r/ and results in epenthesis after /r/ (given left-to-right directionality at the postlexical level).

Perhaps one of the greatest shortcomings of derivational analyses like Crowhurst's (1992) is their failure to account for epenthesis in the diminutives (and augmentatives) of diphthong-final disyllabic bases, such as *tapiecita* [tapi̯esita] (*tapia*) versus *iglesita* (*iglesia*). Crowhurst tries to explain the contrast by means of two Double /i/ Repair rules: Repair I, which delinks the rightmost /i/, and Repair II, which delinks the leftmost one. Although there is independent evidence for a restriction on contiguous high segments in Spanish, it is not clear what the motivation is for postulating two repair rules. Furthermore, the same contrast appears in the augmentative (*-sote, -sota*) despite that fact that Double /i/ Repair would not apply: *tapiesota* [tapi̯esota] (*tapia*) versus *iglesota* (*iglesia*). The OT account shows that, although misalignment due to the need to avoid two identical segments may not be at stake any more, the same output-to-output effects associated with the prosodic-word level attachment of *-citV* (PrWdMin) found in the diminutive—namely, preservation of the moraic structure of the diphthong and the minimal word—are responsible for epenthesis in disyllabic bases in the augmentative.

5.2 DELETION AND NEUTRALIZATION OF CONTRAST

Most dialects of Spanish have word-medial and word-final deletion of a member of a consonant cluster (section 2.2.2.1.3), except in the plural, where epenthesis takes place in the context of an output-to-output correspondence relation. They also exhibit coda consonant deletion or featural neutralization, depending on dialect and register (both in word-medial and word-final positions) (sections 2.2.2.1.1 and 2.2.2.1.2).

An optimality-theoretic account of deletion of coda consonants was presented in sections 2.2.2.1.1 and 2.2.2.1.2. Despite the fact that the focus of that chapter was on the phonotactics—that is, on showing that the mechanisms of constraint interaction and output evaluation can capture in a direct fashion the descriptive generalizations regarding acceptable segments in the coda—the OT account offered also explained the repair mechanisms affecting ill-formed segments. This is yet another advantage of a parallel optimality-theoretic approach, as it simultaneously accounts for well-formed and ill-formed segments and for the outputs corresponding to potentially illegal segments. However, the OT approach, because of its parallel nature, also has some presentational drawbacks, as a certain degree of repetitiveness will inevitably follow from the need to go back to parts of the analysis that have to be presented sequentially but appear simultaneously in the phonology. This will become evident at this point in the book, where, for the sake of the reader, and risking a certain degree of repetitiveness, I summarize the account of coda consonant deletion, featural neutralization, and cluster reduction (deletion) in word-medial and word-final position from section 2.2.2.1. This time the focus is on the repair mechanisms: namely, deletion (violation of MAX-IO) or neutralization (IDENT violations).

An OT analysis captures the common motivation behind several processes of coda deletion and neutralization, along with various degrees of permissiveness in various dialects. The more restrictive goal is to avoid codas and thus to give preference to unmarked CV syllables. All dialects of Spanish allow some codas (sonorants), a fact captured by exploding the *CODA into consonant classes according to sonority. Some dialects and styles ban coda obstruents, allowing sonorants only. Thus, *CODA/obstruent is ranked above faithfulness, while *CODA/sonorant is ranked below faithfulness. Since obstruents are deleted, the relevant faithfulness constraint must be MAX-IO. Dialects and registers with obstruent neutralization satisfy restrictions on the coda (e.g., no voice and point of articulation specifications) by modifying certain features, rather than by deleting the entire segment; in other words, by attempting to satisfy conditions on the coda while salvaging as much of the original segment as possible. Obstruent neutralization reflects the domination of faithfulness over *CODA/obstruent, *CODA/voice, and CODA COND, which in turn dominate IDENT constraints. Usually voicing and continuancy are neutralized in coda obstruents, as voiced obstruents are generally more marked than their voiceless counterparts; at the same time voiced segments are also preferred in the coda due to their higher sonority. In addition, the voice feature of a coda consonant could be licensed through the onset, resulting in voicing assimilation in the coda. Continuancy distinctions tend to be neutralized in favor of fricatives, as fricatives, being more sonorous than stops, make better codas. Consonant clusters are reduced in favor of the most sonorous member of the cluster. The point of articulation of nasals is generally licensed through the following onset, resulting in assimilation.

Overview of processes involving coda deletion or neutralization: OT account can capture the shared motivation behind these processes

Example 5.66 Coda obstruent deletion
/obsoleto/ [osoleto]

	*CODA/obstruent	DEP-IO	MAX-IO
a. ☞ o.so.le.to			*
b. ob.so.le.to	*!		
c. o.be.so.le.to		*!	

Example 5.67 Coda obstruent retention[14]
/obsoleto/ [oBsoleto]

	MAX-IO	DEP-IO	*CODA/obstruent
a. o.so.le.to	*!		
b. ☞ oB.so.le.to			*
c. o.Be.so.le.to		*!	

Example 5.68   Obstruent devoicing in coda position[15]
/digno/ [diKno]

	*CODA[+voice]	IDENT(voice)
a. ☞ diK.no		*
b. diG.no	*!	

Example 5.69   Regressive voice assimilation of coda obstruents[16]
/futbol/ [fuDβol]

	AGREE(voice)	IDENT(voice)
a. ☞ fuDβol		*
b. fuTβol	*!	

Example 5.70   Continuancy neutralization (with voice assimilation)
/futbol/ [fuðβol]

	*CODA/stop	*CODA/fricative	IDENT(continuant)
a. ☞ fuðβol		*	*
b. fudβol	*!		

Example 5.71   Stops preferred in prominent positions (with voice assimilation)
/futbol/ [fudβol]

	PROMINENCE [−cont]	*CODA/stop	*CODA/fricative	IDENT(continuant)
a. fuðβol	*!		*	*
b. ☞ fudβol		*		

Example 5.72   Nasal assimilation. Place features obtained and licensed through the onset
/tango/ [taŋgo]

	IDENT^{OBSTR}(place)	HAVE PLACE	CODA COND	IDENT(place)
a. ☞ taŋgo				*
b. tango			*!	
c. tamgo			*!	*

Example 5.73   Word-final codas

Noncoronal coda obstruents are deleted (rather than altering place features). Coronal coda obstruents are retained.

*CODA/obstruent, DEP-IO >> MAX-IO

IDENT^{OBSTR}(place), HAVE PLACE >> *DOR >> *LABIAL >> MAX-IO >> *CORONAL, IDENT(place)

Clusters are usually simplified (example 5.74). Selection of the target of deletion is according to the universal sonority constraint hierarchy (the least sonorous consonant) (example 5.75).

Example 5.74   **Complex codas**

*COMPLEX CODA >> MAX-IO

Example 5.75

*COMPLEX CODA, DEP-IO >> *CODA/stop >> MAX-IO >> *CODA/s >> *CODA/nasal >> *CODA/liquid >> *CODA/glide

Example 5.76   /biseps/ [bises]

	*COMPLEX CODA	DEP-IO	*CODA/ stop	MAX-IO	*CODA/s	*CODA/ nasal	*CODA/ liquid
a. ☞ bises				*	*		
b. bisep			*!	*			
c. biseps	*!		*		*		
d. bisepes		*!			*		

Example 5.77   /eskulptor/ [eskul̩tor][17]

	*COMPLEX CODA	DEP-IO	*CODA/ stop	MAX-IO	*CODA/s	*CODA/ nasal	*CODA/ liquid
a. ☞ eskultor				*	*		**
b. eskuptor			*!	*	*		*
c. eskulptor	*!		*		*		**
d. eskuleptor		*!	*		*		*
e. eskulpetor		*!			*		**

5.3 SUMMARY

This chapter focused on epenthesis and deletion phenomena, such as those traditionally known as final epenthesis, plural epenthesis (in standard and nonstandard dialects), initial epenthesis, diminutive epenthesis, and deletion and neutralization of coda consonants. OT accounts were proposed and their advantages over serial analyses highlighted.

    The chapter presented evidence against an active process of final epenthesis, arguing instead for word-final coda deletion or neutralization, in accordance with the constraints and constraint ranking presented in chapter 2 and summarized in section 5.2. Colina (2006a) argues that plural epenthesis reflects the emergence of the unmarked with respect to the constraint against coda consonants (*CODA). *CODA is usually violated in the singular, because of the domination of DEP-IO (input-to-output faithfulness) over *CODA (markedness). In the plural, however, since the relevant correspondence relation is of the output-to-output type, DEP-IO is trivially satisfied, and domination of *CODA over DEP-OO results in epenthesis. This account of the plural is shown to be superior to derivational accounts because (1) it explains plural epenthesis with clusters that appear to be well-formed in the singular by the emergence of OO constraints (DEP-OO); (2) it emphasizes the difference between plural epenthesis (exceptional and morphological) and initial epenthesis (unexceptional and phonological); (3) it relies on universal constraints that are independently motivated for Spanish and other languages; and (4) it accounts for apparently odd types of pluralization, such as the so-called double plural of Dominican Spanish, without having to resort to separate rules or special mechanisms.

Building on the constraints and constraint ranking proposed for standard dialects, it is shown that an OT analysis of Dominican plurals, in particular double plurals (like Colina 2006a), can explain the pluralization facts in a direct way through general mechanisms of syllabification and pluralization, thus revealing the connection between double plurals and syllabification mechanisms in Dominican. The apparently redundant attachment of the plural morpheme results from the restrictions on coda obstruents found in Dominican (/s/-deletion and -aspiration) in combination with the need for overt realization of morphemes in prominent positions. The difference between the regular plural and the double plural (focused) is that in the latter case a highly ranked constraint requires that the plural in focused positions have morphological exponence. In more general terms, [se] is the output realization of plural /s/ followed by epenthetic [e] in intonationally prominent (focus) positions. Serial accounts miss this insight and are therefore forced to propose a separate allomorph for the double plural of Dominican.

Within a broader OT analysis of diminutive formation (Colina 2003b) that also accounts for dialectal variation, epenthesis in diminutives is shown to respond to the need to improve the prosodic form of the output through allomorph selection. In *clas-e* 'class,' for instance, most dialects have the diminutive *clase-cita*, rather than the expected *clas-it-a*. This is because *-cita* selection results in two binary feet with all syllables parsed *(clàse)-(cíta)*, whereas selection of *-it-a* would result in either non-binary feet or unparsed syllables, *(cla) (síta)*, **cla(síta)*. Segmental identity of the final vowel and the default epenthetic vowel [e] is crucial and explains the difference in behavior observed in disyllables ending in *-a* and *–o*: *cas-a*, *ca(s-íta)* versus **(càs-e-) (cíta)*. Although allomorph selection is generally dependent on the morphological class of the base (TE-final or not), the preference of diminutive suffixes in Spanish for word-level attachment introduces phonological principles of markedness relative to the prosodic word, which could determine the selection of the alternative allomorph. The notion of output-to-output correspondence in OT directly captures identity requirements between the form of the output of the base and those observed in the diminutive form, as well as the emergence of unmarked forms (the disyllabic prosodic word) in the context of diminutivization. In addition, an OT model of phonology that relies on constraint interaction is particularly well suited to account for the complex interaction of morphological and phonological factors responsible for epenthesis in diminutives.

STUDY QUESTIONS

1. What are the arguments for word-final epenthesis in Spanish? What are the arguments against it?

2. What is the relevance of the status of word-final *-e* for the morpho-phonology of Spanish?

3. What does word-final *-e* have in common with other terminal elements? How is it also different from terminal elements?

4. What are the main approaches to plural formation in the Spanish phonology literature?

5. What are the arguments for word-level attachment of the plural morpheme? How is this connected to an output-to-output account?

6. How is [e] in the plural different from and similar to final [e] in the singular?

7. How does pluralization interact with the phonology in Dominican Spanish?

8. Summarize the role of the phonology and that of the morphology in Colina's (2003b) account of diminutive formation. What about in Crowhurst's (1992) account?

9. What is the role of output-to-output constraints in diminutives according to Colina (2003b)?

GOING BACK TO THE SOURCES

Colina 2003a:

The status of word-final [e] in Spanish. *The Southwest Journal of Linguistics* 22:87–108.

Colina 2003b:

Diminutives in Spanish: A morphophonological account. *The Southwest Journal of Linguistics* 22:45–88.

Colina 2006a:

No "double plurals" in Dominican Spanish: An optimality-theoretic account. *Linguistics* 44:541–68.

Colina 2006b:

Output-to-output correspondence and the emergence of the unmarked in Spanish plural formation. *New Analyses in Romance Linguistics*. Ed. Jean-Pierre Montreuil. Philadelphia: John Benjamins.

Crowhurst 1992:

Diminutives and augmentatives in Mexican Spanish: A prosodic analysis. *Phonology* 9:221–53.

Harris 1986a:

Epenthesis processes in Spanish. *Studies in Romance Languages*. Ed. Carol Neidle and Rafael A. Núñez-Cedeño. Dordrecht: Foris.

Harris 1999:

Nasal depalatalization no, morphological well-formedness sí: The structure of Spanish word classes. *MIT Working Papers in Linguistics* 33:47–82.

ADDITIONAL RECOMMENDED READINGS

These entries contain relevant sections on word classes, final epenthesis, plural epenthesis, and diminutives.

Bermúdez-Otero, Ricardo. 2006. Morphological structure and phonological domains in Spanish denominal derivation. *Optimality-Theoretic Studies in Spanish Phonology.* Ed. Fernando Martínez-Gil and Sonia Colina. Philadelphia: John Benjamins.

Bermúdez-Otero, Ricardo. 2007. Spanish pseudoplurals: Phonological cues in the acquisition of a syntax-morphology mismatch. *Deponency and Morphological Mismatches* (Proceedings of the British Academy 145). Ed. Matthew Baerman, Greville Corbett, Dunstan Brown, and Andrew Hippisley. Oxford: Oxford University Press.

Bonet, Eulàlia. 2006. Gender allomorphy and epenthesis in Spanish. *Optimality-Theoretic Studies in Spanish Phonology.* Ed. Fernando Martínez-Gil and Sonia Colina. Philadelphia: John Benjamins.

Harris, James W. 1991b. The exponence of gender in Spanish. *Linguistic Inquiry* 22:27–62.

Lloret, María Rosa and Mascaró, Joan. 2006. Depalatalization revisited. *Optimality-Theoretic Studies in Spanish Phonology.* Ed. Fernando Martínez-Gil and Sonia Colina. Philadelphia: John Benjamins.

KEY TOPICS

SPANISH PHONOLOGY

pluralization; plural formation

morphology; in plural formation, in diminutive formation

double plurals

terminal elements (word markers, theme vowels, desinence, stem formatives)

word classes

final epenthesis

initial epenthesis

final deletion

final clusters

initial clusters (/s/ + C)

Dominican Spanish

Peninsular Spanish

Mexican (Sonoran) Spanish

PHONOLOGICAL THEORY/OT

 output-to-output constraints

 emergence of the unmarked

 morphology-phonology interface

TOPICS FOR FURTHER RESEARCH

1. Compare the analyses of plural epenthesis by Harris (1999), Colina (2003a, 2006a, 2006b), and Bonet (2006).

2. The account of plural forms did not cover exceptions such as *lunes, lunes* versus *lápis, lápises*. In generative phonology, the usual assumption is that the role of any account is to explain generalizations, not exceptions. As long as the analysis covers the main generalizations, the job is done. Considering exceptions, however, may be illustrative in a process that is argued to be morphological and to rely on the morphological structure of the base. How could one account for these exceptions? Do they offer any insights that may be beneficial to the analysis of pluralization?

3. The current chapter argues that the presence of *-e* after unsyllabifiable consonants is the result of a process of epenthesis earlier in the history of the language, which is no longer active. List two more instances of surface generalizations in Spanish that have recently been argued to be the result of a historical process (against traditional generative analysis). Comment or reflect on the implications of this debate for phonological theory. Does every surface/observable generalization in a language constitute part of the linguistic competence of the speaker? How could experimental linguistics contribute to the resolution of these issues?

4. How does the OT analysis of diminutive formation proposed here account for dialectal variation (see Colina 2003b)? Are you familiar with additional data (from other dialects) that could offer evidence for or against the analysis proposed?

5. Is there something in the phonetic nature of /s/ that makes its preservation in word-initial position a common phenomenon across languages?

NOTES

1. A terminal element (also known as a word marker, class marker, desinence, theme vowel) is a final, unstressed vowel that appears in word-final position in a large number of Spanish words. The TEs of Spanish are *-a, -o*, and, in some analyses, like the one presented here, *-e*. TEs are deleted before most suffixes.

2. Although much of the variation between [es] and [s] can occur within speakers, for some forms the alternation is across dialects.

3. In (d) in example 5.19 and (a) in example 5.20, the glide is parsed in the onset and realized as a fricative. The details of this have no bearing on the analysis proposed for plural epenthesis. For this reason and for ease

of presentation, evaluation of the segmental content of output candidates for /i/ is not considered in these tableaux.

4. The data are from Núñez-Cedeño (2003).

5. The facts concerning consonants in Dominican are in fact more complicated. Obstruents may sometimes vocalize (instead of deleting). While sonorants are usually retained, liquid sonorants often vocalize, and nasals assimilate to a following consonant or velarize (Jiménez-Sabater 1975; Núñez-Cedeño 1980). For the purposes of this book, I simply refer to the general asymmetry between obstruents and sonorants: whereas obstruents delete regularly, sonorants are often preserved.

6. (&) indicates the output of the singular. The output of the plural is indicated in brackets without (&).

7. ☞ indicates a candidate incorrectly selected as optimal.

8. Notice that (e) incurs three DEP-OO violations because of two epenthetic [e]s.

9. As the reader will recall, /f/ is the only fricative that can be parsed as the first member of a consonant cluster *[slaβo] versus [flako]. /f/ lacks an underlying specification for [continuant] and is therefore grouped with the stops (versus other fricatives). Martínez-Gil (2000) argues that the presence of the feature [continuant] contributes to the sonority of segments in Spanish.

10. Under Richness of the Base, /psikoloxía/ must be considered as a possible underlying representation.

11. In languages like English, where the cluster is preserved, MAX-IO #s would dominate both MSD and the faithfulness constraints responsible for epenthesis and deletion.

12. Colina's analysis (2003b) is presented with a few minor modifications.

13. Note that it could be argued that the base does not behave like a prosodic word (cf. the members of a compound) because it does not retain its primary stress: canción + cíta, càncioncíta (*cancióncíta). However, such behavior can be explained as the result of the domination of a more highly ranked constraint that forces the downgrading of the primary stress of the base to secondary (faithfulness violation). More work is needed to determine the nature of this constraint, but one could speculate that it is related to prosodic structure requirements that demand the incorporation of the base and the diminutive suffix into one unique Prosodic Word, in a structure similar to that proposed for prefixes in chapter 4 (example 4.14).

14. B is a voiced bilabial obstruent, unspecified for continuancy.

15. K is a voiceless velar obstruent, unspecified for continuancy; G is a voiced velar obstruent, unspecified for continuancy.

16. D is a voiced dental obstruent, unspecified for continuancy; T is a voiceless dental obstruent, unspecified for continuancy.

17. All candidates have at least one *CODA/liquid violation incurred by the final rhotic.

6

Conclusion

As stated in the introduction, the primary goal of this monograph is to improve upon our current understanding of important topics in Spanish phonology by addressing a wide range of phonological and morphophonological phenomena from a variety of dialects of Spanish: syllable types, syllabification algorithms, syllable repair mechanisms, syllable mergers, nasal assimilation, obstruent vocalization and spirantization, obstruent neutralization, glide formation, onset strengthening, aspiration, /r/ realizations, velarization, plural formation, word classes, and diminutives. In what follows I first summarize what I consider to be some of the successes of the optimality-theoretic analyses presented. Then, I point out some challenging areas for OT in Spanish phonology, as well as new directions for research.

In OT, the basic syllable types of Spanish are accounted for by means of universal faithfulness and markedness constraints; the main advantage of an OT analysis is that the basic syllabic typology of Spanish is obtained by permutations of a few basic universal constraints (e.g., ONSET, *CODA, *COMPLEX ONSET, *COMPLEX CODA) rather than a listing of syllable types or language-specific templates. OT also captures generalizations about the specific segments parsed in each syllabic position, in terms of sonority hierarchies and syllabic markedness constraints. In serial phonology, the role of sonority was recognized, but sonority scales could not be formalized into the theory, therefore constituting separate, external mechanisms. An optimality-theoretic framework, however, captures the generalizations that relate syllabic positions with sonority classes in a straightforward manner by means of universal scales and constraint hierarchies.

Perhaps one of the biggest problems encountered by serial analyses of Spanish syllabification is that syllabification rules are not sufficient to explain the data, as additional descriptive statements must be added that list the consonants that are well-formed in the onset, nucleus, and coda. In OT, no additional mechanisms or stipulations are necessary: The parsing of segments into syllabic positions as well as the parsing of only licit segments are the result of constraint interaction.

One final advantage of an OT analysis of Spanish phonotactics is its ability to reveal the common purpose in apparently unrelated phenomena. For example, the various modifications affecting consonants in the coda: deletion, featural neutralizations in voice and continuancy, and voice and place asssimilation. An OT analysis shows that these are all strategies to avoid coda segments: attempts to create less marked structures by being unfaithful to the input (faithfulness violations) in a position in which contrast preservation is not as crucial as it is in the onset.

Regarding resyllabification and across-the-word diphthongization, OT and its system of minimally violable constraints bring forth an important insight: Alignment of the syllable with the word can be sacrificed in order to provide an onset for a vowel-initial word; however, when the word already has an onset (i.e., it is consonant initial), there is no need to resyllabify a second consonant, since this resyllabification would unnecessarily misalign the syllable and the word. A serial account, in which a Complex Onset Rule applies only at the lexical level and an Onset Rule applies lexically and postlexically, cannot capture the true motivation of the phenomenon.

OT analyses of diphthongization in Peninsular and Chicano are shown to be able to incorporate dialectal differences (gliding of mid vowels versus raising of mid vowels; gliding of only the first vowel in the sequence versus gliding of the least sonorous vowel) in a direct way not available to derivational analyses. Serial analyses of Chicano diphthongization (e.g., Martínez-Gil 2000) suffer from some deficiencies not encountered in an OT framework. For instance, the diphthongization rule is a language-specific rule that does not provide any insight into why such a rule should exist.

An OT account of Chicano diphthongization reveals the motivation behind the phenomenon: the universal tendency (expressed through a universal constraint) to avoid onsetless syllables. It also highlights typological differences with regard to diphthongization: While some languages tolerate onsetless syllables (in order to be faithful to the input), others resort to various strategies to improve upon the syllable type. Peninsular and Chicano Spanish belong to this last type of language, despite the fact that they make use of different strategies. In doing so, they exhibit variation in the ranking of faithfulness over markedness constraints. Chicano allows modification of input specification for [high], while Peninsular has faithfulness ranked higher than markedness, allowing for the more marked mid glide, rather than being unfaithful to the input by making it high. Peninsular also does not permit vowel deletion. Chicano, on the other hand, values unmarked syllable structure more than faithfulness, thus deleting a low vowel rather than creating a syllable with a coda.

Another problem with derivational accounts is that they do not provide a true explanation of why Peninsular Spanish allows mid glides and Chicano does not; similarly, they do not fully explain why mid vowels become high glides in Chicano but not in Peninsular. The real issue is that a derivational account cannot capture the connection between the raising of the mid vowels as a strategy to avoid a mid glide (in Chicano) and the gliding of the mid vowel to avoid being unfaithful to the featural specification of the vowel (in Peninsular).

An OT account can incorporate all this directly into the analysis through the hierarchy of constraints, because it is the result of the tension between faithfulness to the underlying representation and markedness (more or less marked glides according to sonority). Derivational accounts (Martínez-Gil 2000) use rule simplification to account for the fact that the second vowel in the sequence is never the target of diphthongization and deletion. A rule like the one existing in Peninsular can apply to both vowels (rule and mirror image application). In Chicano, however, the rule has lost its mirror image. While this works, it does not provide a true explanation of why this should be so. In an OT analysis, a universal *CODA constraint explains why only the first vocoid is affected by diphthongization, deletion, coalescence, or raising.

The effects of *CODA in this dialect can also be seen in its more stringent restrictions on coda consonants (compared to Peninsular, see section 2.2.2.1.1).

In a derivational model of phonology, rules apply sequentially and within certain domains; thus, rule-based models of syllabification need to specify the domain of syllabification and the order of syllabification rules with respect to other phonological rules, as well as morphological operations, such as suffix-ation, prefixation, and compounding. On the basis of resyllabification, aspiration, and onset strengthening data, Hualde (1989b, 1991) convincingly argues that the domain of syllabification in Spanish is a unit smaller than the word, as syllabifi-cation seems to apply before the adjunction of prefixes and before compounding, but after suffixation. It is also necessary to establish rule ordering with respect to morphological operations.

An OT account obviates the need to define domain of syllabification through the use of general mechanisms, namely, universal constraints and a language-spe-cific ranking previously motivated for the language. No extrinsic ordering of pho-nological rules and morphological operations is necessary either. An important family of constraints that captures the interaction between morphology and pho-nology is the ALIGN family, which requires alignment of the edges (right or left) of morphological units (root, stem, word, suffix, prefix) with the edges (right or left) of phonological components (segment, onset, coda, syllable, prosodic word). In Spanish, ALIGN constraints are shown to be relevant to the interaction of mor-phological phenomena (suffixation, prefixation, and compounding), with phono-logical phenomena (/s/-aspiration, /n/-velarization, /r/-strengthening, and onset strengthening).

The notion of correspondence theory in OT and, in particular, the difference between IO and OO faithfulness sheds new light on Spanish pluralization, while also explaining nonstandard forms of plural formation, such as the double plural of Dominican Spanish. Plural epenthesis is shown to reflect the emergence of the unmarked with respect to the constraint against coda consonants (*CODA). *CODA is usually violated in the singular, because of the domination of DEP-IO (input-to-output faithfulness) over *CODA (markedness). In the plural, however, since the relevant correspondence relation is of the output-to-output type, DEP-IO is trivi-ally satisfied, and domination of *CODA over DEP-OO results in epenthesis. An optimality-theoretic account of the plural explains plural epenthesis with clusters that appear to be well-formed in the singular (*vals* **vales* **valse* 'waltz'; *solsticio* **solesticio* 'solstice' versus *sol-es* **sols* 'suns'); it relies on constraints that are independently motivated for Spanish and other languages; and it accounts for seemingly odd types of pluralization, such as the double plural of Dominican, without having to resort to separate rules or special templates.

As was just mentioned, building on the constraints and constraint ranking proposed for standard dialects, an OT analysis of Dominican plurals can explain the pluralization facts in a direct way through general mechanisms of syllabifica-tion and pluralization, revealing the connection between double plurals and syl-labification mechanisms in Dominican. The apparently redundant attachment of the plural morpheme results from the restrictions on coda obstruents found in Dominican (/s/-deletion and -aspiration) combined with the need for overt real-ization of morphemes in prominent positions. The difference between the regular plural and the double plural is that, in the latter case, a highly ranked constraint requires that the plural in focused positions have morphological exponence. In more general terms, [se] is the output realization of plural /s/ followed by epen-thetic [e] in intonationally prominent (focus) positions. Serial accounts miss this insight and are therefore forced to propose a separate allomorph for the double plural of Dominican.

An additional advantage of an optimality-theoretic analysis of Spanish syllabification lies in its treatment of dialectal variation. While a serial approach proposes different rules and rule ordering for different dialects, dialectal variation in OT is the result of variation in the ranking of the same set of universal constraints. This mechanism allows the theory to make and test predictions relative to the patterns of variation that could be encountered (factorial typology). Perhaps more importantly, an optimality-theoretic approach to dialectal variation brings forth the connections between various cross-dialectal processes that can now be seen as alternative strategies (on the basis of the same set of constraints) for the resolution of conflicts between markedness and faithfulness. OT's superior treatment of dialectal variation becomes clear when analyzing a language like Spanish, with numerous dialects in use throughout the world.

As shown in the previous chapters, OT can successfully account for the following:

- Diphthongization across words in Peninsular and in Chicano dialects, as well as the source of the variation (alternative strategies for creating a diphthong that agrees with the sonority hierarchy and is faithful to underlyingly specified features).

- The differences between standard pluralization and the so-called double plurals in Dominican, which can now be understood as a consequence of specific features of the phonology of Dominican (/s/-deletion) and their interaction with pluralization in intonationally prominent positions.

- The patterns of variation regarding aspiration across prefixes, compounds, and phrases in aspirating varieties of Spanish, and the lack thereof with regard to suffixes, which are explained by resorting to anti-allomorphy constraints on the form of the prosodic word.

- Coda deletion and coda featural neutralizations, which are shown to be alternative strategies for producing less marked syllable structure by improving on coda types or eliminating them completely.

Finally, a nonderivational analysis of Spanish syllabification offers a comprehensive view of many areas of the phonology and the interaction of various syllabification processes with the rest of the phonology.

Despite the overall accomplishments, OT also faces some challenges. Before concluding this section I would like to bring them to the attention of the reader, as they constitute directions for further research. Of these, perhaps the biggest challenge is determining whether strata are necessary in an optimality-theoretic model of phonology, and whether such a move compromises the parallel nature of the theory. Chapter 4 shows that some Spanish processes that have been traditionally accounted for through cyclic application of rules can be accounted for in a parallel fashion by resorting to ALIGN constraints (see, however, Roca 2005 for a Stratal OT account of sections of those data). It has been pointed out, however, that not all Spanish data lend themselves to a nonstratal approach; for instance, Bermúdez-Otero (2006) argues that a version of OT without stratal divisions gives rise to a stratification paradox with regard to diphthongization and depalatalization in Spanish nominal stem formatives. Empirical evidence for the need for strata within OT in other languages can be found in analyses by Booij (1997), Rubach (1997), Itô and Mester (2003), and Kiparsky (2003).

Another challenge for OT is accounting for noncategorical variation. As mentioned in chapter 1, most (if not all) formal analyses generally face significant difficulties when trying to explain noncategorical variation. OT, however, fares much better than previous rule-based models of phonology, which often considered noncategorical variation outside their purview. In accordance with the partial ordering theory (Reynolds 1994; Anttilla and Cho 1997; Nagy and Reynolds 1997; McCarthy 2002 and references therein), a particular grammar is seen as a partial ordering of constraints in which constraints that conflict may be in free ranking with respect to one another, leading to variation in the output. Free ranking does not imply that ranking selection is totally unpredictable, only that it is not governed by grammatical principles; instead, a wide range of extragrammatical factors may affect the choice of ranking (e.g., sociolinguistic variables) (Kager 1999, 404). More specifically, each input-to-output mapping is obtained by applying a totally ordered hierarchy of constraints that is randomly sampled from the total orderings that are consistent with the grammar. If the sampling is uniform (each ordering has equal likelihood of being chosen each time), then each total ordering will be in force fifty percent of the time (McCarthy 2002, 227). However, if the sampling is not uniform, some rankings may be in force more often than others (they will have a higher likelihood of being chosen each time).

Each one of the rankings can be associated with a probabilistic weight that indicates the likelihood that a particular ranking will be chosen on the basis of external constraints. The probabilistic weights can be determined statistically (see Díaz-Campos and Colina 2006 for an application to Spanish). The unranked-constraint (free-ranking) approach preserves strict domination by having one main grammar split into sub-hierarchies (each with strict domination) at the point of variation (for the unranked constraints) (Kager 1999, 404); probabilistic weights reflect the likelihood of selecting one branch or ranking versus another.

The Gradual Learning Algorithm (GLA) (Boersma 1998; Boersma and Hayes 2001), a constraint-ranking algorithm for learning optimality-theoretic grammars, offers a formal proposal for explaining the selection of one ranking over another in accordance with its likelihood of being enforced. Two crucial concepts for the GLA are continuous ranking scales and stochastic evaluation (Boersma 1998; Boersma and Hayes 2001).[1] In the GLA, at evaluation time, the position of each constraint is temporarily perturbed by a random positive or negative value (stochastic evaluation); thus, constraints are said to be associated with ranges of values rather than single points on a continuous ranking scale. The value used at evaluation is called the selection point and the value more often associated with a constraint is the ranking value (higher-ranked constraints have higher-ranking values than lower-ranked ones). When the ranges covered by the selection points (constraint ranges) do not overlap, the result is categorical ranking (no variation). However, if the ranges overlap, there will be variation in ranking and outputs, as a selection point for the lower-ranked constraint could be selected toward the high end of the range at the same time a selection point for the higher-ranked constraint is chosen at the lower end of the range, thus effectively reversing the ranking. The closer the ranking value of two constraints, the greater the likelihood of ranking reversal (i.e., variation) (Boersma and Hayes 2001, 47–50).

OT is faced with the possibility and the challenge of tackling noncategorical variation in phonology. This may in turn encourage researchers to begin empirical research that quantifies variation in processes that may have been wrongly considered categorical or that were known to be noncategorical but were difficult to account for in previous models of phonology. Some of the syllabification phenomena covered in this book are good candidates for this type of research, such as coda consonant deletion and feature neutralization processes (chapter 2), /s/-aspiration (chapter 4), and realization of coda rhotics (chapter 2).[2]

NOTES

1. Continuous ranking scales are also proposed in Zubritskaya (1997) where probabilistic weights are associated and attached to individual constraints.

2. For more on OT's potential for dealing with noncategorical variation see Colina 2008 and the references therein.

Glossary of Constraints

FAITHFULNESS CONSTRAINTS

MAX-IO: Every segment present in the input must have a correspondent in the output.

DEP-IO: Every segment present in the output must have a correspondent in the input.

MAX-IOμ: Every mora present in the input must correspond to a mora in the output.

DEP-IOμ: Every mora present in the output must correspond to a mora in the input.

DEP-OO: Every segment present in the output of the plural must have a correspondent in the output of the singular.

MAX-OO: Every segment present in the output of the singular must have a correspondent in the output of the plural.

MAX-IO(PA): All PA nodes present in the input must be in the output.

MAX-IO(SL): All supralaryngeal nodes present in the input must be in the output.

MAX-V: A vowel present in the input must have a correspondent in the output.

MAX-IO #s: Every word-initial /s/ in the input must have a correspondent in the output.

MAX-Stress: Stress present in the input (lexical) should be present in the output (do not delete stress).

DEP-Bsf: Every element of the suffix (Sf) has a correspondent in the base (B).

REALIZE MORPHEME (RM): All morphemes must be realized. A morpheme is realized if its input has a correspondent in the output.

RM/FOC: All morphemes must be realized overtly in focus position (intonationally or otherwise strong position).

IDENT(feature): A segment's input specification for a specific feature must match that of the output.

IDENT(cons): A segment's input specification for the feature [consonantal] must match that of the output.

IDENT(voice): A segment's input specification for [voice] must match that of the output.

IDENT(continuant): A segment's input specification for [continuant] must match that of the output.

IDENT(high): The [high] specification for the input must be identical to that of the output.

IDENT(low): The [low] specification for the input must be identical to that of the output.

IDENT(back): The [back] specification for the input must be identical to that of the output.

IDENT^{OBSTR}(place): The place features of an obstruent in the input must match those of the output.

IDENT-PROMINENCE[–cont]: Stops are preferred in prominent positions.

IDENT-Stress: Stress is associated to the same stress bearer in the input as it is in the output (no stress shift).

IDENT /R/: A trill in the input must correspond with a trill in the output; a flap in the input must correspond with a flap in the output.

IDENT-BA(R): Let α be a segment in the base (B), and β a correspondent of α in a morphologically derived form (A). If α is a trill, β is a trill; if α is a flap, β is a flap.

IDENT-PrWd(PA): The output PA of a prosodic word must be identical to that of its correspondent (no allomorphy of the prosodic word with regard to the PA node).

IDENT-PrWd(R): The output of a prosodic word must be identical to that of its correspondent with regard to rhotic realization (no allomorphy of the prosodic word with respect to rhotic allophones).

IDENT-PrWd(SL): The output SL of a prosodic word must be identical to that of its correspondent (no allomorphy of the prosodic word with regard to the SL node).

IDENT.Seg B-Sf: A segment in a PrWd in B is identical to its correspondent in Sf.

IDENTμ B-Sf: A moraic segment in a PrWd in the base (B) will have as its correspondent a moraic segment in the corresponding PrWd in the suffixed form (Sf), and a nonmoraic segment will correspond to a nonmoraic one.

MARKEDNESS CONSTRAINTS

ONSET: No vowel-initial syllables.

*CODA: Syllables cannot end in a coda.

*COMPLEX ONSET: No more than one segment in the onset.

*COMPLEX CODA: No more than one segment in the coda.

*COMPLEX NUCLEUS: No more than one segment in the nucleus.

MSD: Possible onset segments must maximize their sonority distance.

NO-LONG: No contiguous identical segments.

*GEM: No geminates.

UNIFORMITY: No coalescence.

*X/y: Do not parse y in X.

    *NUC/vowel: Do not parse a vowel in the nucleus.

    *NUC/glide: Do not parse a glide in the nucleus.

    *NUC/liquid: Do not parse a liquid in the nucleus.

    *NUC/nasal: Do not parse a nasal in the nucleus.

    *NUC/obstruent: Do not parse an obstruent in the nucleus.

    *ONSET/vowel: Do not parse a vowel in the onset.

    *ONSET/glide: Do not parse a glide in the onset.

    *ONSET/liquid: Do not parse a liquid in the onset.

    *ONSET/nasal: Do not parse a nasal in the onset.

    *ONSET/obstruent: Do not parse an obstruent in the onset.

    *CODA/vowel: Do not parse a vowel in the coda.

    *CODA/glide: Do not parse a glide in the coda.

    *CODA/liquid: Do not parse a liquid in the coda.

    *CODA/nasal: Do not parse a nasal in the coda.

    *CODA/obstruent: Do not parse an obstruent in the coda.

    *CODA/stop: Do not parse a stop in the coda.

    *CODA/fricative: Do not parse a fricative in the coda.

    *CODA/s: Do not parse [s] in the coda.

*CODA[+voice]: Codas are voiceless.

*SONORANT[–voice]: Sonorants are voiced.

*PA/coda: No PA in coda position.

*I[ɾ]: No [ɾ] in stem-initial position.

*[ɾ]/onset: No [ɾ] in onset position.

*[r]/onset: No [r] in onset position.

*[r]/coda: No [r] in coda position.

*hi/μ: Do not associate a high vocoid with a mora.

*mid/μ: Do not associate a mid vocoid with a mora.

*low/μ: Do not associate a low vocoid with a mora.

hi/μ: High vocoids are associated with a mora.

mid/μ: Mid vocoids are associated with a mora.

low/μ: Low vocoids are associated with a mora.

*TE-: No terminal elements in positions other than word final. In alignment format: the right edge of a terminal element must be aligned with the right edge of a word.

AGREEPA(–cont): Shared PA nodes also share the [continuant] node.

AGREE(voice): Adjacent segments share the same specification for the feature [voice] (Lombardi 1999).

CODA COND: A coda cannot license place features.

HAVE PLACE: All segments must have place features.

*DORSAL: No dorsal segments.

*LABIAL: No labial segments.

*CORONAL: No coronal segments

Stress/M: Stress bearers must be moraic.

FTFORM (TROCH): The preferred foot type is a (syllabic) trochee.

Prosodic Word-Minimal Word (PrWd-MinWd): Cover term for the combined effects of prosodic constraints that require that all prosodic words be minimally disyllabic (Colina 2003b, 59; for details).

ALIGNMENT CONSTRAINTS

ALIGN-L(σ,C): Every syllable must have a consonant at its left edge.

ALIGN-R(σ,V): Every syllable must have a vowel at its right edge.

ALIGN-L(C,σ): Every consonant must be aligned with the left edge of the syllable.

ALIGN-R(V,σ): Every vowel must be aligned with the right edge of the syllable.

ALIGN-L: The left edge of the grammatical word coincides with the left edge of the prosodic word.

ALIGN (Stem, L, Syllable, L) (ALIGN-LST): Align the left edge of the syllable with the left edge of the stem.

ALIGN (Word, R, Syllable, R) (ALIGN-R): The right edge of a morphological word coincides with the right edge of a syllable.

ALIGN-L(PW, σ) and ALIGN-R(PW, σ): The left/right edge of the word and syllable coincide. (For every PW there must be some syllable such that the left/right edge of the PW and left/right edge of the syllable align.)

ALIGN (Pl, R, Wd, R) (ALIGN-PL): The right edge of the plural morpheme must be aligned with the right edge of the word.

-citV to PrWd: The left edge of the suffix -citV must be aligned with the right edge of the prosodic word (PrWd).

DIM to PrWd: The left edge of the diminutive affix (DIM) must be aligned with the right edge of the prosodic word.

ALIGN (-it-, L, Stem, R) (ALIGN-it-R): The left edge of the diminutive allomorph -it- must be aligned with the right edge of the stem.

-it- to V$_{TE}$: The right edge of the -it- allomorph must be aligned with the left edge of a [+syllabic] TE of the base.

Summary of Constraint Rankings

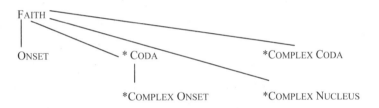

Descriptive facts/process	Ranking
coda clusters	FAITH >> *COMPLEX CODA
complex nuclei	FAITH >> *COMPLEX NUCLEUS
onset maximization	*CODA >> *COMPLEX ONSET
onsetless syllables	FAITH >> ONSET
V.CV	ONSET, *CODA

Figure B.1

BASIC SYLLABLE TYPES (INCLUDING GLIDES)

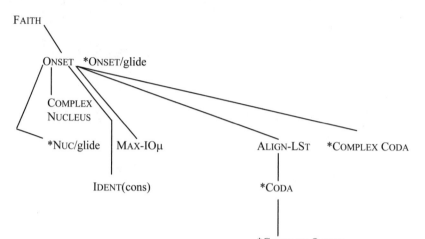

Figure B.2

OBSTRUENT CODA DELETION
/obsoleto/   [osoleto]
*CODA/obstruent, DEP-IO >> MAX-IO

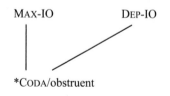

Figure B.3

OBSTRUENT CODA RETENTION
/obsoleto/   [oBsoleto]
DEP-IO, MAX-IO >> *CODA/obstruent

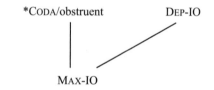

Figure B.4

OBSTRUENT DEVOICING IN CODA POSITION
/futbol/   [fuTβol]
*CODA[+voice] >> AGREE(voice) >> IDENT(voice)

*CODA[+voice]

|

AGREE(voice)

|

IDENT(voice)

Figure B.5

REGRESSIVE VOICE ASSIMILATION OF CODA OBSTRUENTS
/futbol/   [fuDβol]
AGREE(voice) >> *CODA[+voice] >> IDENT(voice)

AGREE(voice)

|

*CODA[+voice]

|

IDENT(voice)

Figure B.6

NEUTRALIZATION OF CONTINUANCY. STOPS IN EMPHATIC POSITIONS.
/futbol/   [fuðβol] ~ [futβol]
IDENT-PROMINENCE[–cont] >> *CODA/stop >> *CODA/fricative, IDENT(continuant)

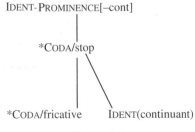

IDENT-PROMINENCE[–cont]

|

*CODA/stop

*CODA/fricative   IDENT(continuant)

Figure B.7

NASAL AND LATERAL ASSIMILATION
/tango/   [taŋgo]
IDENT^{OBSTR}(place), HAVE PLACE >> CODA COND >> IDENT(place)

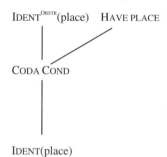

Figure B.8

WORD-FINAL CODAS
NONCORONAL CODA OBSTRUENTS DELETED. CORONAL CODA OBSTRUENTS RETAINED.
/klub/   [klú]   /mes/   [mes]
IDENT^{OBSTR}(place), HAVE PLACE >> *DOR >> *LABIAL >> MAX-IO >>
*CORONAL, IDENT(place)

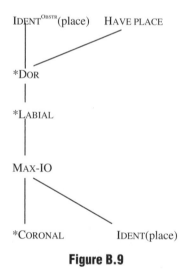

Figure B.9

COMPLEX CODAS
/biseps/ [bises]
*COMPLEX CODA >> *CODA/stop >> MAX-IO >> *CODA/fricative >>
*CODA/nasal >> *CODA/liquid >> *CODA/glide

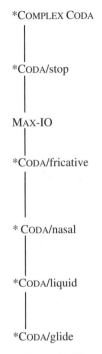

*COMPLEX CODA

*CODA/stop

MAX-IO

*CODA/fricative

* CODA/nasal

*CODA/liquid

*CODA/glide

Figure B.10

RESYLLABIFICATION
/masosos/ [ma.so.sos]
ONSET >> ALIGN-LST >> *CODA

ONSET

ALIGN-LST

*CODA

Figure B.11

DIPHTHONGIZATION (WITHIN AND ACROSS WORDS)
/pierde/ [piér.ðe] /miamigo/ [mi̯a.mi.ɣo]
*ONSET/glide, ONSET >> *COMPLEX NUCLEUS, *NUC/glide, MAX-IOμ

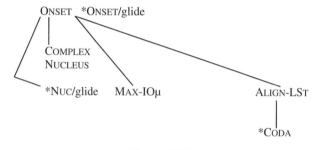

Figure B.12

GLIDE FORMATION AND VOWEL HEIGHT IN PENINSULAR SPANISH: HIGH AND MID GLIDES (NO LOW GLIDES); GLIDE SELECTED ACCORDING TO SONORITY
m[i̯a]*migo t*[eu̯]*tiliza tod*[ae̯]*spaña t*[e̯a]*maré*

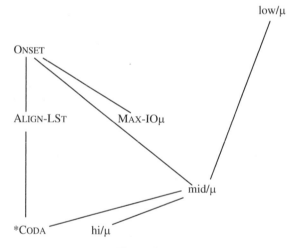

Figure B.13

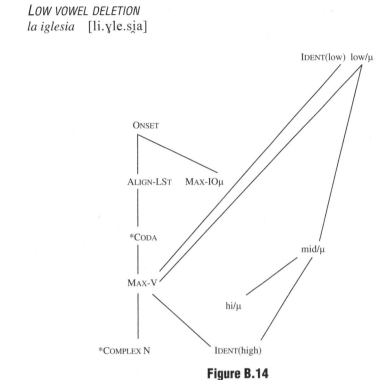

LOW VOWEL DELETION
la iglesia [li.ɣle.si̯a]

Figure B.14

GLIDE FORMATION AND VOWEL HEIGHT IN CHICANO SPANISH: HIGH GLIDES (NO LOW OR MID GLIDES); THE GLIDE IS THE FIRST VOCOID IN THE SEQUENCE
mi ultima [mi̯ul̯.ti.ma]

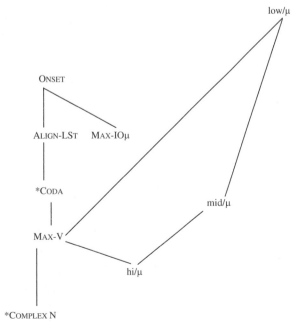

Figure B.15

MID VOWEL RAISING IN CHICANO
me urge   [m̥i̯ur.xe]

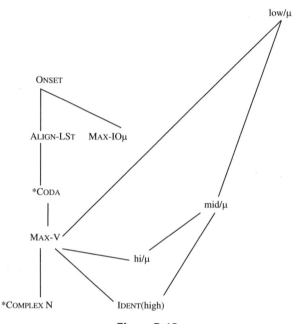

Figure B.16

COALESCENCE UNDER IDENTITY
mi hijo   [mi.xo]
MID VOWEL DOES NOT SURFACE
se hinca   [siŋ.ka]

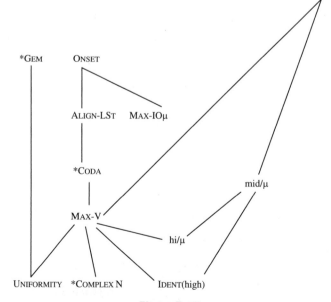

Figure B.17

DIPHTHONGIZATION IN SPANISH: CHICANO AND PENINSULAR COMPARED

PENINSULAR SPANISH

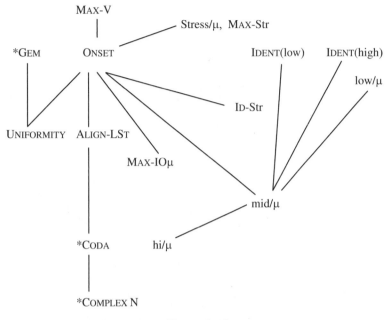

Figure B.18

CHICANO SPANISH

Figure B.19

ASPIRATION IN CARIBBEAN I
/des + ečo/   [de.he.čo]
ASPIRATION IN CARIBBEAN II (PREFIXES ARE NOT PROSODIC WORDS)
/des + ečo/   [de.se.čo]
F, *CODA/s >> IDENT-PrWd(SL) >> MAX-IO(SL)

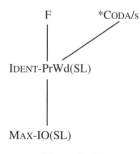

Figure B.20

ASPIRATION IN DIALECTS WITH NO ASPIRATION IN PREFIXAL OR PHRASAL PREVOCALIC CONTEXTS
/des + ečo /   [de.se.čo]
/mes + asul/   [me.sa.sul]
F, *CODA/s >> MAX-IO(SL) >> IDENT-PrWd(SL)

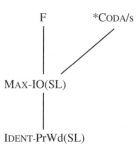

Figure B.21

NASAL VELARIZATION
/in + humano/   [iŋ.u.ma.no]
F, *PA/coda >> IDENT-PrWd(PA) >> MAX-IO(PA)

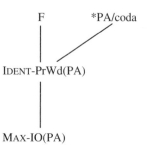

Figure B.22

ONSET STRENGTHENING AND RESYLLABIFICATION
[dez.ye.lo]   *[de.sie.lo]
*ONSET/glide, ONSET >> MAX-IOμ, IDENT(cons)
ONSET >> ALIGN-LST

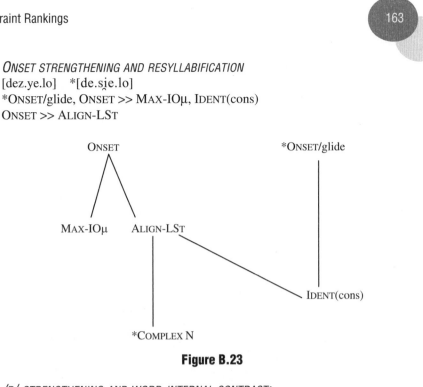

Figure B.23

/R/-STRENGTHENING AND WORD-INTERNAL CONTRAST:
[ma.ta. ra.tas]   [ka.ro]   [ka.ɾo]   [be.ɾlo.sas]
*l[r], AGREEPA(–cont), *[r]/coda, IDENT-PrWd(R) >> IDENT /R/ >>
*[r]/onset, *[ɾ]/onset

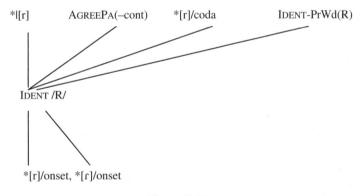

Figure B.24

STANDARD PLURALS

Consonant-final singulars

*sol *sole*

MAX-IO, DEP-IO >> *CODA

Plurals of consonant-final singulars

bals versus *soles, *sols*

RM, ALIGN-PL, MAX-IO, DEP-IO >> *CODA >> DEP-OO

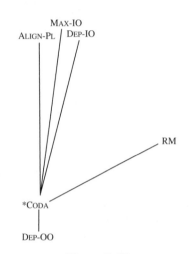

Figure B.25

DOMINICAN PLURALS

/s/-final singulars   [uteðe]

*CODA/obstruent, DEP-IO >> MAX-IO

Plurals of consonant-final singulars [muheɾe]

*CODA/obstruent >> ALIGN-PL >> RM, *CODA >> DEP-OO

Double plurals   [muheɾese]

RM/FOC, *CODA/obstruent >> ALIGN-PL >> RM, *CODA >> DEP-OO

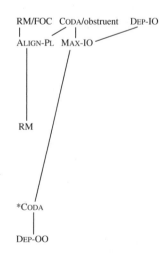

Figure B.26

WORD-INITIAL EPENTHESIS

/slabo/   [ezlaβo]

MSD, MAX-IO #S >> DEP-IO >> *CODA/stop >> MAX-IO >> *CODA/s

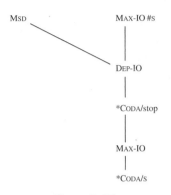

Figure B.27

DIMINUTIVES

DISYLLABIC e-FINAL BASES

clas-e + DIM   *clas-e-cita*

*TE, PrWd-MinWd, -citV to PrWd >> DIM to PrWd >> DEP-Bsf

DISYLLABIC -a AND -o BASES

cas-a + DIM   *cas-it-a*

*TE, PrWd-MinWd, IDENT.Seg B-Sf , -citV to PrWd >> DIM to PrWd >> DEP-Bsf

LONGER-THAN-DISYLLABIC e-FINAL BASES

estuch-e + DIM   *estuch-it-o*

*TE, PrWd-MinWd, IDENT.Seg B-Sf, -citV to PrWd >> DIM to PrWd >> DEP-Bsf

DISYLLABIC, DIPHTHONG-FINAL BASES

tapi-a DIM   *tapi-e-cita*

*TE, PrWd-MinWd, IDENTμ B-Sf >> ALIGN-it-R >> IDENT.Seg B-Sf >> -citV to PrWd >> DIM to PrWd >> DEP-Bsf

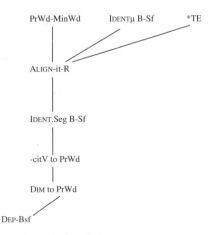

Figure B.28

References

Alarcos Llorach, Emilio. 1965. *Fonología española*. Madrid: Gredos.

Alonso, Amado. 1945. Una ley fonológica del español. *Hispanic Review* 13:91–101.

Alvar, Manuel. 1996. *Manual de dialectología hispánica*. Barcelona: Ariel.

Anttila, Arto, and Young-mee Yu Cho. 1998. Variation and Change in Optimality Theory. *Lingua* 104:31–56.

Baković, Eric. 1994. Strong onsets and Spanish fortition. *MIT Working Papers in Linguistics* 23:21–39. (Available online at ROA 96, Rutgers Optimality Archive, http://roa.rutgers.edu/)

Baković, Eric. 2006. Hiatus Resolution and Incomplete Identity. *Optimality-Theoretic Studies in Spanish Phonology*. Ed. Fernando Martínez-Gil and Sonia Colina. Philadelphia: John Benjamins.

Beckman, Jill. 1997. Positional faithfulness. Ph.D. diss., University of Massachusetts, Amherst.

Benua, Laura. 1995. Identity Effects in Morphological Truncation. *University of Massachusetts Occasional Papers in Linguistics 18: Papers in Optimality Theory*. Ed. Jill Beckman, Laura Walsh, and Suzanne Urbanczyk. Amherst, MA: Graduate Linguistic Student Association.

Bermúdez-Otero, Ricardo. 1999. Constraint interaction in language change: Quantity in English and Germanic. Ph.D. diss., University of Manchester and Universidad de Santiago de Compostela. (Available online at http://www.bermudez-otero.com/PhD.pdf/)

———. 2003. The acquisition of phonological opacity. *Proceedings of the Stockholm Workshop on Variation within Optimality Theory*. Ed. Jennifer Spenader, Anders Eriksson, and Östen Dahl. Stockholm: Department of Linguistics, Stockholm University. (Expanded version available online at ROA 593, Rutgers Optimality Archive, http://roa.rutgers.edu/)

———. 2006. Morphological structure and phonological domains in Spanish denominal derivation. *Optimality-Theoretic Studies in Spanish Phonology*. Ed. Fernando Martínez-Gil and Sonia Colina. Philadelphia: John Benjamins.

———. 2007. Spanish pseudoplurals: Phonological cues in the acquisition of a syntax-morphology mismatch. *Deponency and Morphological Mismatches* (Proceedings of the British Academy 145). Ed. Matthew Baerman, Greville Corbett, Dunstan Brown, and Andrew Hippisley. Oxford: Oxford University Press.

———. In press. *Stratal Optimality Theory.* Oxford: Oxford University Press. (Excerpts available online at http://www.bermudez-otero.com/ Stratal_Optimality_Theory.htm/)

Boersma, Paul. 1998. *Functional Phonology: Formalizing the Interaction between Articulatory and Perceptual Drives.* The Hague: Holland Academic Graphics.

Boersma, Paul, and Bruce Hayes. 2001. Empirical tests of the gradual learning algorithm. *Linguistic Inquiry* 32:45–86.

Bonet, Eulàlia. 2006. Gender allomorphy and epenthesis in Spanish. *Optimality-Theoretic Studies in Spanish Phonology.* Ed. Fernando Martínez-Gil and Sonia Colina. Philadelphia: John Benjamins.

Bonet, Eulàlia, and Joan Mascaró. 1997. On the representation of contrasting rhotics. *Issues in the Phonology and Morphology of the Major Iberian Languages.* Ed. Fernando Martínez-Gil and Alfonso Morales-Front. Washington, DC: Georgetown University Press.

Booij, Geert. 1997. Non-derivational phonology meets lexical phonology. *Derivations and Constraints in Phonology.* Ed. Iggy Roca. Oxford: Clarendon Press.

Booij, Geert, and Jerzy Rubach. 1984. Morphological and prosodic domains in lexical phonology. *Phonology Yearbook* 1:1–27.

Bradley, Travis. 2006. Spanish rhotics and Dominican hypercorrect /s/. *Probus* 18:1–33.

Breen, Gavan, and Rob Pensalfini. 1999. Arrernte: A language with no syllable onsets. *Linguistic Inquiry* 30:1–25.

Bybee, Joan. 2001. *Phonology and Language Use.* Oxford: Oxford University Press.

Canfield, Lincoln. 1981. *Spanish Pronunciation in the Americas.* Chicago: University of Chicago Press.

Carreira, María. 1988. The representation of diphthongs in Spanish. *Studies in the Linguistic Sciences* 18:1–24.

Clements, George N. 1985. The geometry of phonological features. *Phonology Yearbook* 2:225–52.

———. 1986. Syllabification and epenthesis in the Barra dialect of Gaelic. *The Phonological Representation of Suprasegmentals: Studies Offered to John M. Steward on his 60th Birthday.* Ed. Koen Bogers, Harry Van der Hulst, and Maarten Mous. Dordrecht: Foris.

———. 1990. The role of sonority in core syllabification. *Papers in Laboratory Phonology I: Between the Grammar and Physics of Speech.* Ed. John Kingston and Mary Beckman. Cambridge: Cambridge University Press.

Colina, Sonia. 1995. A constraint-based approach to syllabification in Spanish, Galician and Catalan. Ph.D. diss., University of Illinois, Urbana-Champaign.

———. 1996. Spanish noun truncation: The emergence of the unmarked. *Linguistics* 34:1199–1218.

———. 1997. Identity constraints and Spanish resyllabification. *Lingua* 103:1–23.

———. 1999. Reexamining Spanish glides: Analogically conditioned variation in vocoid sequences in Spanish dialects. *Advances in Hispanic Linguistics: Papers from the Second Hispanic Linguistics Symposium.* Ed. Javier Gutiérrez-Rexach and Fernando Martínez-Gil. Somerville, MA: Cascadilla Press.

———. 2002. Interdialectal variation in Spanish /s/ aspiration. *Structure, Meaning and Acquisition in Spanish.* Ed. James Lee, Kimberly Geeslin, and Clancy Clements. Somerville, MA: Cascadilla Press.

———. 2003a. The status of word-final [e] in Spanish. *The Southwest Journal of Linguistics* 22:87–108.

———. 2003b. Diminutives in Spanish: A morphophonological account. *The Southwest Journal of Linguistics* 22:45–88.

———. 2006a. No "double plurals" in Dominican Spanish: An optimality-theoretic account. *Linguistics* 44:541–68.

———. 2006b. Output-to-output correspondence and the emergence of the unmarked in Spanish plural formation. *New Analyses in Romance Linguistics.* Ed. Jean-Pierre Montreuil. Philadelphia: John Benjamins.

———. 2006c. Optimality-theoretic advances in our understanding of Spanish syllabic structure. *Optimality-Theoretic Studies in Spanish Phonology.* Ed. Fernando Martínez-Gil and Sonia Colina. Philadelphia: John Benjamins.

———. 2008. The role of language variation in mental grammars: An optimality-theoretic perspective. *Studies in Hispanic and Lusophone Linguistics* 1:435–446.

———. In press. Sibilant voicing in Ecuadorian Spanish. *Studies in Hispanic and Lusophone Linguistics* 2(1).

Contreras, Heles. 1977. Spanish epenthesis and stress. *Working Papers in Linguistics* 3:9–33. Seattle: University of Washington.

Crowhurst, Megan. 1992. Diminutives and augmentatives in Mexican Spanish: A prosodic analysis. *Phonology* 9:221–53.

Díaz-Campos, Manuel, and Sonia Colina. 2006. The interaction between faithfulness constraints and sociolinguistic variation: The acquisition of phonological variation in first language speakers. *Optimality-Theoretic Studies in Spanish Phonology.* Ed. Fernando Martínez-Gil and Sonia Colina. Philadelphia: John Benjamins.

Eddington, David. 1992. Word-medial epenthesis in Spanish: A lexical phonological approach. *The Southwest Journal of Linguistics* 11:14–28.

Face, Timothy. 1998. Re-examining Spanish "resyllabification." Manuscript. Ohio State University. (Available online at ROA 291, Rutgers Optimality Archive, http://roa.rutgers.edu/)

Foley, James. 1967. Spanish plural formation. *Language* 43:486–93.

Halle, Morris. 1995. Feature geometry and feature spreading. *Linguistic Inquiry* 26:1–46.

Harris, James W. 1969. *Spanish Phonology.* Cambridge, MA: MIT Press.

———. 1970. A note on Spanish plural formation. *Language* 46:928–30.

———. 1980. Nonconcatenative morphology and Spanish plurals. *Journal of Linguistic Research* 1:15–31.

———. 1983. *Syllable Structure and Stress in Spanish.* Cambridge, MA: MIT Press.

———. 1985. Spanish diphthongisation and stress: A paradox resolved. *Phonology Yearbook* 2:31–45.

———. 1986a. Epenthesis processes in Spanish. *Studies in Romance Languages.* Ed. Carol Neidle and Rafael A. Núñez-Cedeño. Dordrecht: Foris.

———. 1986b. El modelo multidimensional de la fonología y la dialectología caribeña. *Estudios sobre la fonología del español del Caribe.* Ed. Rafael Núñez-Cedeño, Iraset Páez, and Jorge Guitart. Caracas: Ediciones La Casa de Bello.

———. 1989a. Sonority and syllabification in Spanish. *Studies in Romance Linguistics.* Ed. Carl Kirschner and Janet DeCesaris. Philadelphia: John Benjamins.

———. 1989b. Our present understanding of Spanish syllable structure. *American Spanish Pronunciation.* Ed. Peter C. Bjarkman and Robert M. Hammond. Washington, DC: Georgetown University Press.

———. 1991a. The form classes of Spanish substantives. *Yearbook of Morphology.* Ed. Geert Booij and Jaap van Marle. Dordrecht: Kluwer.

———. 1991b. The exponence of gender in Spanish. *Linguistic Inquiry* 22:27–62.

———. 1994. The OCP, prosodic morphology and Sonoran Spanish diminutives: A reply to Crowhurst. *Phonology* 11:179–90.

———. 1999. Nasal depalatalization no, morphological well-formedness sí: The structure of Spanish word classes. *MIT Working Papers in Linguistics* 33:47–82.

———. 2002. Flaps, trills and syllable structure in Spanish. *MIT Working Papers in Linguistics* 42:81–108.

Harris, James W., and Ellen Kaisse. 1999. Palatal vowels, glides and obstruents in Argentinian Spanish. *Phonology* 16:117–90.

Holt, D. Eric. 2006. Optimality Theory and language change in Spanish. *Optimality-Theoretic Studies in Spanish Phonology.* Ed. Fernando Martínez-Gil and Sonia Colina. Philadelphia: John Benjamins.

Hooper, Joan B. 1976. *An Introduction to Natural Generative Phonology.* New York: Academic Press.

Hualde, José I. 1989a. Procesos consonánticos y estructuras geométricas en español. *Lingüística* 1:7–44.

———. 1989b. Silabeo y estructura morfémica en español. *Hispania* 72:821–31.

———. 1991. On Spanish syllabification. *Current Studies in Spanish Linguistics.* Ed. Héctor Campos and Fernando Martínez-Gil. Washington, DC: Georgetown University Press.

———. 1994. La contracción silábica en español. *Gramática del español*. Ed. Violeta Demonte. México: El Colegio de México (Nueva Revista de Filología Hispánica VI).

———. 1997. Spanish /i/ and related sounds: An exercise in phonemic analysis. *Studies in the Linguistic Sciences* 27:61–79.

———. 1999a. La silabificación en español. *Fonología de la lengua española contemporánea*. Ed. Rafael Núñez-Cedeño and Alfonso Morales-Front. Washington, DC: Georgetown University Press.

———. 1999b. Patterns in the lexicon: Hiatus with unstressed high vowels in Spanish. *Advances in Hispanic Linguistics*. *Papers from the Second Hispanic Linguistics Symposium*. Ed. Javier Gutiérrez-Rexach and Fernando Martínez-Gil. Somerville, MA: Cascadilla Press.

———. 2002. On the diphthong/hiatus contrast in Spanish: Some experimental results. *Linguistics* 40:217–34.

———. 2004. Quasi-phonemic contrasts in Spanish. *Proceedings of the 23rd West Coast Conference on Formal Linguistics*. Ed. Vineeta Chand, Ann Kelleher, Angelo Rodríguez, and Benjamin Schmeiser. Somerville, MA: Cascadilla Press.

———. 2005. *The Sounds of Spanish*. Cambridge: Cambridge University Press.

Itô, Junko. 1986. Syllable theory in prosodic phonology. Ph.D. diss., University of Massachusetts, Amherst. (Published by Garland, New York, 1988.)

———. 1989. A prosodic theory of epenthesis. *Natural Language and Linguistic Theory* 7:217–60.

Itô, Junko, and Armin Mester. 1994. Reflections on CodaCond and alignment. *Phonology at Santa Cruz III*. Ed. Jason Merchant, Jaye Padgett, and Rachel Walker. Santa Cruz: Linguistic Research Center.

———. 2003. On the sources of opacity in OT: Coda processes in German. *The Syllable in Optimality Theory*. Ed. Caroline Féry and Ruben Van de Vijver. Cambridge: Cambridge University Press.

Jaeggli, Osvaldo. 1978. Spanish diminutives. *Contemporary Studies in Romance Languages*. Ed. Frank H. Nuessel. Bloomington, IN: Indiana University Linguistics Club.

Jiménez Sabater, Max A. 1975. *Más datos sobre el español de la República Dominicana*. Santo Domingo: Ediciones Intec.

Kager, Renè. 1999. *Optimality Theory*. Cambridge: Cambridge University Press.

Kahn, Daniel. 1976. *Syllable-Based Generalizations in English Phonology*. Cambridge, MA: MIT Press.

Kaisse, Ellen M. 1997. Aspiration and resyllabification in Argentinian Spanish. *University of Washington Working Papers in Linguistics* 15:199–209.

———. 1998. Resyllabification: Evidence from Argentinian Spanish. *Formal Perspectives on Romance linguistics*. Ed. J. Marc Authier, Barbara E. Bullock, and Lisa A. Reed. Philadelphia: John Benjamins.

Kenstowicz, Michael. 1996. Base identity and uniform exponence: Alternatives to cyclity. *Current Trends in Phonology: Models and Methods*. Ed. Jacques Durand and Bernard Laks. Salford, UK: University of Salford Publications.

Kenstowicz, Michael, and Charles Kisseberth. 1979. *Generative Phonology*. San Diego: Academic Press.

Kiparsky, Paul. 1973. Phonological representations. *Three Dimensions of Linguistic Theory*. Ed. Osamu Fujimura. Tokyo: TEC.

———. 1982. Lexical phonology and morphology. *Linguistics in the Morning Calm*. Ed. In-Seok Yang. Seoul: Hanshin.

———. 1985. Some consequences of lexical phonology. *Phonology Yearbook* 2:85–138.

———. 2003. Syllables and moras in Arabic. *The Syllable in Optimality Theory*. Ed. Caroline Féry and Ruben van de Vijver. Cambridge: Cambridge University Press.

Kurisu, Kazutaka. 2001. The phonology of morpheme realization. Ph.D. diss., University of California at Santa Cruz. (Available online at ROA 490, Rutgers Optimality Archive, http://roa.rutgers.edu/)

Lipski, John. 1989. /s/-Voicing in Ecuadoran Spanish. *Lingua* 79:49–71.

Lloret, María Rosa, and Mascaró, Joan. 2006. Depalatalization revisited. *Optimality-Theoretic Studies in Spanish Phonology*. Ed. Fernando Martínez-Gil and Sonia Colina. Philadelphia: John Benjamins.

Lombardi, Linda. 1999. Positional faithfulness and voicing assimilation in Optimality Theory. *Natural Language and Linguistic Theory* 17:267–302.

Martínez-Gil, Fernando. 1996. El principio de la *distancia mínima de sonoridad* y el problema de la vocalización consonántica en el español dialectal de Chile. *Hispanic Linguistics* 8:201–46.

———. 1997. Obstruent vocalization in Chilean Spanish: A serial versus a constraint-based approach. *Probus* 9:165–200.

———. 2000. La estructura prosódica y la especificación vocálica en español: el problema de la sinalefa en ciertas variedades de la lengua coloquial contemporánea. *Panorama de la fonología española actual*. Ed. Juana Gil Fernández. Madrid: Arco Libros.

———. 2001. Sonority as a primitive phonological feature: Evidence from Spanish complex onset phonotactics. *Features and Interfaces in Romance: Essays in Honor of Heles Contreras*. Ed. Julia Herschensohn, Enrique Mallén, and Karen Zagona. Philadelphia: John Benjamins.

———. 2004. Hiatus resolution in Chicano Spanish. Paper presented at the 34th Linguistics Symposium on Romance Languages, University of Utah, Salt Lake City.

Martínez-Gil, Fernando, and Sonia Colina. 2006. *Optimality-Theoretic Studies in Spanish Phonology*. Philadelphia: John Benjamins.

McCarthy, John. 2002. *A Thematic Guide to Optimality Theory*. Cambridge: Cambridge University Press.

———. 2007. *Hidden Generalizations*. London: Equinox.

McCarthy, John, and Alan Prince. 1993a. Generalized alignment. *Yearbook of Morphology*. Ed. Geert Booij and Jaap van Maarle. Dordrecht: Kluwer.

―――. 1993b. *Prosodic Morphology: Constraint Interaction and Satisfaction*. New Brunswick, NJ: Rutgers University Center for Cognitive Science. (Available online at ROA 482, Rutgers Optimality Archive, http://roa.rutgers.edu/)

―――. 1994. The emergence of the unmarked. *Proceedings of the North East Linguistic Society 24*. Ed. Mercè Gonzàlez. Amherst, MA: Graduate Linguistic Student Association.

―――. 1995. Faithfulness and reduplicative identity. *University of Massachusetts Occasional Papers in Linguistics 18: Papers in Optimality Theory*. Ed. Jill Beckman, Laura Walsh, and Suzanne Urbanczyk. Amherst, MA: Graduate Linguistic Student Assocation.

Miranda, Inés. 1999. An optimality theoretic analysis of Nicaraguan Spanish diminutivization: Results of a field survey. Ph.D. diss., University of Washington, Seattle.

Mohanan, Karuvannur P. 1986. *The Theory of Lexical Phonology*. Dordrecht: Reidel.

Morales-Front, Alfonso. 1994. A constraint-based approach to Spanish phonology. Ph.D. diss., University of Illinois, Urbana-Champaign.

Morin, Regina. 1999. Spanish substantives: How many classes? *Advances in Hispanic linguistics*. Ed. Javier Gutiérrez-Rexach and Fernando Martínez-Gil. Somerville, MA: Cascadilla Press.

Moyna, Irene, and Carolina Wiltshire. 2000. Spanish plurals: Why [s] isn't always optimal. *Hispanic Linguistics at the Turn of the Millenium. Papers from the Third Hispanic Linguistics Symposium*. Ed. Héctor Campos, Elena Herburger, Alfonso Morales-Front, and Thomas J. Walsh. Somerville, MA: Cascadilla Press.

Nagy, Naomi, and William Reynolds. 1997. Optimality Theory and variable word-final deletion in Faetar. *Language Variation and Change* 9:37–55.

Navarro Tomás, Tomás. 1980. *Manual de pronunciación española*. Madrid: Consejo Superior de Investigaciones Científicas. (Orig. pub. 1918.)

Nespor, Marina. 1999. Stress domains. *Prosodic Systems in the Languages of Europe*. Ed. Harry Van del Hulst. New York: Mouton de Gruyter.

Nespor, Marina, and Irene Vogel. 1986. *Prosodic Phonology*. Dordrecht: Foris.

Núñez-Cedeño, Rafael A. 1980. *La fonología moderna y el español de Santo Domingo*. Santo Domingo: Taller.

―――. 2003. Double plurals in Dominican: A morpho-pragmatic sccount. *Theory, Practice, and Acquisition: Papers from the 6th Hispanic Linguistics Symposium and the 5th Conference on the Acquisition of Spanish*. Ed. Paula Kempchinsky and Carlos-Eduardo Piñeros. Somerville, MA: Cascadilla Press.

Núñez-Cedeño, Rafael A., and Alfonso Morales-Front. 1999. *Fonología generativa contemporánea de la lengua española*. Washington, DC: Georgetown University Press.

Ohala, John, and Manjari Ohala. 1993. The phonetics of nasal phonology: Theorems and data. *Nasals, Nasalization and the Velum*. Ed. Marie K. Huffman and Rena Krakow. San Diego: Academic Press.

Padgett, Jaye. 1994. Stricture and nasal place assimilation. *Natural Language and Linguistic Theory* 12:465–513.

Penny, Ralph. 1991. *A History of the Spanish Language*. Cambridge: Cambridge University Press.

Peperkamp, Sharon. 1994. Prosodic constraints in the derivational morphology of Italian. *Yearbook of Morphology*. Ed. Geert Booij and Jaap van Marle. Dordrecht: Kluwer Academic Publishers.

———. 1996. The prosodic representation of clitics. *Interfaces in Phonology*. Ed. Ursula Kleinhenz. Berlin: Akademie Verlag.

Piñeros, Carlos-Eduardo. 2000. Prosodic and segmental unmarkedness in Spanish truncation. *Linguistics* 38:63–98.

———. 2001. Segment-to-segment alignment and vocalization in Chilean Spanish. *Lingua* 111:163–88.

———. 2006. The phonology of nasal consonants in five Spanish dialects. An alignment-based account of coda effects in a Caribbean Spanish dialect. *Optimality-Theoretic Studies in Spanish Phonology*. Ed. Fernando Martínez-Gil and Sonia Colina. Philadelphia: John Benjamins.

Prieto, Pilar. 1992. Morphophonology of the Spanish diminutive formation: A case for prosodic sensitivity. *Hispanic Linguistics* 5:169–205.

Prince, Alan and Paul Smolensky. 1993. *Optimality Theory: Constraint Interaction in Generative Grammar*. Rutgers, NJ: Rutgers University Center for Cognitive Science.

Quilis, Antonio. 1981. *Fonética acústica de la lengua española*. Madrid: Gredos.

———. 1993. *Tratado de fonética y fonología españolas*. Madrid: Gredos.

Reynolds, William. 1994. Variation and phonological theory. Ph.D. diss., University of Pennsylvania, Philadelphia.

Robinson, Kimball. 1979. On the voicing of intervocalic /s/ in the Ecuadorian Highlands. *Romance Philology* 33:1.

Roca, Iggy. 1988. Theoretical implications of Spanish stress. *Linguistic Inquiry* 19:393–423.

———. 1991. Stress and syllables in Spanish. *Current Studies in Spanish Linguistics*. Ed. Héctor Campos and Fernando Martínez-Gil. Washington, DC: Georgetown University Press.

———. 1996. Phonology-morphology interface in Spanish plural formation: An optimality analysis. *Interfaces in Phonology*. Ed. Ursula Kleinhenz. Berlin: Akademie Verlag.

———. 1997. There are no glides, at least in Spanish. *Probus* 9:233–65.

———. 2005. Strata, yes; Structure preservation, no. Evidence from Spanish. *Romance Languages and Linguistic Theory 2003*. Ed. Twan Geerts, Ivo van Ginneken, and Haike Jacobs. Philadelphia: John Benjamins.

———. 2006. The Spanish stress window. *Optimality-Theoretic Studies in Spanish Phonology*. Ed. Fernando Martínez-Gil and Sonia Colina. Philadelphia: John Benjamins.

Rosenthall, Samuel. 1994. *Vowel/Glide Alternation in a Theory of Constraint Interaction*. New York: Garland.

Rubach, Jerzy. 1997. Extrasyllabic consonants in Polish: Derivational Optimality Theory. *Derivations and Constraints in Phonology*. Ed. Iggy Roca. Oxford: Clarendon Press.

Sagey, Elizabeth. 1986. The representation of features and relations in nonlinear phonology. Ph.D. diss., MIT, Cambridge, MA.

Saltarelli, Mario. 1970. Spanish plural formation: Apocope or epenthesis. *Language* 46:89–96.

Samek-Lodovici, Vieri. 1993. A unified analysis of crosslinguistic morphological gemination. Ph.D. diss., Rutgers University, New Brunswick, NJ.

Terrell, Tracy D. 1986. La desparición de /s/ posnuclear a nivel léxico en el habla dominicana. *Estudios sobre la fonología del español del Caribe*. Ed. Rafael Núñez-Cedeño, Iraset Páez, and Jorge Guitart. Caracas: Ediciones La Casa de Bello.

Trigo, Lorenza. 1988. On the phonological derivation and behavior of nasal glides. Ph.D. diss., MIT, Cambridge, MA.

Wiltshire, Caroline. 2006. Prefix boundaries in Spanish varieties: A non-derivational OT account. *Optimality-Theoretic Studies in Spanish Phonology*. Ed. Fernando Martínez-Gil and Sonia Colina. Philadelphia: John Benjamins.

Zubritskaya, Katya. 1997. Mechanism of sound change in Optimality Theory. *Language Variation and Change* 9:121–48.

Index